UGARITIC AND HEBREW POETIC PARALLELISM

A TRIAL CUT

(ʿ*nt* I and Proverbs 2)

SUPPLEMENTS
TO
VETUS TESTAMENTUM

EDITED BY
THE BOARD OF THE QUARTERLY

VOLUME XXXIX

UGARITIC AND HEBREW POETIC PARALLELISM

A TRIAL CUT
(ʿ*nt* I and Proverbs 2)

BY

DENNIS PARDEE

E.J. BRILL
LEIDEN • NEW YORK • KØBENHAVN • KÖLN
1988

Library of Congress Cataloging-in-Publication Data

Pardee, Dennis.
Ugaritic and Hebrew poetic parallelism.
(Supplements to Vetus testamentum, ISSN 0083-5889; v. 39)
Includes bibliographical references and index.
1. Bible. O.T. Proverbs II—Language, style.
2. Ugaritic language—Parallelism. 3. Ugaritic literature—Relation to the Old Testament. I. Title.
II. Series.
BS410.V452 vol. 39 221 s [809'.9352237] 87-20933
[BS1465.5]
ISBN 90-04-08368-5

ISSN 0083-5889
ISBN 90 04 08368 5

PRINTED IN THE NETHERLANDS BY E.J. BRILL

Peters thought at the speed of an arthritic tortoise and acted with the decisiveness of a soporific sloth.

Colin Dexter
The Silent World of Nicholas Quinn

CONTENTS

ABBREVIATIONS

AAAS	*Annales Archéologiques Arabes Syriennes*
AfO	*Archiv für Orientforschung*
AOAT	Alter Orient und Altes Testament
BiOr	*Bibliotheca Orientalis*
BSOAS	*Bulletin of the School of Oriental and African Studies*
CBQ	*Catholic Biblical Quarterly*
De Moor, *Seasonal Pattern*	J. C. de Moor, *The Seasonal Pattern in the Ugaritic Myth of Baʿlu According to the Version of Ilimilku*. AOAT 16. Kevelaer: Butzon & Bercker, Neukirchen-Vluyn: Neukirchener Verlag, 1971
HAR	*Hebrew Annual Review*
HUCA	*Hebrew Union College Annual*
JANES	*Journal of the Ancient Near Eastern Society of Columbia University*
JAOS	*Journal of the American Oriental Society*
JBL	*Journal of Biblical Literature*
JNES	*Journal of Near Eastern Studies*
JSOT	*Journal for the Study of the Old Testament*
JSS	*Journal of Semitic Studies*
JTS	*Journal of Theological Studies*
OED	*Oxford English Dictionary*
RSP	*Ras Shamra Parallels*
SEL	*Studi Epigrafici e Linguistici sul Vicino Oriente antico*
TO	A. Caquot, M. Sznycer, A. Herdner, *Textes ougaritiques*. Tome 1. *Mythes et légendes*. Litteratures Anciennes du Proche Orient. Paris: Cerf, 1974
UF	*Ugarit-Forschungen*
UT	C. H. Gordon, *Ugaritic Textbook*. Analecta Orientalia 38. Rome: Pontifical Biblical Institute, 1965
VT	*Vetus Testamentum*
Whitaker	Richard E. Whitaker, *A Concordance of the Ugaritic Literature*. Cambridge, MA: Harvard University Press, 1972
ZAW	*Zeitschrift für die Alttestamentliche Wissenschaft*

FOREWORD

The present work began as spadework for an oral paper that was intended to be delivered in Fall of 1980 at the First International Symposium of Palestine Antiquities on the topic of Ugaritic and Hebrew poetic parallelism. The first chapter, on the Ugaritic *ʿnt* text, was basically completed by June of 1980. The symposium was deferred until 1981 and in the intervening year my analysis of the biblical text was completed, during the course of a stay in Syria. The pressures of a heavy teaching load and and of publishing the collations of Ugaritic tables which I made in Syria have made the actual preparation for publication of the manuscript a long one. Some revisions to the manuscript itself have been possible and some of the more recent bibliography has been registered in the footnotes. The basic body of the text represents research accomplished in 1980-1981, however, and is thus both original in that some of my ideas had not yet been stated in print by my colleagues working in this area and somewhat outdated in that some of these ideas have since been stated in print. I have endeavored to refer to these statements in the footnotes. Two preliminary papers are included here as appendices: 1) The original oral paper for the Aleppo Colloquium; * 2) an oral paper prepared for the Annual Meeting of the Society of Biblical Literature, December 1982. They contain a certain amount of repetition in comparison with the main text but are included in order to show the development of my thought in interaction with that of my colleagues.

The present work should, at the least, be useful to students of Ugaritic and Hebrew poetry in that I utilize, explain, compare, and criticize several of the most important systems of analysis of these poetries which have been proposed in the last decade and it can be used as a sort of companion to or further illustration of those methods. In addition to this descriptive aspect, I propose a systematic analysis of parallelism as a structural device which permeates all levels of a Ugaritic or Hebrew poem. This call to a consistent, systematic analysis of parallelistic structures and the examples given of some aspects of this analysis may, I hope, serve as an incentive to further studies on the structure of Ugaritic and Hebrew poetry and hence as a stepping-stone on the path to a more complete understanding of these poems.

My thanks for research facilities and the possibility of publication are here rendered to: the Fulbright-Hays Fellowship, which funded my stay

* Also to be published in the acts of the colloquium in *AAAS*.

in Syria; Jacques and Elisabeth Lagarce, who furnished me with research facilities during the course of a lectureship in Paris; Stuart M. Tave, Dean of the Division of Humanities of the University of Chicago, who provided a generous subsidy to make this publication possible; Eduard Nielsen, editor of this series, for accepting a very difficult manuscript for publication.

INTRODUCTION

This opuscule grew out of preparations for a much briefer paper entitled "Ugaritic and Hebrew Poetry: Parallelism."[1] It attempts an analysis of two trial texts according to several of the methods and systems of analysis adopted for Hebrew poetry over the past few years.[2] It is thus not so much a new notational system as it is a trial of existing ones. What is new here is the systematic notation of the distributions of types of parallelism over a given poem. A brief introduction to the study of distributions may be found in my paper mentioned above and the present study includes comments on each distribution as it is listed and summary comments on how the various types of parallelism (repetitive, semantic, grammatical, and phonetic) function in each of the distributions (half-line, regular, near, and distant).

I have become convinced in the course of this study that recognition and analysis of the distributions of the various types of parallelism is

[1] To be published in the acts of The First International Symposium of Palestine Antiquities, which took place at the University of Aleppo, September 1981 (to appear in *AAAS*; see here Appendix I). Various theoretical discussions are taken up there which are not repeated here. The most important recent contribution to the major theoretical topic ("thesaurus of fixed pairs" vs. natural association) is Adele Berlin's paper "Word Pairs and Parallelism" at the 1982 Society of Biblical Literature Annual Meeting, the major results of which have now been published as "Parallel Word Pairs: A Linguistic Explanation," *UF* 15 (1983) 7-16 (see also F. Landy's references to the oral paper in "Poetics and Parallelism: Some Comments on James Kugel's *The Idea of Biblical Poetry*," *JSOT* 28 [1984] 61-87, esp. p. 63 and notes 16, 17, and 19, and now Berlin's much more extensive work *The Dynamics of Biblical Parallelism* [Bloomington, IN: Indiana University Press, 1985]). For a recent overview of parallelism in Ugaritic poetry, see S. Segert, "Parallelism in Ugaritic Poetry," *JAOS* 103 (1983) 295-306.

[2] The two primary systems studied here are those of Terence Collins, in *Line-Forms in Hebrew Poetry. A Grammatical Approach to the Stylistic Study of the Hebrew Prophets* (Studia Pohl: Series Maior, vol. 7. Rome: Pontifical Biblical Institute, 1978) and Stephen A. Geller, in *Parallelism in Early Biblical Poetry* (Harvard Semitic Monographs, vol. 20. Chico, CA: Scholars Press, 1979). M. O'Connor's book *Hebrew Verse Structure* (Winona Lake, IN: Eisenbrauns, 1980) reached me only after the manuscript for this book was complete, but I was able to insert analyses of the two sample texts according to O'Connor's syntactic analysis into the final draft. Many other studies of Ugaritic and Hebrew poetry which are either less complete or else differently oriented have appeared in the years during which this manuscript was being written and typed (see especially James L. Kugel, *The Idea of Biblical Poetry. Parallelism and Its History*. New Haven, CT: Yale, 1981). Some of these studies will be referred to in the course of the present research. My major concern, however, was with systems of analysis and it is these that are treated in detail here. For an extensive treatment which is oriented towards the techniques at the disposal of the ancient poet (rather than towards the techniques of analysis at the disposal of the modern critic, which is my perspective), see W. G. E. Watson, *Classical Hebrew Poetry: A Guide to Its Techniques* (JSOT Supplements 26; Sheffield: JSOT Press, 1984 [actually appeared in 1985 and still unavailable to me when the present manuscript was completed]).

essential for the comprehension of the poetic structure of a given work. Any notion that a poem may be studied, as a piece of poetry, only by reference to the individual poetic units (bicola or tricola) must, if still alive anywhere, be abandoned. Though it will be abundantly evident from my own analyses and comments here below that I consider the bicolon or tricolon to be the building-block of poetic structure, I hope that it will be equally evident that I consider it as insignificant to study only these building-blocks as it would be to study, say, only the individual stones of the Parthenon. Because of the bulk of any complete study, I remain uncertain as to how to go about producing the type of study advocated here, but am no less convinced that all facets of parallelism must be the purview of any study aiming at comprehensiveness.

The texts chosen for this "trial cut"—a deep and detailed analysis of a comparatively narrow sampling—were selected somewhat at random, but not completely so. The texts needed to be separate, or at least separable, ones. The Ugaritic text is physically separable in that the tablet on which it is found is broken at the beginning and end of this column and its links with the surrounding material have thus disappeared. As for the biblical text, a more obvious candidate would have been a psalm; but I had previously taught Prov. 1-9 as part of a course on biblical Hebrew poetry and was then impressed by the relative discreteness of each of the chapters as well as by the regularity of the poetic structure. One of these chapters appeared, therefore, to provide an ideal foil over against the archaic Ugaritic sample text. In the conclusions below, the reader can see outlined the points of dissimilarity between the two poetic structures, but also the many points of similarity.

CHAPTER ONE

THE PARALLELISTIC STRUCTURE OF *ʿnt* I[3]

1.00

Text[4]	*Vocalization*[5]
2) … *ʿbd . ʾalʾ̊i[yn]*	I. *ʿabada ʾalʾiyāna baʿla*
3) *bʿl . sʾid . zbl . bʿl*	*saʾida zabūla baʿla ʾarṣi*

[3] Column I of the text known in C. H. Gordon's grammars as "*ʿnt*" (cf. *UT*, 1965). The latest edition of the text itself is in M. Dietrich, O. Loretz, and J. Sanmartín, *Die keilalphabetischen Texte aus Ugarit* (AOAT 24/I. Kevelaer: Butzon & Bercker, Neukirchen-Vluyn: Neukirchener Verlag, 1976), text 1.3. For photographs and hand copies one must turn to the official editions by Ch. Virolleaud, *La Déesse ʿAnat* (Bibliothèque Archéologique et Historique, vol. 28. Paris: Geuthner, 1938) and A. Herdner, in *Corpus des tablettes en cunéiformes alphabétiques découvertes à Ras Shamra-Ugarit de 1929 à 1939* (Mission de Ras Shamra, vol. 10. Paris: Imprimerie National & Geuthner, 1963), text 3. Ugaritic texts are cited in this study by Herdner's numbers whenever possible.

[4] I was able to collate this tablet in 1980-1981 (my thanks to the Fulbright-Hays fellowship, to the Syrian Department of Antiquities, and to the Mission de Ras Shamra for facilities and the permission to study the tablet). I hope eventually to publish a full epigraphic, philological, and poetic study of this text. My readings are incorporated into the text given here, but I have purposely avoided discussing philological details that do not have a direct effect on the poetic analysis, this in order to concentrate on the poetic aspects of the text. (The same will be true of the analysis of Proverbs 2, below). Though alternative philological analyses would produce differences of poetic analysis, I believe that the form of the text used here is at least one defensible form and that it is valid as a basis for discussion of the poetics of the text. My further studies of this text will not be able to go into the excruciating detail of poetic analysis to be found in this study, where the systems of analysis being examined are followed rather closely and my own notions are occasionally added. My own final poetic analysis of *ʿnt* I will be linked with the epigraphic and philological analyses just mentioned and for matters of method, procedure, and comparison with other systems will have to refer back to this study. Note that the first word of line 2, *prdmn*, is not included in any of the analyses below because it apparently belonged to the end of the preceding poetic unit—though we cannot be certain of this because of the damaged state of the tablet.

[5] The vocalized text must be accompanied by the usual disclaimers regarding the largely conjectural nature of any reconstruction of the Ugaritic phonetic system (cf. Pardee, *UF* 15 [1983] 140, n. 64). Such a reconstruction is very useful at some stage of a grammatical analysis (as an aid to the critic in getting the grammar worked out coherently) and in publication as well, as a sort of shorthand expression of the critic's grammatical analysis addressed to other scholars. However hypothetical a vocalized text may be, it is almost a necessity for an analysis of poetics, for no system of analysis of modern poetry of which I am aware dispenses totally with the phonetic aspect of the poetic structure. The critic must not, of course, lose sight of the fact that the phonetic structure is to some degree his own creation, but as long as the system is followed consistently and to the extent that it is based on the ancient evidence that is at our disposal and not on individual whim, the pursuit is both necessary and valid.

4) *ʾarṣ . qm . yṯʿr*
5) *w . yšlḥmnh*
6) *ybrd . ṯd . lpnwh*
7) *bḥrb . mlḥt*
8) *qṣ . mrʾi . ndd*
9) *yʿšr . wyšqynh*
10) *ytn . ks . bdh*
11) *krpn . bklʾat . ydh*
12) *bkrb . ʿẓm . rʾidn*
13) *mt . šmm . ks . qdš*
14) *ltphnh . ʾaṯt . krpn*
15) *ltʿn . ʾaṯrt . ʾalp*
16) *kd . yqḥ . bḫmr*
17) *rbt . ymsk . bmskh*
18) *qm . ybd . wyšr*
19) *mṣltm . bd . nʿm*
20) *yšr . ǵzr . ṭb . ql*
21) *ʿl . bʿl . bṣrt*
22) *ṣpn . ytmr . bʿl*
23) *bnth . yʿn . pdry*
24) *bt . ʾar . ʾapn . ṭly*
25) *b̊[t .] rb . pdr . ydʿ*

II. *qama yaṯʿuru*
wayašalḥimannahu
III. *yabrudu ṯada lêpanīhu*
biḥarbi malūḥati qiṣṣa marīʾi
IV. *nadada yaʿšuru*
wayašaqqiyannahu
V. *yattinu kāsa badihu*
karpana bikilʾatê yadêhu
VI. *bīka rabba ʿaẓuma ruʾí*
dā numāti šamīma
VII. *kāsa qudši lātiphânnahu ʾaṯṯatu*
karpana lātaʿīnu ʾaṯiratu
VIII. *ʾalpa kaddi yiqqaḥu biḫamri*
rabbāta yamsuku bimaskihu
IX. *qama yabuddu wayašīru*
maṣiltâma badê naʿīmi
X. *yašīru ǵazru ṭābu qāli*
ʿalê baʿli biṣarīrati ṣapāni
XI. *yîtamiru baʿlu binātihu*
yaʿīnu pidraya bitta ʾāri
XII.[6]

1.01 *Translation*

I. He serves mighty Baal,
Regales the Prince, lord of the earth.
II. He arises, prepares,
And causes him to eat.
III. He cuts the breast(-cut) before him,
With a salted knife (does he cut) a slice of fatling.
IV. He arises, serves,
and causes him to drink.
V. He puts a cup in his hand,
A goblet in his two hands;

[6] Because the text is severely damaged after *ydʿ*, it is uncertain to what unit the preceding words belong. It is very possible that *ʾapn ṭly bt rb* is the third segment of § XI, which would then be a tricolon. If *pdr* is a divine name as several scholars have suggested (e.g., *TO* [1974] 156), then the analysis of the preceding words as belonging to § XI becomes very likely. In any case, my division of the present text into only bicola should not be interpreted as reflecting a bias against larger poetic units; I simply do not see them occurring here. On §§ II-V as possible tricola, see discussion below.

VI. A large vessel, mighty to look upon,
Belonging to the furnishings of the heavens.
VII. A holy cup (which) women may not see,
A goblet (which) ʾAṯirat (herself) may not eye.
VIII. One thousand *kd*-measures he takes from the *ḫmr*-wine,
Ten thousand he mixes into his mixture.
IX. He arises, chants, and sings,
Cymbals (being) in the hands of the goodly one.
X. The good-voiced youth sings
For Baal in the heights of Ṣapan.
XI. Baal sees his daughters,
Eyes Pidray, daughter of Dew …

1.02 *Sense Units*

		Serving Food	I.	*ʿbd . ʾalʾiyn* ^{3}*bʿl*
				sʾid . zbl . bʿl ^{4}*ʾarṣ*
			II.	*qm . yṯʿr*
				^{5}*w . yšlḥmnh*
			III.	^{6}*ybrd . ṯd . lpnwh*
				^{7}*bḥrb . mlḥt* ^{8}*qṣ . mrʾi .*
Drinking	Cup	Serving Drink	IV.	*ndd* ^{9}*yʿšr .*
				wyšqynh
			V.	^{10}*ytn . ks . bdh*
				^{11}*krpn . bklʾat . ydh*
		Cup	VI.	^{12}*bk rb . ʿẓm . rʾi*
				dn^{13}*mt . šmm .*
			VII.	*ks . qdš* ^{14}*ltphnh . ʾaṯt .*
				krpn ^{15}*ltʿn . ʾaṯrt .*
		Drink	VIII.	*ʾalp* ^{16}*kd . yqḥ . bḫmr*
				^{17}*rbt . ymsk . bmskh*
		Serving-Song	IX.	^{18}*qm . ybd . wyšr*
				^{19}*mṣltm . bd . nʿm*
			X.	^{20}*yšr . ǵzr . ṭb . ql*
				^{21}*ʿl . bʿl . bṣrrt* ^{22}*ṣpn .*
		?	XI.	*ytmr . bʿl* ^{23}*bnth .*
				yʿn . pdry ^{24}*bt . ʾar .*

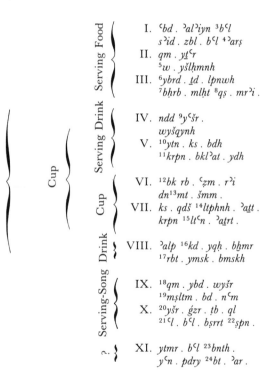

1.1 *Quantitative Analysis*[7]

	Word Count	Syllable Count	Consonant Count[8]	"Vocable" Count[9]	"Verse-units"[10]
I.	3 // 4	9 // 10	11 // 12	21 // 23	3 // 3
II.	2 // 1	5 // 7	6 // 8	12 // 16	2 // 2[11]
III.	3 // 4	9 // 12	11 (10!) // 13	21 // 28	3 // 3
IV.	2 // 1	6 // 7	7 // 7	13 // 16	2 // 2
V.	3 // 3	8 // 10	8 // 12	18 // 24	3 // 3
VI.	4 // 2	9 // 7	9 // 7	21 // 17	4 (2 + 2) // 2
VII.	4 // 3	12 // 11	14 // 12	31 // 25	4 (2 + 2) // 3
VIII.	4 // 3	10 // 10	12 // 12	24 // 24	3 // 3
IX.	3 // 3	9 // 9	9 // 10	21 // 22	3 // 3
X.	4 // 4	9 // 12	10 // 13	22 // 28	3 // 3
XI.	3 // 4	10 // 10	11 // 11	23 // 24	3 // 3

[7] Quantitative considerations do not figure largely in the present study because it is intended to be a follow-up of my previous studies of meter in Hebrew and Ugaritic poetry ("Ugaritic and Hebrew Metrics," in *Ugarit in Retrospect. 50 Years of Ugarit and Ugaritic*, ed. G. D. Young, Winona Lake, IN: 1981, pp. 113-130; review [of B. Margalit's book *A Matter of "Life" and "Death"*], *AfO* 28 [1981-1982] 267-70; and, a study of a particular text, "A Philological and Prosodic Analysis of the Ugaritic Serpent Incantation *UT* 607," *JANES* 10 [1978] 73-108). Quantitative notations only become important in the assessment of "deletion-compensation" and then only within my stated definition of the quantitative constraint as "approximately comparable length of line" (*JANES* 10 [1978] 102; *ZAW* 91 [1979] 403-5, n. 21). Since the publication of these studies, critiques of meter in Hebrew poetry which are much more extensive and convincing than mine have appeared in the works by O'Connor and Kugel cited above in Introduction, note 2 (see my review of O'Connor in *JNES* 42 [1983] 298-301, esp. p. 299, n. 3). It should be noted here that Geller's system of notation, which is discussed in detail below under the rubrics of semantic and grammatical parallelism, includes a notation of metrical balance based on syllable count. Because of my scepticism regarding the presence of meter in Ugaritic poetry and because the purpose of the present study is to separate parallelistic considerations from quantitative ones (these two aspects only overlap in my study in the analysis of "deletion-compensation"), I have not included Geller's metrical notations in my analysis of the two sample texts by his system.

[8] O. Loretz is the only major scholar of whom I am aware who gauges line-length by consonant count. This is a regular feature of his analyses of poetic texts and has been defended at some length: "Die Analyse der ugaritischen und hebräischen Poesie mittels Stichometrie und Konsonantenzählung," *UF* 7 (1975) 265-69. It is, of course, a very "conservative" system of notation in that it is not based on any form of reconstruction. On the other hand, by taking into consideration only consonants, it precludes a complete phonetic analysis, an important aspect of modern systems of poetic analysis (see above Ch. I, note 5 and Pardee, *JNES* 42 [1983] 301). Moreover, balance of consonant count is often attained by emendation in Loretz' work, when "vocable" count shows that the actual production time of the line was well balanced. *Vice versa*, a line that is well balanced in consonants or syllables can have an unbalanced "vocable" count. So one could only emend on the basis of consonant count *if it were established that consonant count was the ancient poet's criterion of line length*, a very unlikely proposition. Though Loretz makes no claim that consonant count reflects meter, and I can only agree with that aspect of his system, I do not, on the other hand, find that the system describes the length of line more meaningfully than do syllable count or vocable count. As a perfectly valid alternative, however, it cannot be faulted. Indeed, glancing down the columns of the chart one notes that in the expression of relationships between the two half-lines of a bicolon the

consonant is sometimes more closely related to syllable count than to vocable count (§ XI: 10 // 10, 11 // 11, 23 // 24—though the difference of one vocable count is minimal), sometimes it is more closely related to vocable count than to syllable count (§ V: 8 // 10, 8 // 12, 18 // 24), sometimes the three express the same relationship (§ VIII: 10 // 10, 12 // 12, 24 // 24), but that they usually express approximately the same relationship (e.g., § I: 9 // 10, 11 // 12, 21 // 23). In no case does consonant count go radically its own way and not approximate one of the other two notations.

[9] Vocable count was invented by D. N. Freedman ("Strophe and Meter in Exodus 15," in *A Light Unto My Path: Old Testament Studies in Honor of Jacob M. Myers*, eds., H. N. Bream et al., Philadelphia: Temple University Press, 1974, pp. 163-203, esp. 169) in an effort "to secure an exact calculation of the time-span of a poetic unit" ("Pottery, Poetry, and Prophecy: An Essay on Biblical Poetry," *JBL* 96 [1977] 5-26, quotation from p. 12) but he dropped the method shortly thereafter (in the lines following the preceding quotation). It consists of counting each vowel and consonant, giving two counts to a long vowel (*melek* = 5, *mālak* = 6). If, in defense of the method, one is not seeking a metrical system, but only a means of noting length relationships between line sigments, it is no less valid than syllable counting or than consonant counting (except, with respect to the latter, for the conjectural nature of the reconstructed vowels in the vocable count), and though it is not "an exact calculation of time-span" it does take into account the differences between long and short syllables that do not show up in a simple syllable count.

[10] B. Margalit has up-dated the Ley-Sievers metrical system and applied it to a large number of Ugaritic poems or segments of poems. The system is defended at length in "Studia Ugaritica I: 'Introduction to Ugaritic Prosody'," *UF* 7 (1975) 289-313, and put to its longest test in *A Matter of "Life" and "Death": A Study of the Baal-Mot Epic (CTA 4-5-6)*, AOAT 206 (Kevelaer: Butzon & Bercker, Neukirchen-Vluyn: Neukirchener Verlag, 1980). For my criticisms of the system, see articles and review cited above, Ch. I, note 7. Though I cannot guarantee it, I hope that my counts reflect adequately Margalit's system, which is based on counting "verse-units," which are in turn based essentially on accentual patterns (see my review cited in Ch. I, note 7), though the rules as stated are based on various considerations of word type, word length and relationships between words. I have borrowed one of Margalit's rules, not counting proclitic particles as "words," in my "Word Count" in column I of this table.

[11] If §§ II-III and IV-V are analyzed as tricola the counts are as follows:

§§ II-III:	3 // 3 // 4	12 // 9 // 12	14 // 11 // 13	28 // 21 // 28	4 // 3 // 3
§§ IV-V:	3 // 3 // 3	13 // 8 // 10	14 // 8 // 12	29 // 18 // 24	4 // 3 // 3

To the extent that quantitative considerations have affected my decision to divide these lines as bicola, it is especially the counts that result from taking § IV as a half-line that dissuade, for, by all the counts of micro-elements, that line segment would be the longest in this section of *ʿnt*. This consideration cannot be considered decisive, however, for even longer line segments are found in later columns of this text. Another negative consideration with regard to the tricolon hypothesis is the relative imbalance of the three segments of both tricola (long // short // long). More research is necessary into the structure of tricola in Ugaritic before this factor can be weighed.

1.2 *Parallelism: Repetitive Parallelism*[12]

I. *ʿbd . ʾalʾiyn [3]bʿl* *sʾid . zbl . bʿl [4]ʾarṣ*	*bʿl* *bʿl*												
II. *qm . yṯʿr* *[5]w . yšlḥmnh*		*qm*	 *w*	 *-nh*									
III. *[6]ybrd . ṯd . lpnwh* *[7]bḥrb . mlḥt [8]qṣ . mrʾi .*				*-h*			 *b*						
IV. *ndd [9]yʿšr .* *wyšqynh*			 *w*	 *-nh*									
V. *[10]ytn . ks . bdh* *[11]krpn . bklʾat . ydh*				*-h* *-h*	*ks*	 *krpn*	*b* *b*	*-d* *yd*					
VI. *[12]bk rb . ʿẓm . rʾi* *dn[13]mt . šmm .*													
VII. *ka . qdš [14]ltphnh . ʾaṯt .* *krpn [15]ltʿn . ʾaṯrt .*				*-nh*	*ks*	 *krpn*			*l* *l*	 *tʿn*			
VIII. *ʾalp [16]kd . yqḥ . bḫmr* *[17]rbt . ymsk . bmskh*				 *-h*			*b* *b*				 *ymsk* *bmsk-*		
IX. *[18]qm . ybd . wyšr* *[19]mṣltm . bd . nʿm*		*qm*	*w*				 *b*	 *-d*				*yšr*	
X. *[20]yšr . ǵzr . ṭb . ql* *[21]ʿl . bʿl . bṣrrt [22]ṣpn .*	 *bʿl*						 *b*					*yšr*	
XI. *ytmr . bʿl [23]bnth .* *yʿn . pdry [24]bt . ʾar*	*bʿl*			*-h*						 *yʿn*			*bnt* *bt*
XII.													*b̊[t*

1.2.1 *Repetitive Parallelism: Distribution*[13]

A. Half-line

ymsk (*b*)*msk-* (VIII)

---

[12] For the problem of the proper definition of "repetitive" parallelism see my article cited in Introduction, note 1. Here I have included under "repetitive" parallelism both verbatim repetition and root parallelism. O'Connor (ref. above, Introduction, note 2) prefers to limit the term to verbatim parallelism (p. 109). There is no doubt that root parallelism occupies a middle ground between verbatim repetition and simple paronomasia, but in my estimation it is more closely related to the former than to the latter. On the inclusion of "minor elements" in this list, see sections below on parallelism of minor elements. An important study of repetition in large structures (several psalms) is that of J. Magne, "Répétitions de mots et exégèse dans quelques psaumes et le Pater," *Biblica 39* (1958) 177-97. He charts the distributions of both major and minor lexical elements and draws conclusions for the structure of each psalm. Even so purposely brief a note as this one cannot pass over the many studies of the structure of individual poems by P. Auffret, where lexical repetition plays a role in charting lexical structure.

[13] For the four distributions listed here, see my article cited in Introduction, note 1. Many critics have, of course, studied poetic structures other than those that exist between line-segments. Just a sampling from relatively recent studies: A. R. Ceresko, "A Note on Psalm 63: A Psalm of Vigil," *ZAW* 92 (1980) 435-36 (distant repetitive parallelism as *inclusio*); idem, "A Poetic Analysis of Ps 105, with Attention to Its Use of Irony," *Biblica* 64 (1983) 20-46 ("distant parallelism" mentioned alongside "key words, chiasmus, merismus, inclusion" on p. 20); M. Dahood, *RSP* III (1981) 6 ("distant parallelism"—

with a reference to Y. Avishur's Jerusalem dissertation—see below, this note); Landy, *JSOT* 28 (1984) 74-75 (Kugel is criticized for ignoring larger units); F. Rousseau, "Structure de Qohelet I 4-11 et plan du livre," *VT* 31 (1981) 200-17 (discusses regular, near, and distant distributions, but not according to my "types" [repetitive, semantic, grammatical, phonetic]); H. W. M. van Grol, "Paired Tricola in the Psalms, Isaiah and Jeremiah," *JSOT* 25 (1983) 55-73 (on p. 66 uses "external parallelism" as criterion for defining "strophe"—following P. van der Lugt, *Strofische Structuren in de Bijbels-Hebreeuwse Poëzie*, Dissertationes Neerlandicae, Series Theologica; Kampen: Kol, 1980); W. G. E. Watson, Review, *Orientalia* n.s. 45 (1976) 434-42 (on p. 435 "distant" parallelism is mentioned, and S. Gevirtz, *Orientalia* n.s. 42 [1973] 167, is cited, who exploits the principle without using the term); idem, "Internal Parallelism in Ugaritic Verse," *SEL* 1 (1984) 53-67 ("internal" is what I have termed "half-line" distribution—the purpose of my more cumbersome term is to avoid the possible confusion wherein "internal" would mean "internal to the line," rather than "internal to the half-line"); G. A. Yee, "An Analysis of Prov 8 22-31 According to Style and Structure," *ZAW* 94 (1982) 58-66 (discusses near and distant structures). The high point of the study of word-pairs as such is Avishur's Jerusalem dissertation, now published as *Stylistic Studies of Word-Pairs in Biblical and Ancient Semitic Literatures* (AOAT 210; Kevelaer: Butzon & Bercker, Neukirchen-Vluyn: Neukirchener Verlag, 1984), wherein he considers word-pairs in all of the distributions studied here. What I see as my contribution is the insistance that the possible distributions be classified systematically in any study of the macrostructure of a given poem and that all types of parallelism (repetitive, semantic, grammatical [including morphological and syntactic], and phonetic) be systematically sought in each of these distributions.

To date, the most comprehensive presentation of distributions of parallelism is O'Connor's, but his study of grammatical parallelism (his syntactic "constraints") is limited to the bicolon (and organized around the half-line), whereas his study of the "near" distribution is practically limited to semantic parallelism ("tropes"), and that of distant distribution to large repetitive structures (see my observations in the review cited above in Ch. I, note 7). Watson ("A Review of Kugel's *The Idea of Biblical Poetry*," *JSOT* 28 [1984] 89-98) has given a preview of the "types" of parallelism which are discussed in his book (reference here above, Introduction, note 2) which includes both what I call "types" (grammatical and semantic, no mention of phonetic, repetitive is located under "structural"—I am uncertain whether he is referring to microparallelism or to macroparallelism or to both) and what I call "distributions" ("structures," of which there are eleven, including chiasmus and staircase parallelism alongside internal and distant parallelism). I believe that it is worthwhile to keep the four "distributions" as I have listed them separate from these other structures, for one finds the various structures in all four distributions (e.g., chiasmus can occur in the half-line, the line, between lines, or in distant structures [chiastic "strophes" or even complete works]). The only one of these structures that has emerged clearly in my two sample texts is chiasmus, not a regular feature of *ᶜnt* I but definitely one in Proverbs 2 (see "Semantic Parallelism: Arrangements" in part II). On the topic of chiasmus, see John W. Welch, ed., *Chiasmus in Antiquity: Structures, Analyses, Exegesis* (Hildesheim: Gerstenberg, 1981), especially the chapters by Welch on "Chiasmus in Ugaritic" (pp. 36-49) and by Watson on "Chiastic Patterns in Biblical Hebrew Poetry" (pp. 118-168). Another important presentation of "types" of parallelism (my term), but without an explicit charting of distributions, is by G. M. Schramm, "Poetic Patterning in biblical Hebrew," in *Michigan Oriental Studies in Honor of George C. Cameron* (ed. L. L. Orlin; Ann Arbor, MI: University of Michigan, 1976) 167-91. Schramm sums up his study in the following sentences: "Poetic structures in biblical Hebrew share in common the feature of parallelism expressed semantically, syntactically, morphologically and phonologically. The higher the incidence of parallelism and the larger the componential sources for its expression, the more embellished the result" (p. 191). Note that repetitive parallelism is missing from this list and that I emphasize not only the concentration of parallelism but how the various types and distributions interrelate to bolster even apparently "unembellished" units.

B. Regular
1) *bᶜl* // *bᶜl* (I)
2) *-h* // *-h* (V)
3) *b* // *b* (V, VIII)
4) *-d* // *yd* (V)
5) *l* // *l* (VII)
6) *bnt-* // *bt* (XI)

C. Near
1) *-(n)h . . . -h . . . -(n)h . . . -h* // *-h* (II, III, IV, V); *-(n)h . . . -h* *(VII, VIII)*
2) *b* // *b . . . b . . . b* (VIII, IX, X)
3) *yšr . . . yšr* (IX, X)
4) *bᶜl . . . bᶜl* (X, XI)
5) *bnt* // *bt . . . b̊[t]* (XI, XIII)[14]

D. Distant
1) *bᶜl* // *bᶜl . . . bᶜl . . . bᶜl* (I, X, XI)
2) *qm . . . qm* (II, IX)
3) *w . . . w . . . w* (II, IV, IX)
4) *-(n)h . . . -h . . . -(n)h . . . -h* // *-h . . . -(n)h . . . -h . . . -h* (II, III, IV, V, VII, VIII, XI)
5) *ks* // *krpn . . . ks* // *krpn* (V, VII)
6) *ks* // *krpn . . . ks* // *krpn* (V, VII)
7) *b . . . b* // *b . . . b* // *b . . . b . . . b* (III, V, VIII, IX, X)
8) *-d* // *yd . . . -d* (V, IX)
9) *tᶜn . . . yᶜn* (VII, XI)

E. Combinations
1) *bᶜl* (regular, near, distant)
2) *-(n)h* (regular, near, distant)
3) *b* (regular, near, distant)
4) *(y)d* (regular, distant)
5) *b(n)t* (regular, near)

1.2.2 *Repetitive Parallelism: Grammatical Relationships*

A. Complete Repetition
1) *bᶜl* // *bᶜl* (I, X, XI)
2) *qm* // *qm* (II, IX)

---

[14] The partial restoration *b̊[t]* at the beginning of line 25 is quite likely. The further continuation of that line seems to indicate, however, that we have only two of the canonical list of three daughters (*pdry bt ʾar*, *ṭly bt rb*, and *ʾarṣy bt yᶜbdr* (the third is also omitted in 5 V 10-11). Thus the parallelism seems to be *bnt* // *bt . . . bt* rather than *bnt* // *bt . . . bt* // *bt*. On this text and 5 V 10-11, see *TO* (1974) 77-80, 156, 248.

3) *w . . . w . . . w* (II, IV, IX)
4) *-h . . . -h // -h . . . -h . . . -h* (III, V, VIII, XI)
5) *-nh . . . -nh . . . -nh* (II, IV, VII)
6) *ks // krpn . . . ks // krpn* (V, VII)
7) *b . . . b // b . . . b // b . . . b . . . b* (III, V, VIII, IX, X)
8) *l // l* (VII)
9) *bt . . . b[t]* (XI, XII)

B. Minor Differences
1) *-(n)h* (## 4 & 5 above): suffix on energic form of verb versus suffix on nouns, singular, dual, and plural
2) *(y)d*: different prefixes, suffixes, and form of noun (V, IX)
3) *tˁn . . . yˁn*: different person and gender (VII, XI)
4) *bnt // bt*: different number (XI)

C. Different Grammatical Category
ymsk (b)msk-: verb versus noun (VIII)

1.3 *Parallelism: Semantic Parallelism*[15]

		Without minor elements[16]	Including minor elements
ˁbd . ʾalʾiyn ^{3}*bˁl*	$a\ b^{2}\ (=x+y)$	$1\ I^{1}\ 2\ I^{1}+3^{1}$	$1\ I^{1}\ 2\ I^{1}+3^{1}$
sʾid . zbl . bˁl ^{4}*ʾarṣ*	$a'\ b'^{3}\ (=x'+y+z)$	$1\ II^{1}\ 2\ II^{1}+3^{2}+4\ I^{1}$	$1\ II^{1}\ 2\ II^{1}+3^{2}+4\ I^{1}$
qm . yṯˁr	$a\ b$	$5\ I^{1}\ 1\ III^{1}$	$5\ I^{1}\ 1\ III^{1}$
^{5}*w . yšlḥmnh*	b'	$1\ IV^{1}$	$6^{1}+1\ IV^{1}+7^{1}$
^{6}*ybrd . ṯd . lpnwh*	$a\ b\ c$	$6^{1}\ 7^{1}\ 8^{1}$	$8^{1}\ 9^{1}\ 10^{1}+11^{1}+7^{2}$
^{7}*bḥrb . mlḥt* ^{8}*qṣ . mrʾi .*	$d^{2}\ b'^{2}\ (=b'+x)$	$9^{1}+10^{1}\ 11^{1}+12^{1}$	$12^{1}+13^{1}+14^{1}\ 15^{1}+16^{1}$
ndd ^{9}*yˁšr .*	$a\ b$	$5\ II^{1}\ 1\ V^{1}$	$5\ II^{1}\ 1\ V^{1}$
wyšqynh	b'	$1\ VI^{1}$	$6^{2}+1\ VI^{1}+7^{3}$
^{10}*ytn . ks . bdh*	$a\ b\ c$	$13\ I^{1}+14\ I^{1}\ 15^{1}$	$17\ I^{1}+18\ I^{1}\ 12^{2}+19^{1}+7^{4}$
^{11}*krpn . bklʾat . ydh*	$b'\ c'^{2}\ (=x+c)$	$14\ II^{1}\ 16^{1}+15^{2}$	$18\ II^{1}\ 12^{3}+20^{1}+19^{2}+7^{5}$
^{12}*bk rb . ˁẓm . rʾi*	$a^{2}\ (=x+y)\ b\ (=y')\ c$	$14\ III^{1}+17\ I^{1}\ 17\ II^{1}\ 18\ I^{1}$	$18\ III^{1}+21\ I^{1}\ 21\ II^{1}\ 22\ I^{1}$
dn^{13}*mt . šmm .*	$d\ e$	$19^{1}\ 4\ II^{1}$	$23^{1}+24^{1}\ 4\ II^{1}$
ks . qdš ^{14}*ltphnh . ʾaṯt*	$a^{2}\ (=x+y)\ b\ c$	$14\ I^{2}+20^{1}\ 18\ II^{1}\ 21\ I^{1}$	$18\ I^{2}+25^{1}\ 26^{1}+22\ II^{1}+7^{6}\ 27\ I^{1}$
krpn ^{15}*ltˁn . ʾaṯrt .*	$a'\ (=x')\ b'\ c'$	$14\ II^{2}\ 18\ III^{1}\ 21\ II^{1}$	$18\ II^{2}\ 26^{2}+22\ III^{1}\ 27\ II^{1}$
ʾalp ^{16}*kd . yqḥ . bḫmr*	$a^{2}\ (=x+y)\ b\ c$	$22\ I^{1}+14\ IV^{1}\ 13\ II^{1}\ 23\ I^{1}$	$28\ I^{1}+18\ IV^{1}\ 17\ I^{1}\ 12^{4}+29\ I^{1}$
^{17}*rbt . ymsk . bmskh*	$a'\ (=x')\ d\ c'\ (=d)$	$22\ II^{1}\ 23\ II^{1}\ 23\ II^{2}$	$28\ II^{1}\ 29\ II^{1}\ 12^{5}+29\ II^{2}$
^{18}*qm . ybd . wyšr*	$a\ b\ b'$	$5\ I^{2}\ 24\ I^{1}\ 24\ II^{1}$	$5\ I^{2}\ 30\ I^{1}\ 6^{3}+30\ II^{1}$
^{19}*mṣltm . bd . nˁm*	$c\ d\ e$	$25^{1}\ 15^{3}\ 26\ I^{1}$	$31^{1}\ 12^{6}+19^{3}\ 26\ I^{1}$
^{20}*yšr . ǵzr . ṭb . ql*	$a\ b^{3}$	$24\ II^{2}\ 27^{1}+26\ II^{1}+28^{1}$	$30\ II^{2}\ 33^{1}+32\ II^{1}+34^{1}$
^{21}*ˁl . bˁl . bṣrrt* ^{22}*ṣpn .*	$c\ d^{2}$	$3^{3}\ 29^{1}+30^{1}$	$35^{1}+3^{3}\ 12^{7}+36^{1}+37^{1}$
ytmr . bˁl ^{23}*bnth .*	$a\ b\ c$	$18\ IV^{1}\ 3^{4}\ 31^{1}$	$22\ IV^{1}\ 3^{4}\ 38^{1}+7^{8}$
yˁn . pdry ^{24}*bt . ʾar .*	$a'\ b'^{3}\ (=x+c+y)$	$18\ III^{2}\ 32^{1}+31^{2}+33^{1}$	$22\ III^{2}\ 39^{1}+38^{2}+40^{1}$

[15] The first column is a traditionally formatted analysis of semantic parallelism, bicolon by bicolon. The only significant difference from traditional analyses of this type is that I have tried rigorously to separate semantic analysis from grammatical analysis. Thus, for example, *yqḥ // ymsk* in § VIII are here given different letters (b // d) because of the semantic disparity between 'taking' and 'mixing'. Superscript numbers in this col-

1.3.1 *List of Words as Semantic Parallels*

Without minor elements

1 I *ˁBD* (I^{1})[17]
II *Sʾ D* (I^{1})
III *ṮˁR: yṯˁr* (II^{1})
IV *LḤM: yšlḥmnh* (II^{1})
V *ˁŠR: yˁšr* (IV^{1})
VI *ŠQY: yšqynh* (IV^{1})
2 I *ʾalʾiyn* (I^{1})
II *ZBL* (I^{1})
3 *bˁl* (I^{1,2}, X^{3}, XI^{4})
4 I *ʾRṢ* (I^{1})
II *ŠMM* (VI^{1})
5 I *QM* (II^{1}, IX^{2})
II *NDD* (IV^{1})

Including minor elements

1 I *ˁBD* (I^{1})
II *Sʾ D* (I^{1})
III *ṮˁR: yṯˁr* (II^{1})
IV *LḤM: yšlḥmnh* (II^{1})
V *ˁŠR: yˁšr* (IV^{1})
VI *ŠQY: yšqynh* (IV^{1})
2 I *ʾalʾiyn* (I^{1})
II *ZBL* (I^{1})
3 *bˁl* (I^{1,2}, X^{3}, XI^{4})
4 I *ʾRṢ* (I^{1})
II *ŠMM* (VI^{1})
5 I *QM* (II^{1}, IX^{2})
II *NDD* (IV^{1})

---

umn represent the number of words in an entity identified by means of a given letter (e.g., "b^{2}" in § I means that the semantic compound *ʾalʾiyn bˁl* consists of two words). The last two columns represent an attempt to note the semantic analysis of an entire poem. In this notation, the first number (Arabic) indicates the concept (semantic group), the second number (Roman) indicates a member of the group, and the third (superscript Arabic) indicates the occurrence of the individual member. For example, "18 III^{2}" in col. III for § XI means that *yˁn* is a member of the eighteenth semantic group (which began with "18 I^{1}" in § VI), the third member thereof (the first two were 18 I = *rʾy* and 18 II = *phy*), and the second occurrence of the root *ˁn*. As an experiment (already dropped in the analysis of Proverbs 2, where the attempt simply became too cumbersome) I have tried setting up columns which do and do not include minor elements. There are seven of these minor elements and the final column has, therefore, seven more entries than does column III: *w-*, # 6; *-h*, # 7; *l-*, # 10 (preposition); *b-*, # 12; *d-*, # 23; *l-*, # 26 (negative adverb); *ˁl*, # 35. In the following chart, all words are listed as semantic groups (i.e., arranged according to the first number of the notation in the final two columns of this chart). For another example of this notation with a longer (and quite pessimistic!) introduction, see Pardee, "The Semantic Parallelism of Psalm 89," in *In the Shelter of Elyon. Essays on Ancient Palestinian Life and Literature in Honor of G. W. Ahlström*, eds., W. B. Barrick and J. R. Spencer (*JSOT* Supplement 31; Sheffield: JSOT Press, 1984) 121-37.

[16] Not counting minor elements there are sixty-four total words, which are here reduced to thirty-three semantic groups. Counting minor elements there are eighty-one total terms (plus eight suffixes), reduced to thirty-nine parallel terms plus the 3 m.s. suffix (= thirty-three major elements plus seven minor elements).

[17] As in the previous chart the first number (Arabic) denotes the semantic group and corresponds to the first number of each identification in the preceding chart, the second number (Roman) indicates the member of the semantic group and corresponds to the second number of each identification in the preceding chart; the numbers in parentheses indicate the section of *ˁnt* I (the Roman numeral) and the number of occurrence of the individual word (superscript Arabic, corresponding to the superscript number in the last two columns of the preceding chart). The same notation was used in the study of Psalm 89 cited in the preceding note, with the exception that verse numbers were indicated by Arabic numbers, rather than Roman numerals as here.

6 *BRD: ybrd* (III^{1})
7 *ṮD* (III^{1})

8 *PNY: pnwh* (III^{1})

9 *ḤRB* (III^{1})
10 *MLḤ: mlḥt* (III^{1})
11 *QṢṢ: qṣ* (III^{1})
12 *MRʾ: mrʾi* (III^{1})
13 I *YTN* (V^{1})
II *LQḤ: yqḥ* (VIII^{1})
14 I *KS* (V^{1}, VII^{2})
II *KRPN* (V^{1}, VII^{2})
III *BK* (VI^{1})
IV *KD* (VIII^{1})
15 (*YD*): *-dh* (V^{1})
ydh (V^{2})
-d (IX^{3})
16 *KLʾ: klʾat* (V^{1})
17 I *RBB: rb* (VI^{1})
[cf. *rbt* #22 II]
II *ʿẒM* (VI^{1})
18 I *Rʾ Y: rʾi* (VI^{1})
II *PHY: tphnh* (VII^{1})
III *ʿYN: tʿn* (VII^{1})
yʿn (XI^{2})
IV *ʾMR: ytmr* (XI^{1})

19 *NMT* (VI^{1})
20 *QDŠ* (VII^{1})

21 I *ʾṮṮ: ʾaṯṯ* (VII^{1})
II *ʾaṯrt* (VII^{1})
22 I *ʾLP* (VIII^{1})
II *RBB/Y: rbt* (VIII^{1})
23 I *ḪMR* (VIII^{1})
II *MSK: ymsk* (VIII^{1})
msk (VIII^{2})

6 *w* (II^{1}, IV^{2}, IX^{3})
7 *-h* (II^{1}, III^{2}, IV^{3}, V^{4,5}, VII^{6}, VIII^{7}, XI^{8})
8 *BRD: ybrd* (III^{1})
9 *ṮD* (III^{1})
10 *l* (III^{1})
11 *PNY: pnwh* (III^{1})
12 *b* (III^{1}, V^{2,3}, VIII^{4,5}, IX^{6}, X^{7})
13 *ḤRB* (III^{1})
14 *MLḤ: mlḥt* (III^{1})
15 *QṢṢ: qṣ* (III^{1})
16 *MRʾ: mrʾi* (III^{1})
17 I *YTN* (V^{1})
II *LQḤ: yqḥ* (VIII^{1})
18 I *KS* (V^{1}, VII^{2})
II KRPN (V^{1}, VII^{2})
III *BK* (VI^{1})
IV *KD* (VIII^{1})
19 (*Y*)*D*: *-dh* (V^{1})
ydh (V^{2})
-d (IX^{3})
20 *KLʾ: klʾat* (V^{1})
21 I *RBB: rb* (VI^{1})
[cf. *rbt* #28 II]
II *ʿẒM* (VI^{1})
22 I *RʾY: rʾi* (VI^{1})
II *tphnh* (VII^{1})
III *ʿYN: tʿn* (VII^{1})
yʿn (XI^{2})
IV *ʾMR: ytmr* (XI^{1})
23 *d* (VI^{1})
24 *NMT* (VI^{1})
25 *QDŠ* (VII^{1})
26 *l* (VII^{1,2})
27 I *ʾṮṮ: ʾaṯṯ* (VII^{1})
II *ʾaṯrt* (VII^{1})
28 I *ʾLP* (VIII^{1})
II *RBB/Y: rbt* (VIII^{1})
29 I *ḪMR* (VIII^{1})
II *MSK: ymsk* (VIII^{1})
msk (VIII^{2})

24 I *BDD: ybd* (IX^1)
II *ŠR: yšr* (IX^1, X^2)
25 *ṢLL: mṣltm* (IX^1)
26 I *NʿM* (IX^1)
II *ṬB* (X^1)
27 *ǴZR* (X^1)
28 *QL* (X^1)

29 *ṢRR: ṣrrt* (X^1)
30 *ṣpn* (X^1)
31 *BN: bnth* (XI^1)
bt (XI^2)
32 *pdry* (XI^1)
33 *ʾar* (XI^1)

30 I *BDD: bdd* (IX^1)
II *ŠR: yšr* (IX^1, X^2)
31 *ṢLL: mṣltm* (IX^1)
32 I *NʿM* (IX^1)
II *ṬB* (X^1)
33 *ǴZR* (X^1)
34 *QL* (X^1)
35 *ʿl* (X^1)
36 *ṢRR: ṣrrt* (X^1)
37 *ṣpn* (X^1)
38 *BN: bnth* (XI^1)
bt (XI^2)
39 *pdry* (XI^1)
40 *ʾar* (XI^1)

1.3.2 *Semantic Parallelism: Distribution*[18]

A. Half-line
1) *rb* + *ʿẓm* (VI) (synonymous)
2) *ybd* + *yšr* (IX) (synonymous)

B. Regular
I. Same Relative Position
1) *ʿbd* // *sʾid* (I) (synonymous)
2) *ʾalʾiyn* // *zbl* (I) (synonymous)
3) *yṯʿr* // *yšlḥmnh* (II) (list [?])
4) *yʿšr* // *yšqynh* (IV) (list [?])
5) *ks* // *krpn* (V, VII) (list [?])
6) (*b*)*d*(*h*) // (*b*)*klʾat* (*ydh*) (V) (part-whole)
7) *tphnh* // *tʿn* (VII) (synonymous)
8) *ʾaṯt* // *ʾaṯrt* (VII) (whole-part; proper name)
9) *ʾalp* // *rbt* (VIII) (number)

---

[18] Semantic categories which roughly follow Geller's (see Geller [reference above, Introduction, note 2], pp. 31-40) are given in parentheses. Note that (1) the parallel pairs in "regular" distribution are all in the same relative position in their bicola: there are no simple chiastic structures (the only exception being the chiastic grammatical parallelism of prepositional phrases in § III, which produces chiastic distribution of *ṯd* and *qṣ mrʾi*); (2) All the parallelisms in half-line, regular, and near distributions are various forms of the larger category of "synonymous" parallelism, here broken down into Geller's categories; only the distant parallel *ytn . . . lqḥ* (§§ V, VIII) may be considered antithetic; (3) A rigorous separation of grammatical from semantic parallelism reveals some strong grammatical parallels that have no intrinsic semantic component (e.g., *lpnwh* // *bḥrb mlḥt* [§ III], *yqḥ* // *ymsk* [§ VII]); (4) So-called "synthetic" parallelism (i.e., not strongly marked by synonymity or antonymity) is an important feature of this poem, with three sections thus characterized (§§ VI, IX, X).

10) *ḫmr // msk* (VIII) (part-whole)
11) *ytmr // yʿn* (XI) (synonymous)
12) *bnth // pdry bt ʾar* (XI) (whole-part; proper name; epithet)

II. Chiastic

1) *ṯd + lpnwh // bḥrb mlḥt + qṣ mrʾi* (III) (*ṯd // qṣ mrʾi* = part-whole)

C. Near

1) *ʿbd // sʾid . . . yṯʿr // yšlḥmnh* (I, II) (list)
2) *yʿšr // yšqynh . . . ytn ks* (IV, V) (list)
3) *ks // krpn . . . bk . . . ks // krpn . . . kd* (V, VI, VII, VIII)
4) *rʾi . . . tphnh // tʿn* (VI, VII) (synonymous)
5) *ybd + yšr . . . yšr* (IX, X) (synonymous)
6) *nʿm . . . ṭb* (IX, X) (synonymous)

D. Distant

1) *ʾrṣ . . . šmm* (I, VI) (synonymous [merismus])
2) *qm . . . ndd . . . qm* (II, IV, IX) (synonymous)
3) *yṯʿr // yšlḥmnh . . . yʿšr // yšqynh* (II, IV) (list)
4) *ytn (ks) . . . (kd) yqḥ* (V, VIII) (antonymic)
5) *rʾi . . . tphnh // tʿn . . . ytmr // yʿn* (VI, VII, XI)

E. Combinations

1) *ʿbd // sʾid . . . yṯʿr // yšlḥmnh . . . yʿšr // yšqynh . . . ytn ks* (I, II, IV, V) (regular, near, distant)
2) *ks // krpn . . . bk . . . ks // krpn . . . kd* (V, VI, VII, VIII) (regular, near)
3) *rʾi . . . tphnh // tʿn . . . ytmr // yʿn* (VI, VII, XI) (regular, near, distant)
4) *ybd + yšr . . . yšr* (IX, X) (half-line, near)

1.3.3 *Semantic Parallelism: Semantic Relationships*[19]

A. Synonymous

1) *ʿbd // sʾid* (I)
2) *ʾalʾiyn // zbl* (I)

---

19 The purpose of this chart is to show the varieties of semantic relationships between elements in parallel in "regular" distribution. It includes considerations of a grammatical nature in order to show that nouns that are semantically parallel need not be grammatically so and *vice versa*. The chart which follows this one is intended to classify the grammatical parallelisms according to three ranges of similarity and dissimilarity. For a comparison of the results of these two charts for the two sample texts, see Ch. II, note 16, below. Note that § X shows no semantic nor grammatical parallelism between the two half-lines (here below D, 2). This is also to some extent true of §§ VI and IX but those lines can be analyzed as including weak semantic parallelism but little or no

3) *bʿl* // *bʿl ʾarṣ* (I) (includes repetitive element)
4) *yṯʿr* // *yšlḥmnh* (II)
5) *ṯd* // *qṣ mrʾi* (III) (part-whole)
6) *yʿšr* // *yšqynh* (IV)
7) *ks* // *krpn* (V, VII)
8) *bdh* // *bklʾat ydh* (V) (includes repetitive element)
9) *tphnh* // *tʿn* (VII)
10) *ʾaṯt* // *ʾaṯrt* (VII)
11) *ʾalp* // *rbt* (VIII)
12) *ytmr* // *yʿn* (XI)
13) *bnth* // *pdry bt ʾar* (XI) (whole-part)

B. Antonymic
No examples

C. Grammatical but not Semantic[20]
1) *lpnwh* // *bḥrb mlḥt* (III) (prepositional phrases)
2) *yqḥ* // *ymsk* (VIII)
3) *bḫmr* // *bmskh* (VIII)

D. Neither Grammatical nor Semantic
1) *rb*, *ʿṣm*, *rʾi* // *šmm* (VI)
2) § X

E. Semantic but not Grammatical
1) *bk* // *nmt* (VI) (part-whole)
2) *ybd* + *yšr* // *mṣltm* (IX) (whole-part [?])

1.3.4 *Semantic Parallelism: Grammatical Relationships*[21]

A. Same Grammatical Form
1) *ʿbd* // *sʾid* (I)
2) *ʾalʾiyn* // *zbl* (I)

---

grammatical parallelism: *bk* // *nmt* in § VI and *ybd* + *yšr* // *mṣltm* in § IX. (Note that these weak semantic parallelisms are classified as of "C" rank below in "Semantic Parallelism: Geller's Categories," and do not appear, therefore, in the previous lists. I have included them in the present chart and in the following one in order to give the full range of relationships between semantic and grammatical parallelism; this range shows up more clearly in Proverbs 2—see corresponding charts below).

[20] For a notation of the grades of grammatical parallelism separate from semantic parallelism, see next chart.

[21] The categories are here the same as for "Repetitive Parallelism: Grammatical Relationships," except that "same grammatical form" here replaces "complete repetition." This list is limited to forms in "regular" distribution because of the many permutations that would result from considering all distributions simultaneously. Moreover, there has been no indication from this section (nor from Proverbs 2) that grammatical parallelism apart from semantic parallelism can function beyond the near distribution. Nouns that differ only in gender are listed, perhaps somewhat arbitrarily, under "same grammatical form." For the two main perspectives on grammatical parallelism, see below Ch. I, note 39 (I have noted in this and the following chart both grammatical similarities and dissimilarities).

3) *l* // *b* (III)
4) *t̠d* // *qṣ mrʾi* (III)[22]
5) *ks* // *krpn* (V, VII)
6) *ʾat̠t* // *ʾat̠rt* (VII)
7) *ʾalp* // *rbt* (VIII)
8) *yqḥ* // *ymsk* (VIII) (semantically dissimilar)

B. Similar Grammatical Form
1) *yt̠ᶜr* // *yšlḥmnh* (II) (indicative // energic; only second has suffix)
2) *yᶜšr* // *yšqynh* (IV) (same as previous)
3) (*b*)*d*(*h*) // (*b*)*klʾat* (*ydh*) (V) (probably different number, cf. Hebrew *kilʾayim*)
4) *tphnh* // *tᶜn* (VII) (energic // indicative; only first has suffix, i.e. mirror-image of first two entries)
5) *ḫmr* // *mskh* (VIII) (semantically dissimilar; pronominal suffix only on second)
6) *ytmr* // *yᶜn* (XI) (Gt versus G)
7) *bnth* // *pdry* (*bt ʾar*) (XI) (different number)

C. Different Grammatical Form
1) *bk* // *nmt* (VI) (noun, singular, accusative // noun, plural, genitive)
2) *ybd* + *yšr* // *mṣltm* (IX) (verbs // noun)

1.3.5 *Semantic Parallelism: Geller's Categories*[23]

I. *ᶜbd . ʾalʾiyn ³bᶜl*	$a\ b^2\ (= x + y)$	Verb + compound (= epithet + PN)

---

[22] *t̠d* and *qṣ* are the same grammatical form (singular noun, accusative case); the different case of *mrʾi* is, of course, owing to its position as second element in the compound.

[23] This is not Geller's form of notation, but his categories of semantic analysis are here adopted more or less directly. The first two columns give the text then my notation of it according to more or less traditional forms. The third column gives Geller's categories. I follow Geller in using upper-case Roman letters to represent semantic grades: A = close semantic parallels, B = distant semantic parallels, C = positional/grammatical parallels without intrinsic semantic proximity, D = identical (repetitive parallelism). I have adapted this system only to the extent of using A exclusively for attested parallel pairs and B for non-attested pairs (which Geller suggests [p. 42] as a possible adaptation of his system). For purposes of comparing the traditional semantic notation with Geller's, the conventions observed in the column with traditional notation are the following: I use a same letter to indicate repetitive parallelism (a // a = D), primed values to indicate primary or secondary semantic parallelism (a // a′ = A or B) and a different letter to denote very weak semantic or non-semantic parallelism (a // b = C). (Upper-case letters are also used in discussions of parallelism, according to standing convention, for macro-semantic statements, e.g., *qm . . . ndd . . . qm* = ABA.) If repetitive parallelism is contained within a compound, the repetitive element will only show up in my notation of

sʾid. zbl. bᶜl [4]*ʾarṣ* *a′ b′*[3] (= *x′* + *y* + *z*) Verb (B) + double compound (epithet [A] + epithet [= PN + noun (Epith-D)])

The conventional semantic analysis shows up the structure of these compounds. The notation "Epith-D" at the end of the second half-line represents Geller's abbreviation for an epithet made up of PN + noun, the PN of which is identical to a PN in the first line. Thus *ʾalʾiyn bᶜl // zbl bᶜl ʾarṣ* consists of two parallel compound phrases; the first word of each phrase forms a parallel pair of primary semantic proximity (the two are elsewhere attested in this formula[24]); the words in second position are identical; the third word in the second phrase is the *rectum* of a construct phrase which itself forms an epithet of Baal. To avoid taking the DN Baal as the *regens* of a construct chain I have interpreted it as 'lord'. If this is correct, the formal repetitive parallelism conceals a subtle play on meanings as reflected in syntax.[25]

II. *qm. yṯᶜr* *a b* Verb$_1$ + verb$_2$ (C to verb$_2$)
[5]*w. yšlḥmnh* *b′* Verb (C to verb$_1$; B to verb$_2$)

Before the introduction of grammatical analysis, one would have been torn between the conventional analyses *a a′ a″* (representing the threefold verbal sequence) and *a b b′* (representing the closer semantic proximity between the second and third elements as compared with the first). Now one can separate out the two features, pointing out the semantic parallelism of the second and third verbs when dealing with semantic parallelism and reserving the grammatical parallelism of all three for the discussion of grammatical parallelism. This is perhaps the best place to point out the structural and semantic parallels which exist

---

the elements of the compound, e.g., § I: a b^2 (= x + y) // a b′^{3} (= x′ + y + z) for *zbl bᶜl ʾarṣ // ʾalʾiyn bᶜl*. In this pair of parallel compounds there is the semantic parallelism of *zbl // ʾalʾiyn* (x // x′), the repetitive parallelism of *bᶜl // bᶜl* (y // y), and the non-parallel unit *ʾarṣ* (z). One weakness of Geller's system may be noted in this respect, viz., a semantic classification is attached to compounds in his system, and not to the elements thereof. This is usually not important because compounds are frequently made up of semantically similar elements, but such is not always the case (cf. below on Proverbs 2: 13 *ʾrḥwt yšr // drky ḥšk*).

[24] A point of debate: Should A be reserved for pairs that occur in more than one idiom? (*ʾalʾiyn* and *zbl* are only attested as a parallel pair in Ugaritic when referring to Baal.)

[25] I do not mean to deny that divine names may occur in construct (cf. G. Tuttle, "*di dit* in Ug 5.2.1.8," *UF* 8 [1976] 465-66; J. A. Emerton, "New Light on Israelite Religion: The Implications of the Inscriptions from Kuntillet ᶜAjrud," *ZAW* 94 [1982] 2-20). But the rarity of the construction in Northwest Semitic permits the perception of such plays on words as the one proposed here.

between the poetic units in §§ II, IV, and IX. First, there is the *A B A* distant parallelism of the first verb in each bicolon (*qm // ndd // qm*).[26] Second, there is the precisely equivalent internal parallelism of *A B B* (no semantic parallelism between the first verb and the other two; the second and third verbs are elsewhere attested as parallel or sequential pairs). The primary difference between the first two units and the third lies in the area of quantitative analysis ("metrics"), for, while the length of the first line in the first two examples is such as to warrant legitimate discussion as to its division and relationship to the following lines, in the third case the first line is too short to be divided into two lines and must either be taken as a monocolon or linked with the following line as a (non-parallel) bicolon. (See below on § IX for further discussion.)

III.	[6]*ybrd . ṯd . lpnwh*	*a b c*	Verb + noun + adverbial (preposition + noun)
	[7]*bḥrb . mlḥt* [8]*qṣ . mrʾi*	d^2 b'^2 (= b' + x)	Compound adverbial (preposition + noun + epithet) + compound (noun + noun [WP/A])

The primary proximity of *ṯd // qṣ* is established by 4(51).3.4; .6.56.[27] The abbreviation WP in Geller's system refers to the "whole vs. part" relationship.[28] Here I have taken the "slice" to be part of the "breast," though both are, of course, parts of the "fatling." The two adverbial phrases are not taken as semantic pairs in spite of the grammatical parallelism because of the great semantic disparity ("face" versus "knife"); moreover the function of the two phrases is quite different (locative versus instrumental).

If §§ II and III were analyzed as a tricolon, the semantic structure would be:

a b b′ Verb_1 + verb_2 (C to verb_1) + verb_3 (C to verb_1, B to verb_2)
b″ c d Verb (C to verb_1, B to $\text{verbs}_{2,3}$), etc.
e^2 c'^2 (= c' + x)

IV.	*ndd* [9]*yʿšr*	*a b*	Verb_1 + verb_2 (C to verb_1)
	wyšqynh	*b′*	Verb (C to verb_1; A to verb_2)

---

[26] On the semantics of *ndd*, see M. H. Pope, Review, *JSS* 11 (1966) 228-41, esp. 232.

[27] The relationship between *ṯd* and *qṣ* is generally taken to be quite different from that of this passage (cf., e.g., *TO* [1974] 202).

[28] For explanations of Geller's terms and abbreviations, see below at "Grammatical Parallelism: Geller."

The parallel structure here is precisely that of §II and of the first half-line of § IX (see remarks above on § II and below on § IX). The parallelism of *yʿšr* and *yšqynh* is here taken as of primary proximity because the two verbs are found in sequential relationship in 17(2 Aqht).6.30-31, in, by the way, precisely the same forms.

V.	10*ytn . ks . bdh*	*a b c*	Verb + noun + adverbial (preposition + noun)
	11*krpn . bklʾat . ydh*	*b′ c′*^{2} (= *x* + *c*)	Noun (A) + compound adverbial (preposition + noun + noun [PW/D]

PW refers to the relationship between one hand and a pair of hands. D, denoting identity in Geller's system, refers to the *-d-* of *bdh*, which is, of course, derived from *yd* 'hand'. Notice that the six-line unit which describes the act of giving the cup, then the cup itself, is bound together by the repetitive parallelism of the semantic pair *ks* // *krpn* (§§ V, VII), further fleshed out by the semantic parallels *bk* in between (§ V) and *kd* in the following unit (§ VIII).

VI.	12*bk . rb . ʿẓm . rʾi*	*a*^{2} (= *x* + *y*) *b* (= *y′*) *c*	Compound noun (noun + adj.) + adjective + verbal noun
	*dn*13*mt . šmm .*	*d e*	Relative pronoun + compound noun (*nmt* to *bk* = C [PW ?]

It is to be noted that conventional analysis is more specific here than is a strict line versus line comparison, in that, at least by the use of parentheses as above, it is able to note the half-line parallelism of *rb* and *ʿẓm* (which are, by the way, a semantically primary parallelism[29]). Indeed, conventional notation may well have represented this half-line as *a b b′ c*, separating the noun/adjective compound and showing the semantic parallelism of the two adjectives. Geller's system, however, puts more emphasis on compounds[30] and would here, in fact, represent quite well the structure of this line in relation to the following lines: I take lines 10-15 (§§V-VII) as enjambed (i.e., line 12 does not begin a new syntactic unit and *bīka* is here indicated as accusative in case, reflecting its syntactic

29 See M. Dahood, *RSP* I (1972) 338.

30 An adjective and the noun it modifies are the same "thing" and thus in a sense identical and thus a stronger semantic pair than two adjectives considered in their relationship to each other.

dependence on *ytn* in line 10). If this analysis is correct, then *bk rb* is a compound object ('He put . . . a large vessel') and *ʿẓm rʾi* is an appositional modifying phrase ('He put . . . a large vessel [which was] mighty to look upon'). For the meaning of *ʿẓm rʾi*, compare I Sam. 16:12 *ṭō*^{w}*b rōʾī*^{y} 'good-looking'.[31] The philological analysis of the bicolon as a whole is basically de Moor's.[32] The parallelism of *bk* and *nmt* is "functional" (the *bk* comes from the heavenly stores) and a form of "part-whole" parallelism, though it is so weak that it is here classified as of "C" ranking.

VII. *ks . qdš* [14]*ltphnh . ʾaṯt .*	a^2 $(=x+y)$ b c	Compound noun (noun_1 + noun_2) + verb + noun
krpn [15]*ltʿn . ʾaṯrt .*	a' $(=x')$ b' c'	Noun (A to noun_1 + verb (A) + noun (WP-PN/B)

ks qdš could be noun + adjective (*kāsa qadāša*—unless, of course, *ks* be feminine as in some later dialects). For the primary parallelism of *phy* and *ʿn*, see 4(51).2.12-14:

bnšʾi ʿnh	*binašāʾi ʿênêha*	(7)[33]	When she lifts her eyes
wtphn hlk bʿl	*watiphânna halaka baʿli*	(9)	She sees the progress of Baal,
ʾaṯrt ktʿn	*ʾaṯiratu kī taʿīnu*	(7)	Even ʾAṯirat does see
hlk btlt ʿnt	*halaka batūlati ʿanati*	(10)	The progress of Girl ʿAnat,
tdrq ybmt lʾimm	*tadriqa yabamati liʾmima*	(10)	The striding of the sister-in-law of Liʾm.

Though some have taken *ʾaṯrt* in the *ʿnt* text as a common noun 'goddess' rather than as a proper noun,[34] the force of the statement is stronger if it is understood to declare that not even the consort of El may look at this particular cup. This notion is, of course, contained in the phrase 'no goddess', but it is stronger if the goddess in question is ʾAṯirat herself. Since ʾAṯirat is contained in the phrase 'no goddess', I see no reason for the philological gymnastics necessary to find a usage of *ʾaṯrt* in Ugaritic which would be common rather than proper. (If we were dealing with Hebrew, it would be different, for the formulation *hāʾăšērā*^{h} shows that the word

---

[31] U. Cassuto, *The Goddess Anath* (Jerusalem: Magnes, 1971 [Eng. ed.]) 110, cited Josh. 22:10 *gādôl l*^{e}*mare*^{h} 'of great appearance' but apparently did not come across the Samuel passage, which furnishes an example of the same syntax as in found is *ʿnt* I with the noun *rŏʿī*^{y}.

[32] De Moor, *Seasonal Pattern* (1971) 67, 74.

[33] Only syllable count is given here as indication of line length.

[34] E.g., de Moor, *Seasonal Pattern* (1971) 67, 75.

has become generic as well as specific in the Bible; witness also the form *ʾšrth* in one of the Hebrew inscriptions from Kuntillet Ajrud,[35] which illustrates the same syntactic and semantic status as biblical *hʾšrh*, i.e., marked rather than inherent definiteness). Thus I take the parallelism of *ʾaṯt* and *ʾaṯrt* as "whole-part" (ʾAṯirat as one female), proper noun versus common noun (PN), of secondary semantic proximity (B—because I have not found the two words elsewhere in parallel). Though not so obviously so, *phy* and *ʿn* may also be "whole-part," in this case, "generic-specific."

VIII.	*ʾalp* [16]*kd . yqḥ . bẖmr*	$a^2\ (= x + y)\ b\ c$	Compound noun (number + noun) + verb + adverbial (prep. + noun)
	[17]*rbt . ymsk . bmskh*	$a'\ (= x')\ d\ c'\ (= d)$	Noun (Num/A + verb (C) + adverbial (prep. + noun [PW/A])

This bicolon illustrates one of the advantages of close analysis and, especially, of the analysis of grammatical parallelism and may furthermore reveal one aspect of the psychology of poetic structure in Ugarit. The crucial point is the parallelism of *yqḥ* and *ymsk*. In my analysis of these lines prepared for class purposes some time before working out the present analysis, I more or less automatically analyzed the parallelism of *yqḥ* and *ymsk* as *b // b′* because of the grammatical and positional parallelism that exists between the two (both verbs, both in second position in the line). Only when forced by Geller's method to distinguish clearly between semantic and grammatical parallelism, did it dawn on me that *lqḥ* and *msk* are only sequentially or functionally parallel. It then became clear that what permits the use of a non-semantic parallel in this case is precisely the structure of the bicolon which led me first to analyze *yqḥ* and *ymsk* as *b // b′*: the form *ymsk* is so locked into the structure of the bicolon by its form and position that semantic parallelism may easily be dispensed with. Moreover, not only is *ymsk* locked in by the two abovementioned features, but the half-line repetitive parallelism with *bmskh* provides it with the strongest form of semantic parallelism, a (partially) repetitive one, which further reduces the need for *ymsk* to be provided with a semantic parallel elsewhere in the bicolon. Whether or not such considerations were consciously in the mind of the poet, something along these lines must have been intuitively present, for so strong and tightly interwoven a structure could hardly be the result of accident.

[35] For bibliography, see the article by Emerton cited in Ch. I, note 23.

As for the other parallelisms: *ʾalp* and *rbt* form a well-attested number parallel ("Num"). *ḫmr*, if a kind of wine, is in the "part-whole" relationship to *msk*; the primary semantic notation ("A") is based on the apparent collocation of the two roots (forms unsure) in Ps. 75:9.[36] For the cognate prepositional phrase *ymsk bmskh* it might be of interest to point out another one of the many literary parallels which occur between the Ugaritic texts and the Book of Revelation, in this case Rev. 18:6: ἐν τῷ ποτηρίῳ ᾧ ἐκέρασεν κεράσατε αὐτῇ διπλοῦν 'In the cup in which she mixed mix for her a double (draught)'. Finally, in the traditional notation by letters, "c′ (= d)" is applied to *bmskh* to make clear its double function in the semantic parallelism (primary parallelism with *ḫmr*, with virtually the same grammatical form and the same function; repetitive parallelism with *ymsk*).

IX.	[18]*qm . ybd . wyšr*	*a b b′*	$\text{Verb}_1 + \text{verb}_2$ (C to verb_1) + verb_3 (C to verb_1, A to verb_2)
	[19]*mṣltm . bd . nʿm*	*c d e*	Noun + compound adverbial (prep. + noun + noun) (*mṣltm* to *ybd wyšr* = C [WP ?])

This bicolon is the third of the three units beginning *qm-ndd-qm* + two verbs. Here the third verb is shorter, according to all methods of quantitative analysis, than in the two previous cases, which makes the grouping of the three verbs into one half-line more plausible than in the previous cases. Moreover, though there is no semantic (nor, for that matter, grammatical) parallelism with the second half-line in this bicolon, the grammatical and semantic structure of the surrounding bicola indicate that we should take lines 18-19 as a bicolon. This is an argument analogous to the one used in explaining the lack of semantic parallelism between *yqḥ* and *ymsk* in § VIII: just as the structure of the bicolon there permitted a loose semantic relationship between the two verbs in question, so the structure of the surrounding bicola (certainly bicola for grammatical and semantic reasons), permits § IX to be structured sequentially only, with neither of the lines being mistaken for members of other poetic units. On the other hand, one might describe the lack of parallelism in § IX in terms of the problem at hand for the poet: whether the two previous examples of the structure of line 18 are analyzed as bicola or tricola, there is little parallelism in either preceding case with what follows the three-verb sequence (*ybrd*, line 6, and *ytn ks*, line 10, do not provide primary parallelisms). If the first two cases are correctly analyzed

[36] Dahood, *RSP* I (1972) 186-87, though the meanings ascribed to the words in question are not correct (see O. Loretz, *UF* 4 [1972] 28).

as bicola, however, the three-verb sequence forms an independent poetic structure; when that structure was repeated in line 18 with a shorter verb in third position the problem was how to fill out the poetic structure. A loose parallelism could have been used, such as *ybrd* or *ytn ks*, but apparently even this concession to inter-line parallelism was felt to be unnecessary. Moreover, the macrostructure of §§ II, III and of §§ V, VI *is* followed in the section under discussion, though here it is much strengthened by being repetitive, rather than weak: *wyšlḥmnh* : *ybrd* :: *wyšqynh* : *ytn ks* :: *wyšr* : *wyšr*! It is to be noted that the verb following the three-verb sequence under discussion is in each case in the next poetic unit. (It is certainly so in the third case, and this may argue for the same being true in the first two cases.) In the first two cases the first three verbs formed an independent bicolon, whereas the brevity of the third verb in the third case required a (positionally, but not semantically) parallel line to intercede between the third verb and the fourth. Finally, it may be noted that the "parallelism" of § IX, though neither strongly semantic nor grammatical, is sequential and presents a unified image: a young man arises and sings, accompanying himself with an instrument. Thus there is a structure, a sequential rather than oppositional one. Non-parallel lines have always been an embarassment to students of Hebrew poetry, whence such terms as 'synthetic' parallelism. R. Jakobson's remarks regarding metrically "orphan lines" are applicable here: "... any word or clause when entering into a poem built on pervasive parallelism is, under the constraint of this system, immediately incorporated into the tenacious array of cohesive grammatical forms and semantic values. The metaphoric image of 'orphan lines' is a contrivance of a detached onlooker to whom the verbal art of continuous correspondences remains aesthetically alien. Orphan lines in poetry of pervasive parallels are a contradiction in terms, since whatever the status of a line, all its structure and functions are indissolubly interlaced with the near and distant verbal environment, and the task of linguistic analysis is to disclose the levers of this coaction. When seen from the inside of the parallelistic system, the supposed orphanhood, like any other componential status, turns into a network of multifarious compelling affinities."[37]

---

[37] "Grammatical Parallelism and Its Russian Facet," *Language* 42 (1966) 399-429, quotation from pp. 428-29. For a study of sequential parallelism (in the specific environment of partial semantic parallelism), see P. D. Miller, Jr., "Synonymous-Sequential Parallelism in the Psalms," *Biblica* 61 (1980) 256-60. On *mṣltm* as a weak semantic parallel (part to whole?) to *ybd wyšr*, see Ch. I, note 19, above. This weak semantic parallelism is, of course, part of the "sequential" parallelism discussed in the present comment.

X.	*[20]yšr . ǵzr . ṭb . ql*	*a b^3*	Verb + compound (noun + adj. + noun)
	[21]ʿl . bʿl . bṣrrt ṣpn .	*c d^2*	Adverbial (prep. + noun) + compound adverbial (prep. + noun + noun [no parallelism])

It is to be noted that, though there is no internal semantic or grammatical parallelism in this bicolon, there is near repetitive parallelism with both the preceding and the following bicola. Again, also, the structure is sequential (as in § IX), here grammatically stronger (prepositional complements rather than apposition). On the basis of the two bicola just discussed, then, one could conclude that what was necessary to create a poetic unit in Ugaritic was not a set form of parallelism in a set distribution, but (usually) some form of parallelism in any distribution. In order to perceive the structure, then, one must be aware of the various types of parallelism and must chart the various distributions.

XI.	*ytmr . bʿl [23]bnth .*	*a b c*	Verb + noun (subj.) + noun (obj.)
	yʿn . pdry [24]bt . ʾar .	*a′ b′* (= *x* + *c* + *y*)	Verb (B) + Compound (noun + noun [+ construct] + noun [WP/PN/epithet/D])

The parallel *ytmr*//*yʿn* is classified here as of secondary semantic proximity because it is not attested elsewhere.[38] From the perspective of semantics alone, however, Geller would probably classify the parallelism as primary, because the two verbs denote the same action, perhaps related to the more frequent nominal whole-part relationship (generic verb 'to see' in parallel with a denominative specific verb 'to eye'). The parallelism *bnth*//*pdry bt ʾar* includes elements of repetitive parallelism (*bnt*//*bt* ["D"]) and is "whole-part" (daughters // one daughter) and contains an epithet (*pdry* = *bt ʾar*).

1.4.1 *Grammatical Parallelism: Collins*[39]

I.	*ʿbd . ʾalʾiyn [3]bʿl*	V O	II C: ii)1
	sʾid . zbl . bʿl [4]ʾarṣ	V O	

---

[38] Dahood has proposed that this pair occurs in Job 22:29 (*RSP* II [1975] 6-7), but the existence of *ʾmr* 'to see' in Hebrew remains dubious.

[39] Reference in Introduction, note 2. I have varied my notation by using S = subject and O = object in place of Collins' NP¹ and NP² (NP = noun phrase), respectively. This is indubitably a travesty on Collins' attempt to base his poetic analysis on a transforma-

This formula denotes that the bicolon consists of two basic sentences of the same kind (line-type II), consisting of (optional) subject + verb + object (sentence-type C; omission of subject = ii; word-order V-O = 1). This specific line-type is attested 42 times in Collins' sample (p. 114), a relatively high number of occurrences.

II. *qm . yṯᶜr*	V V	Variation
[5]*w . yšlḥmnh*	V	

Collins' system deals only with poetic lines that consist of one or two sentences in the deep structure. On pp. 219-223 he deals with the variations from his system which consist of repeated verbs. The type V V // V does not occur in his examples (nor does the type V V V)—though there are types which contain three verbs plus other elements (see p. 222).

III. [6]*ybrd . ṯd . lpnwh*	V O M	III D: ii)1f
[7]*bḥrb . mlḥt* [8]*qṣ . mrʾi .*	M O	

Two basic sentences of the same kind with deletion of one or more elements in the second half-line (III), each consisting of (optional) subject + verb + object + modifer (D; form with subject omitted = ii), here consisting of verb + object + modifier in the first half-line (= 1) and of modifier + object in the second half-line (= f). A noun expressing the subject is usually not expressed in the line-type III D, leaving six possibilities of arrangement of the three remaining constituents (VOM) in the first half-line. Because of possibilities of arrangement plus deletion in the second half-line, there are nine possible forms, which, coupled with the six possibilities of arrangement in the first half-line, result in fifty-four possible line-types in III D (p. 152). Of these fifty-four, twenty are

tional syntactic analysis but, as E. Talstra has shown in his review of Collins (*BiOr* 41 [1984] 453-57), Collins' analyses were not thorough-going transformational analyses; my further simplification into a superficial structural analysis may, therefore, be permitted. Note that, in general, Collins and Geller are observing grammatical *parallelism*, that is, grammatical *likeness*, though grammatical dissimilarities do, of course, stand out clearly in a notation of likenesses. A. Berlin has turned the concept on its head by using the phrase "grammatical parallelism" to describe grammatical *dissimilarity*: "Grammatical Aspects of Biblical Parallelism," *HUCA* 50 (1979) 17-43 (see now also her *Dynamics of Biblical Parallelism* [ref. above Ch. I, note 1]); she has been followed by Watson in this orientation: *JSOT* 28 (1984) 90-91 (a list of types of grammatical dissimilarity). In my estimation, the process of analysis should begin from a perspective like those of Collins and Geller, that is, the critic should study how grammatical parallelism lines up in all its facets, alike, unlike and in between. As seen here in the charts on "Semantic Parallelism: Semantic Relationships" and "Semantic Parallelism: Grammatical Relationships" (for both texts), it is indeed the case that it is the grammatical dissimilarities which provide spice to the poetic structure, but grammatical regularity should no more go unnoticed than should semantic or phonetic regularity.

actually attested in Collins' sample. The two III D sentences in *ʿnt* I (for the second, see § V) are both types cited by Collins: III D: ii)1f is attested three times (Isa. 5:18; 60:18; Joel 3:3), while III D: ii)1e (here § V) is the most frequently attested, with forty-nine examples.

The alternative interpretation of the second half-line, according to which the form *qṣ* is analyzed as a verb,[40] gives a grammatical analysis of V O M // M V O (II D: ii)5), a line-type which is attested, but which is even rarer than the line-type adopted here (twice in Collins' sample: Isa. 11:4; 28:15 [p. 118]).

IV.	*ndd* [9]*yʿšr*.	V V	Variation
	wyšqynh	V	

See on § II, above.

V.	[10]*ytn . ks . bdh*	V O M	III D: ii)1e
	[11]*krpn . bklʾat . ydh*	O M	

For a description of the III D line-type, see note above on § III. III D: ii)1e varies from the type discussed above only in reversing the order of the elements in the second half-line (VOM // OM). As noted above, this is a very frequently attested line-type in Collins's sample, with forty-nine examples.

VI.	[12]*bk rb . ʿẓm . rʾi*	O	Variation
	dn[13]*mt . šmm*	M	

This bicolon is discussed along with § VII in the next note.

VII.	*ks . qdš* [14]*ltphnh . ʾaṯt .*	O (= O + [R] + V + S)	Variation
	krpn [15]*ltʿn . ʾaṯrt .*	O (= O + [R] + V + S)	

The proper notation of the two preceding bicola has caused me a great deal of thought. I at first considered noting § VI according to at least one level of the deep structure, where the relative nature of the phrase *ʿẓm rʾi* is at a higher level than that of *rb* (see note on § VI above in analysis of semantic parallelism), and taking the underlying relative clause as a modifier clause: *bk rb*/*ʿẓm rʾi* = O M(= [R] + NP).[41] This analysis is tempting for it results in a concatenation structure (Collins, pp. 225-26)

[40] De Moor, *Seasonal Pattern* (1971) 71.
[41] R = relative pronoun [here elided]; NP = noun phrase.

in which the extra poetic line is similar to the primary structure (here lines 10-12 = VOM // OM + OM . . . [42]). There are two main difficulties here, however. First, all attributive adjectives are forms of underlying relative clauses (*bk rb* 'the vessel [which is] great') and Collins' system does not note attributives and appositionals as modifier clauses. Second, there are constructions precisely like *ʿẓm rʾi* below in primary poetic units where the construction not only would not be thus noted by Collins but there would be no advantage to do so. I refer to *ṭb ql* in line 20, which is part of an expanded subject phrase, and *bt ʾar* in line 24, which is part of an expanded object phrase. I thus conclude that lines 12-13 are simply expanded forms of object phrases, line 12 consisting of two adjectival phrases (*rb*, *ʿẓm rʾi*), line 13 consisting of an explicit relative clause, genitival in nature, which are thus grammatically enjambed with lines 10-11 and quantitatively sufficient to form an independent bicolon.

The case with § VII is in one sense precisely like that of § VI, in another completely different. To deal first with the similarity: These lines continue as the description of the heavenly cup put into Baal's hand and the structure is a continuation of the grammatical enjambment begun in § VI. Moreover, § VII consists of a noun plus a modifying underlying relative clause, just as line 12 did (with the second half-line dependent on the first). Here is where the difference arises also, however, for the suppressed relative clause here is verbal and Collins' system does not allow for noun phrases which consist of N + V + N. I must confess that I do not now see how Collins would work these lines into his system of analysis. I do not, in any case, believe that we would arrive at anything meaningful by analyzing these lines as though they formed an independent grammatical structure. Such an analysis would give:

O V S 'Women may not see (this) holy cup,
O V S ʾAṯirat may not eye (this) goblet'.

This would be Collins' line-type II C: i)36 (II = two identical sentences; C = sentence-type S + V + O, in any order; i = subject is present; 36 = actual word-order OVS // OVS). This particular line-type is not attested in Collins' sample (pp. 111-112). In fact, of the twelve word-combinations possible with object in first position in the first half-line, only one is attested: OSV // OSV in Isa. 49:25. Though an extensive analysis of Ugaritic line-types would have to be done to validate such a conclusion, it does seem that the absence of this construction and the rarity of its congeners in Hebrew poetry serve as an indication that an

[42] If this analysis were adopted for lines 10-15, the concatenation would continue with only one variation (§ VIb would be M only) to the end of the unit: VOM // OM, OM // M, OM // OM.

analysis of § VII as an independent grammatical unit would be no more useful in Collins' system than it is in a traditional philological analysis. Geller's system employs a much more extensive notation of compounds and thus may be more useful in analyzing the different forms of expansion visible in lines 12-15; we will see, however, in analyzing this unit by Geller's system that the latter is so tied to the individual poetic units that it is of no use, as presently formulated, in analyzing extended structures as macrostructures.

VIII.	*ʾalp* [16]*kd . yqḥ . bḫmr*	O V M	II D: ii)15
	[17]*rbt . ymsk . bmskh*	O V M	

Two basic sentences of the same kind (II), consisting of subject + verb + object + modifier, in any order (D), here with subject omitted (ii), of the specific word-order OVM // OVM (15). In Collins' sampling there are three examples of this particular word-order (pp. 119-20: Ezek. 26:9; Hos. 2:10; 6:4), which, though not a high number, is the highest number of the general type II D: ii with object in first position of the first half-line (twelve possibilities of word worder; five of which are actually attested; with a total of nine attestations).

IX.	[18]*qm . ybd . wyšr*	V V V	Variation
	[19]*mṣltm . bd . nᶜm*	S M	

For a discussion of the structure of this bicolon, in comparison with §§ II and IV, see note above on semantic analysis. The grammatical analysis certainly is not at variance with the one proposed above (§ IX as an expanded form of II and IV), for § IX consists of two of Collins' variational types in juxtaposition: (1) the type which consists of more than one verb in a half-line (pp. 219-223), and (2) a nominal sentence (pp. 215-218). The "parallelism" of these lines is not, therefore, semantic or grammatical but positional (fitted between two otherwise identifiable bicola) and sequential (representing a given situation). For the possible semantic (whole-part?) but non-grammatical parallelism of *ybd yšr* // *mṣltm*, see above, "Semantic Parallelism: Semantic Relationships."

X.	[20]*yšr . ǵzr . ṭb . ql*	V S	I B: i)variation
	[21]*ᶜl . bᶜl . bṣrrt* [22]*ṣpn .*	M M	

One basic sentence (I), consisting of subject + verb + modifier (B), with the subject explicitly stated (i). The variations that Collins lists to this line-form consist of an extra modifier-phrase, with various word-orders (pp. 67-70). The variation which consists of two modifiers (rather than one) appears to be fairly frequent (eight verses listed on p. 68), though all of Collins' examples have the configuration VSM // M rather than VS // MM as here.

XI.	*ytmr . bʿl* [23]*bnth .*	V S O	II C: i)3e
	yʿn . pdry [24]*bt . ʾar .*	V O	

Two basic sentences of the same type with deletion of one or more elements in the second half-line, with the elements subject + verb + object in any order (C), with subject present (i), here in the specific order VSO // VO (3e). It is of interest that several of the III C: i) line-forms fall into what Collins calls "semantic sets," that is, the line-type is used to express rather broadly defined notions of a given type. For example, III C: i) may be divided into two main semantic sets: (1) "the activity of God in relation to man, especially as the judge of good and evil conduct"; (2) "the activity of various classes of persons judged from a moral standpoint" (p. 142). Though the present Ugaritic example apparently evinces no moral overtones (we do not know, of course, what follows), it certainly deals with the activity of a deity. Ugaritic poetry deserves an extensive analysis along the lines suggested by Collins in order to determine, among other things, whether the semantic sets observed in Hebrew line-types emerge in their Ugaritic counterparts.

1.4.1.1 *Conclusions Regarding Collins' Notation of Grammatical Parallelism*
At the end of this analysis of a segment of Ugaritic poetry according to Collins' method, it may be useful to make a few remarks. The first is that the system works and is useful in pointing up structural features and relationships of structures. On the other hand, the elevated number of completely and partially variated structures (6/11) indicated that Collins' system needs to be restated so as to include more forms of lines. The criticism that he voices against traditional semantic analysis, viz., that it tended to see type II forms as somehow paradigmatic (pp. 92-93), may be voiced against his own system. Taking into consideration only subject, verb, object, and modifier phrases, with only one appearance allowed for each, will only account for a minority of attested structures; Collins' figure of "approximately 40%" (p. 215) is remarkably similar to the result of this small sample from Ugaritic (five out of eleven poetic units fall unvaried into Collins' categories, which is about 45%; the percentage goes up to 54 if § X is counted amoung the major types). It is also to be noted that the five bicola which are analyzable by Collins' system all fall into regular categories, as does the variant form in § X. The other main

types of structures which have emerged from this sample as needing regular notations have already been recognized by Collins: units with more than one verb in a half-line and concatenations (pp. 215-26). § X illustrates the need for a regular notation for multiple occurrences of grammatical elements other than verbs. §§ VI, VII, though a concatenation, illustrate the need for an analysis and notation of relative clauses, with the relativization both marked and deleted. Finally, though no independent nominal clauses appeared in this sample, Collins' recognition of this feature and its regular appearance in all the Northwest Semitic languages point up the necessity of a notational system for these sentences which would be more explicit than that proposed briefly by Collins (pp. 215-18).

1.4.2 *Grammatical Parallelism: Geller*[43]

I. *ᶜbd . ᵓalᵓiyn* [3]*bᶜl*
sᵓid . zbl . bᶜl [4]*ᵓarṣ .*

Grammatical structure: a 2 ,=2pn
a 2 ,=2pn-C
Transformation: none
Addition: none
Comparison: a:a::A (Syn)
2 ,=2pn : 2 ,=2pn-C :: A/A̸ (Epith; Epith-D)
Result: Formula: A/A/A̸
Deletion-Compensation: none
Semantic parallelism: Syn; Epith-D
Transformation: none

In the notation of the grammatical structure, a denotes a transitive verb, 2 a direct object, ,=2pn a proper noun (pn) as direct object (2) in apposition with preceding word (,=), and -C the *nomen rectum* of a construct phrase.

Transformation: If any transformation (such as passive to active) is required in order to align the grammatical structure of one half-line with the other, it is noted here.

[43] See above Introduction, note 2 for complete reference and Ch. I, note 23 for differences between my notation of Geller's categories and his own conventions. A further deviation that appears in this chart is the presentation of what Geller calls the "reconstructed sentence." I have only given a reconstruction when the reconstructed form of the verse is significantly different from the actual form in the verse and furthermore have given the reconstruction as a verse rather than as a single sentence with bivalent elements. See example below at § III and Ch. II, note 24 on the notation of the "reconstructed sentence" in the biblical sample text.

Addition: If any addition is necessary to render the grammatical structure of the half-line comparable, it is noted here, e.g., a "deletion" as below in § III.

Comparison: Each grammatical parallelism is now compared for semantic value: a:a::A denotes that the two transitive verbs are in a primary semantic relationship; 2 ,=2pn : 2 ,=2pn-C :: A/A̸ (Epith; Epith-D) denotes that a compound consisting of a direct object in apposition with a proper name is in parallel with a double compound which consists of a direct object in apposition with a proper name which is followed by a noun in the construct relationship. Geller distinguishes three main types of relationships between compounds in the two half-lines of a bi-colon: 1) the elements are interchangeable, both grammatically and semantically; 2) the elements are grammatically interchangeable but semantic constraints make a sentence wherein the interchange is effected nonsensical; 3) the elements are not interchangeable for grammatical reasons (pp. 18-20). He further considers that compounds which are parallel to non-compounds are indivisible (p. 19), one must assume because the zero element in the simple expression precludes interchangeability with an expressed element in the compound, though this is not stated specifically. In Geller's notational system the relationship between various simple and compound phrases is marked by a slash ("virgule") placed with relationship to the letter marking semantic relationship: /A = simple phrase in parallel with a compound phrase; A/ = compound in parallel with simple phrase, etc. When the parallelism is between two compounds, the presence or absence of interchangeability may be indicated: a simple slash indicates interchangeability (A/A); a hyphenated slash indicates semantic constraints (A/̶A); a slash through the letter (A̸) indicates both semantic and grammatical constraints (p. 48). This system of notation has two major ambiguities. The first is that the slash indicates both "compound" and "divisible compound." Thus "/A" indicates simple phrase // compound (which is by nature indivisible—p. 19), while "A/A" indicates compound // compound with interchangeable elements. In the first case, the slash indicates "compound" (which is to be understood from other considerations to be indivisible) while in the second it indicates a divisible relationship between the two compounds. The second ambiguity is directly related to the first: Both a slash and a slash through the letter are used to indicate indivisibility owing to a simple phrase vs. compound relationship. The simple slash is used when the relationship is simple vs. compound (/A = simple // compound, etc.), while the slash through the letter is used when the relationship is compound vs. compound (e.g., A/A̸ = compound vs. double compound). The only way that I can make sense of the latter notation is to interpret it as meaning that two sets of the elements in the compounds are interchangeable, while the constitutive elements of the double compound are not interchangeable with anything in the parallel half-line because there are fewer elements there, i.e., because it is basically a single vs. compound relationship. For example, one of the compound // double compound parallelisms listed on p. 330 is *pʾt mʾb* // *qdqd kl bny št* (Num. 24:17) 'the temples of Moab // the pate of all the sons of Sheth'. This is clearly divisible into

pʾt	*mʾb*
qdqd	*kl bny št*

where the four boxes are interchangeable vertically. The phrase *kl bny št*, however, is indivisible because its relationship to *mʾb* is that of compound vs. simple phrase. Thus both the simple slash (/A) and the slash through a letter (A/A̸) are used to indicate the same basic phenomenon. If one works this through, one soon realizes that it would be impossible to note the indivisibility of an entire compound // double compound relationship because the sign for indivisibility (slash through the letter) has already been used to indicate the indivisibility of one part of that relationship. Thus Geller lists A/A̸ for compound // double compound in which two of the compound elements in each line are interchangeable, and he lists A̸/A̸ for compound // double compound where semantic constraints disallow interchange (p. 49), but there is no listing for indivisibility of an entire compound // double compound, i.e., no way of indicating that not only the embedded simple vs. compound relationship may not be divided, but that the compounds themselves may not be divided and interchanged for both grammatical and semantic reasons. I assume that this system was adopted because in fact no situations arose in Geller's corpus which required that both forms of indivisibility be noted for parallel compounds. This does not, however, permit someone who is proposing a new system to use an ambiguous notational system, for the next person who tries his hand at the system may be confused. (It took me many hours to come up with the solution just given and, since Geller does not explain his notations in detail, even this explanation may be faulty.)

However that may be, the present line of the Ugaritic poem may be divided

ʾalʾiyn	*bᶜl*
zbl	*bᶜl ʾarṣ*

where the four units are grammatically and semantically interchangeable on the vertical plane—indeed, because of the appositional nature of the phrases, the units could be exchanged horizontally (semantically and grammatically). It should be obvious that in this particular case the indivisibility of *bʿl ʾarṣ* is owing uniquely to its parallel position with a simple phrase—there is no semantic or grammatical reason why *ʾarṣ* could not interchange with the blank space after *bʿl* at the end of the first half-line. The reason for the presence of *ʾarṣ* at the end of the second half-line may lie in what Geller calls "compensation," i.e., *zbl* is at least one syllable and perhaps two shorter than *ʾalʾiyn* (depending on the proper vocalization of *zbl*) and *ʾarṣ* thus may function as a space filler. (This function of *ʾarṣ*, if no other, precludes the interchange of Ø and *ʾarṣ*.)

There is a further problem in the notation of this particular line: the partial repetitive parallelism left me uncertain as to whether the proper notation is A/A̸ or A/D̸. I have patterned my notation on *ʾl* // *ʾlhy ʾby* in Exod. 15:2, which Geller analyzes as /A (Epith-"D") (p. 75—the quotation marks around D mark "virtual identity" [p. 37]). Thus *bʿl* // *bʿl ʾarṣ* might be marked as a primary parallelism in Geller's system, with the repetitive parallelism as only a constitutive element.

Result: Finally the results are summed up in four stages: The formula for the parallelism of the two half-lines is given as a summary of the preceding steps: "A" refers to the parallelism of *ʿbd* and *sʾid*; "A/A̸" to the parallelism of *ʾalʾiyn bʿl* and *zbl bʿl ʾarṣ*. Next, any grammatical element which was "deleted" from one or the other of the half-lines is noted, along with the means used to compensate quantitatively in the other half-line (none here; see below for examples). Third, the semantic features of the parallelism are summarized: "Syn" indicated that *ʿbd* and *sʾid* are synonymous; "Epith-D" that *ʾalʾiyn bʿl* and *zbl bʿl ʾarṣ* contain epithets and repetitive parallelism. Fourth, any transformations (passive to active, etc.) required to represent the deep structure of the line are noted (none here; none below; see Geller for examples).

II. *qm . yṯʿr*
[5]*w . yšlḥmnh*
Grammatical structure: b a
ptcl a-s
Transformation: none
Addition: none
Comparison: b a : ptcl a-s :: B/ (list)
Result: Formula: B/
Deletion-Compensation: none
Semantic parallelism: list
Transformation: none

In the notation of grammatical structure, b denotes an intransitive verb, a denotes a transitive verb, and a-s denotes a transitive verb plus pronominal suffix.

Comparison: I am assuming that Geller would consider *qm yṯʿr* to be a form of verbal hendiadys, and thus a compound.[44] I have retained "B" as a notation for parallelisms elsewhere unattested.[45] The slash ("virgule") following the B indicates that the relationship is compound // simple. "List" is one category of parallelism proposed by Geller, corresponding to some extent to the older "synthetic" parallelism. Though *ṯʿr* and *šlḥm* are closely associated and may in one sense be considered synonymous, in another sense they form a sequence of actions, a list, especially when taken together with *qm*. It should be noted that this perception of the semantic parallelism emerges from Geller's grammatical analysis—which led me to analyze *qm yṯʿr* as a compound—and that it is a different perspective on the parallelism than that which emerged from the strictly semantic analysis (semantic: a b // b′; grammatico-semantic: a → b // b′; grammatico-metrico-semantic: a + b // b′). Note further that the length compensation in the longer verb in third position may be included in Geller's formula (cf. pp. 49-51). Finally, an alternative analysis of this bicolon is possible in Geller's system: the first two verbs could be taken as separate entities rather than as elements of a compound; in which case the first verb would be noted as "deleted" in the second half-line:

qm yṯʿr
(*qm*) *wyšlḥmnh*

The syntactic structure of the three-verb sequence, however, with *w* marking the last element, seems to indicate that the sequence was perceived as a list rather than as two separate statements. The basic problem here, of course, is the uniquely verbal structure of the bicolon, which permits semantic variation and parallelism but does not permit deletion/compensation of major grammatical elements. (For Geller's method of notation of deletion/compensation, see note on next bicolon. In "Length Compensation" below, I have noted the "deletion-compensation" according to the semantic analysis just discussed rather than according to the primarily grammatical analysis which here above resulted in taking *qm yṯʿr* as a compound.)

---

[44] For "coordinated . . . verbs" as a category of compounding, see Geller, p. 21.
[45] See above, Ch. I, note 23.

III. [6]*ybrd . ṯd . lpnwh*
[7]*bḥrb . mlḥt* [8]*qṣ . mrʾi .*
Grammatical structure: a 2 3-s
3,-3 2-c
Transformation: none
Addition: + a
Reconstructed sentence: *ybrd ṯd lpnwh*
(*ybrd*) *bḥrb mlḥt qṣ mrʾi*
Comparison: (a : a :: D)
2 : 2-c :: /A (WP)
3-s : 3,-3 :: /C
+ compensation
Result: Formula: /A /C (D)
Deletion-compensation: - a + compensation
Semantic parallelism: WP; none
Transformation: none

For the sigla in the notation of the grammatical structure, a = transitive verb, 2 = (direct) object, 3-s = adverbial phrase + pronominal suffix, 3,-3 = adverial + attributive + adjective, 2-c = (direct) object + *nomen regens*. Geller does not give a separate listing for adjectives, but he does give ",-" as the siglum for attributives (p. 55) and on p. 81 he analyzes *bmym ʾdrm* (Exod. 15:10) "in the terrible waters" in the manner indicated above (3,-3), apparently meaning to state that the attributive adjective is in apposition with the noun it modifies and thus has the same syntactic function.

Addition: "+ a" indicates that the transitive verb *ybrd* is without parallel in the second half-line and is thus considered "deleted" from that half-line and to be restored in the reconstructed sentence.

Reconstructed sentence: Geller gives his reconstructed sentence in the following format:

ybrd *ṯd lpnwh*
bḥrb mlḥt qṣ mrʾi

Comparison: Geller indicates the restored deletion in his "comparison" section. Since the restored word is the same as the one in the explicit half-line, it is of course a repetition and is thus semantically D. Because one of the two like elements is reconstructed, the parallelism x : x :: D is given in parentheses.

/A (WP) = simple // compound in primary semantic relationship, with a relationship of the two phrases of whole to part (see note to § III above at "Semantic Parallelism: Geller's Categories").

/C = simple // compound of dissimilar semantic relationship (on the semantic dissimilarity, see note referred to in preceding paragraph). Geller's method is not especially enlightening on this particular point except in so far as it points up that *lpnwh* and *bḥrb mlḥt* occupy a similar syntactic slot (though even from that perspective, the locative versus instrumental function is a major difference), something that the most cursory philological analysis would show.

+ compensation = the deletion of *ybrd* in the second half-line is compensated for by increased length in the compound phrases in the second half-line.

Result: Deletion-compensation: -a + compensation = a transitive verb has been deleted and "metrical compensation" has taken place elsewhere (here in the two compound phrases in the second half-line parallel to simple phrases in the first half-line).

IV. Same structure, analysis, and problems as in § II.

V. [10]*ytn . ks . bdh*
[11]*krpn . bklᵓat . ydh*

Grammatical structure: a 2 3-s
2 3-C-s
Transformation: none
Addition: + a
Reconstructed sentence: *ytn ks bdh*
(*ytn*) *krpn bklᵓat ydh*
Comparison: (a : a :: D)
2 : 2 :: A (list)
3-s : 3-C-s :: /"D" ("D" = Num)
+ compensation
Result: Formula: A /"D" (D)
Deletion-Compensation: -a + compensation
Semantic parallelism: List; "D" = Num
Transformation: none

In the notation of the grammatical structure, a = transitive verb, 2 = (direct) object, 3-s = adverbial phrase + pronominal suffix, 3-C-s = adverbial phrase + noun in construct relationship + pronominal suffix.

Addition: a transitive verb is "added" to the second half-line, as is noted in the reconstructed sentence.

Comparison: "D" denotes "virtual identity" (p. 37). The "D" is chosen over D here because it is 'hand' vs. 'two hands' (and is thus a "number" relationship, hence the abbreviation "Num") or else 'two hands' (marked by dual) vs. 'two hands' (marked lexically).

Result: Deletion-compensation: the compensation is in the compound form for 'two hands' in the second half-line.

VI. [12]*bk rb . ʿẓm . rʾi*
dn[13]*mt . šmm .*

Grammatical structure: 2 ,-2 ,-2-C
rel. pr. 3-C

Result: Non-parallel sentence (enjambment + nominal clause + relative clause)

In the notation of the grammatical structure, 2 = direct object (here, with enjambment, *bk* is the direct object of *ytn* in the preceding bicolon), ,-2 = attributive adjective (,- = attributive, 2 = direct object, i.e., if I have understood Geller's notation correctly, the attributive is indicated as playing the same major syntactic role as the noun it modifies), ,-2-C = attributive modifier in construct; rel. pr. = relative pronoun, 3-C = adverbial in construct (I am considering the genitive relative to be an adverbial clause).

Result: Non-parallel sentence: This is Geller's notation for sentences that do not have sufficient parallelism to permit analysis according to parallelistic criteria (cf., e.g., pp. 62, 66). Note that this attention to grammatical parallelism glosses over the weak part-whole semantic parallelism of *bk* and *nmt* (see above "Semantic Parallelism: Semantic Relationships" and "Semantic Parallelism: Grammatical Relationships").

VII. *ks . qdš* [14]*ltphnh . ʾaṯt .*
krpn [15]*ltʿn . ʾaṯrt .*

Grammatical structure: 2-C ,-R (neg a-s 1)
2 ,-R (neg a-s 1)

Transformation: none

Addition: none

Comparison: 2-C : 2 :: A/ (list)
,-R (neg a-s 1) : ,-R (neg a-s 1) :: A/B (WP-PN)

Result: Formula: A/ A/B
Deletion-Compensation: none
Semantic parallelism: list; WP-PN
Transformation: none

The sigla in the grammatical structure are: 2-c = direct object (here, of the verb *ytn* in the second preceding bicolon) + noun in construct, ,-R

= relative clause not preceded by a relative pronoun, neg a-s 1 = negative adverb + transitive verb + pronominal suffix + subject. The two half-lines are identical in structure except for the noun *qdš* which modifies *ks* in the first half-line.

Comparison: For a discussion of the semantic relationships in this bicolon, see note above in "Semantic Parallelism: Geller's Categories." There is no "Deletion-Compensation" according to Geller's notational system, for there is no major syntactic entity missing in the second half-line. There is, however, definite "metric" deletion-compensation (in this case compensation-deletion!), in the pair *ks qdš* // *krpn*. As for the suppressed relative clauses, I believe from Geller's statement on p. 20 and from his treatments of Deut. 32:15 and 32:35 (pp. 120, 136), that he would treat clauses as compounds. Thus A/B = (two-word) compound // (two-word) compound, with the second elements unattested elsewhere as a parallel pair.

VIII. *ʾalp* [16]*kd . yqḥ . bḫmr*
[17]*rbt . ymsk . bmskh*

Grammatical structure: 2-C a 3
2 a 3-s

Transformation: none
Addition: none
Comparison: 2-C : 2 :: A/ (Num)
a : a :: C (sequence)
3 : 3-s :: A (PW)
Result: Formula: A/ C A
Deletion-Compensation: none
Semantic parallelism: Num; sequence; PW
Transformation: none

The sigla used in noting the grammatical structure are: 2-C = direct object + noun in construct, a = transitive verb, 3 = adverbial (prepositional) phrase. The second line is similar, with a simple direct object phrase and a pronominal suffix on the adverbial (prepositional) phrase.

Comparison: For the semantic analysis, see above on § VIII in the section "Semantic Parallelism: Geller's Categories"—the term "sequence" is not Geller's; its usage should be clear from the note just cited. It should be remarked that Geller's system has no means of pointing up the half-line repetitive parallelism *ymsk bmskh*.

IX. [18]*qm . ybd . wyšr*
[19]*mṣltm . bd . nʿm*

Grammatical structure: b b b
S 3-C

Result: Non-parallel sentence (VP + VP + VP + NP)

Sigla: b = intransitive verb; S = subject of nominal sentence; 3-C = adverbial phrase + construct noun.

Geller's analysis appears more specific than any discussed so far in that it distinguishes intransitive from transitive verbs. On the other hand, it is no better equipped than is Collins' system to deal with the poetic structure of this bicolon. As shown above (note to § IX in "Semantic Parallelism: Geller's Categories"), only "distant parallelism," which points up the comparable structure of §§ II, IV, and IX, and "positional parallelism," which locks this bicolon in between more tightly structured units, can show the place of this bicolon within the larger structure of the poem.

X. [20]*yšr . ǵzr . ṭb . ql*
[21]*ᶜl . bᶜl . bṣrrt* [22]*ṣpn*

Grammatical structure: b 1 ,-C
3 3-C

Result: Non-parallel sentence (VP + NP + modifier phrases)

The sigla are: b = intransitive verb, 1 = subject of said, ,-C = attributive adjective + construct noun, 3 = adverbial phrase, 3-C = adverbial with construct noun.

XI. *ytmr . bᶜl* [23]*bnth .*
yᶜn . pdry [24]*bt . ʾar .*

Grammatical structure: a 1 2
a 2 ,=2-C
\+ compensation

Transformation: none

Addition: + 1

Reconstructed sentence: *ytmr bᶜl bnth*
yᶜn (bᶜl) pdry bt ʾar

Comparison: a : a :: B (WP)
(1 : 1 :: D)
2 : 2 ,=2-C :: /A̸ (WP-PN "D")
\+ compensation

Result: Formula: B /A̸ (D)
Deletion-Compensation: -1 + compensation
Semantic Parallelism: WP; WP-PN ("D")
Transformation: none

The sigla used in notation of the grammatical structure are: a = transitive verb, 1 = subject of said, 2 = direct object of said, ,=2-C = second direct object in apposition with first direct object in the second half line + construct.

Addition: " + 1" indicates that a subject must be added to the second half-line in order to achieve the reconstructed full sentence. Geller's presentation of this full sentence would be:

ytmr *bʿl* *bnth*
yʿn *pdry bt ʾar*

Comparison: The categories of semantic parallelism assigned here are explained above in "Semantic Parallelism: Geller's Categories." The notation "/A̸" is for simple phrase // double compound (the first slash denotes compound, while its position denotes indivisibility; the second slash denotes the second compound—its position through the letter also denotes indivisibility). The Whole/Part relationship here is of a special type, that of a category followed by the proper name of a member of that category (Geller, pp. 39-40). The repetitive parallelism is noted in the semantic parallelism as "D," i.e., according to Geller's system, virtual identity (the forms *bnt-* and *bt* are different in grammatical number). The compensation for the "missing" subject in the second half-line is, of course, found in the expanded object phrase (*bnth // pdry bt ʾar*).

1.4.2.1 *Frequency of Formulae in ʿnt I as Compared with Geller's Sample*[46]

I. A A/A̸ = minor configuration (one case, Geller, p. 291)
II. B/ = minor configuration (no cases of 2 // 1)
III. /A /C (D) = minor configuration (no cases in Geller)[47]
IV. B/ = II.

[46] Part III of Geller's book deals in part with "Unit Formulae" (pp. 231-94). Much of that classification and discussion concerns the various combinations of grammatical and "metrical" units, the latter element of which is not indicated here. It does appear useful, however, to list the formulae obtained above (without the metrical component of Geller's notation) and to indicate whether the formula is a major or a minor one. A major formula is one attested at least five times in Geller's corpus (p. 231). It is the configuration of parallel elements that is considered major or minor, not the actual distribution of semantic grades. Thus the first listed major formula is "xxx" (p. 235), which may appear as "AAA," "AAB," "DAA," et cetera. The one formula of a major type in *ʿnt* I (§ V) is found with precisely the same formual in Gen. 4:24 (Geller, p. 249), though the grammatical entities which fall into this configuration are different in the Ugaritic and biblical passages. Semantic grades applied to weak semantic and non-grammatical parallels in the section above on "Semantic Parallelism: Geller's Categories" (§§ VI, IX) will not show up here. The combination of semantic weakness and grammatical dissimilarity would probably have caused them to be classified as non-parallel by Geller.

[47] There are three cases in Geller's sample texts for the formula "/A/A(D)": Exod. 15:14 (p. 85); Num. 23:7a (pp. 91-92); 2 Sam. 22:21 (pp. 179-80); for the list, see p. 292.

V. A /"D" (D) = major configuration
VI. Non-parallel
VII. A/ A/B = minor configuration (no cases in Geller)[48]
VIII. A/ C A = minor configuration (no cases in Geller)[49]
IX. Non-parallel
X. Non-parallel
XI. B /X̸ (D) = minor configuration (no cases in Geller)

1.4.2.2 *Summary Conclusions Regarding the Applicability of Geller's System to Ugaritic poetry*

1. The incidence of "minor" configurations leads one to believe that, at least in the matter of compounding, the Ugaritic poet's typical production was different from that of the Hebrew poets studied by Geller.
2. The higher incidence of "B" and "C" grade parallelism indicates less adherence to poetic formulae (though my usage of "B" for poetic pairs that are, however good, simply unattested, resulted in a higher incidence of "B's" than would following Geller's system strictly).
3. There is a much higher incidence of non-parallel configurations in my sample than in Geller's (much larger) sample: 27%, as opposed to 12% (Geller, p. 30).
4. Because Geller's system states parallelism first in terms of grammatical parallelism it can miss semantic parallels that show serious grammatical disparity (§§ VI and XI in *ʿnt* I; one clear example in Proverbs 2). The defect is not, of course, so serious as in Collins's system, which plots only major grammatical constituents and ignores semantic parallelism altogether.

1.4.3 *Grammatical Parallelism: Kaiser*[50]

	Verb	Subject	Object	Modifier
I.	*ʿbd*		*ʾalʾiyn* [3]*bʿl*	
	sʾid		*zbl bʿl* [4]*ʾarṣ*	
II.	*qm*			
	yṯʿr			
	[5]*wyšlḥmnh*			

[48] "/xx/x" exists (Geller, p. 292), as does "x/x/x(D)" (Geller, p. 294), but I have not found the configuration of § VII (compound // simple; compound // compound, grammatically and semantically interchangeable).

[49] The closest configuration to this one that I have been able to find in Geller is "xx/x" (i.e., simple // simple; simple // simple; simple // compound) in Judg. 5:28b and Ps. 89:7 (see pp. 161-62, 219, 294).

[50] The system of notation in the following chart was developed by Barbara Kaiser in an unpublished University of Chicago dissertation entitled "Reconsidering Parallelism: A Study of the Structure of Lamentations 1, 2, and 4" (1983).

	Verb	Subject	Object	Modifier
III.	[6]*ybrd*		*ṯd*	*lpnwh*
				[7]*bḥrb mlḥt*
			[8]*qṣ mrʾi*	
IV.	*ndd*			
	[9]*yʿšr*			
	wyšqynh			
V.	[10]*ytn*		*ks*	*bdh*
			[11]*krpn*	*bklʾat ydh*
VI.			[12]*bk rb ʿẓm rʾi*	
				dn[13]*mt šmm*
VII.			*ks qdš*	
	[14]*ltphnh*[51]	*ʾaṯt*		
			krpn	
	[15]*ltʿn*	*ʾaṯrt*		
VIII.			*ʾalp* [16]*kd*	
	yqḥ			
				bḫmr
			[17]*rbt*	
	ymsk			*bmskh*
IX.	[18]*qm*			
	ybd			
	wyšr			
		[19]*mṣltm*[52]		*bd nʿm*
X.	[20]*yšr*	*ǵzr ṭb ql*		
				[21]*ʿl bʿl*
				bṣrrt ṣpn
XI.	*ytmr*	*bʿl*	[23]*bnth*	
	yʿn		*pdry* [24]*bt ʾar*	

To read this chart, one scans horizontally and reads as many words as are contained in a given line. If the grammatical elements occur in an order different from the arrangement at the top of the page, they are put into more than one horizontal line so that one may constantly read an entire horizontal line then skip to the next, always finding a continuous reading of the Ugaritic text.

Kaiser's system of notation has the advantage of making large trends immediately visible. The most obvious trend here is the small number of entries in the "subject" column. Indeed, even the first three entries that are in that column belong outside the major structure of the poem: *ʾaṯt* and *ʾaṯrt* are both the subject of modifier clauses (relative clauses with the relative pronoun suppressed), while *mṣltm* is the subject of a nominal sentence which stands in opposition to the third of the the three triple-verb sequences of §§ II, IV, and IX (see footnotes 51 and 52). At last,

[51] This verb and its parallel are here listed as verbs, though their place in the larger structure is within relative clauses which serve as modifier clauses to *ks qdš* and *krpn*.

[52] *mṣltm* serves as subject of the complete nominal sentence "cymbals (were) in the hands of the goodly one"; but that nominal sentence also serves as a modifier phrase to the verbs in the first half-line ('he sang with cymbals in his hands').

in line 20, we find a subject stated explicitly (*ǵzr ṭb ql*)—perhaps the same personage as the subject of lines 2-19.[53]

Another obvious conclusion derivable from Kaiser's system as applied to this text is the preponderance of verbs. In this respect *ʿnt* I is somewhat like Kaiser's own first section, Lamentations 2:1-8[b], where *YHWH* or *ʾdny* is always the subject (explicitly mentioned, however, more frequently than is a subject in the text under discussion here, viz., six times in all), with many verbal expression (twenty-nine). The *ʿnt* text has one explicit subject in the first twenty-one lines (*ǵzr ṭb ql*—excluding the relative clauses of § VII), with sixteen verbal expressions (again excluding the verbs of § VII).

One of the major difficulties of Kaiser's notation lies in the order of major constituent elements. V-S-O may be the least marked order for a prose sentence, but should it be made normative for poetry? On the other hand, the real problem lies not so much, perhaps, in deciding what the normative word order is as in imposing any order, for purposes of analysis, on a poem. In standard analysis, and even more so in Geller's system, it is the order of the first half-line of any unit that is of primary importance (e.g., the letters a, b, c, neutral as to word order, are used to indicate parallelisms in standard analysis). Collins' system, which observes the same major constituents as does Kaiser, simply notes them in the order in which they appear and his rendering of § VII is thus much easier to follow (OVS // OVS) than is the staggered notation of Kaiser's system. (One can argue, of course, that the "abnormal" word order that stands out so clearly in Kaiser's notation is owing to the enjambment and relativization of § VII and that her system is thus more illuminating than Collins'.) It is thus somewhat difficult to compare these two notational systems, with Collins stressing first the *presence* of certain elements and only secondarily their order, while the very nature of Kaiser's system necessitates a classification according to order. One major difference between Kaiser's notation and that of both Geller and Collins, is that the latter lead to various kinds of formulae and quantifications of formulae while Kaiser passes directly (and only) to commentary. It is thus a physical reorganization of the text itself, which can be illuminating but which does not, at least as used by Kaiser herself, result in the recognition of grammatical and syntactic patterns with the detail and nicety of Geller's and Collins' systems.

---

[53] Or the subject of the verbs of those lines may be different and it would have been found in the broken section preceding the extant line 1. Some consider *prdmn* to be that subject (cf. *TO* [1974] 153).

1.4.4 *Grammatical Parallelism: O'Connor*[54]

I.	*ʿbd . ʾalʾiyn* [3]*bʿl*	1 clause/2 constituents/3 units[55]
	sʾid . zbl . bʿl [4]*ʾarṣ*	1 clause/2 constituents/4 units
II.	*qm . yṯʿr*	2 clauses/2 constituents/2 units
	[5]*w . yšlḥmnh*	1 clause/1 constituent/1 unit
III.	[6]*ybrd . ṯd . lpnwh*	1 clause/3 constituents/3 units
	[7]*bḥrb . mlḥt* [8]*qṣ . mrʾi*	0 clause/2 constituents/4 units
IV.	*ndd* [9]*yʿšr .*	2 clauses/2 constituents/2 units
	wyšqynh	1 clause/1 constituent/1 unit
V.	[10]*ytn . ks . bdh*	1 clause/3 constituents/3 units
	[11]*krpn . bklʾat . ydh*	0 clause/2 constituents/3 units
VI.	[12]*bk . rb . ʿẓm . rʾi*	0 clause/2 constituents/4 units
	dn[13]*mt . šmm .*	0 clause/2 constituents/2 units
VII.	*ks . qdš* [14]*ltphnh . ʾaṯt .*	1 clause/3 constituents/4 units
	krpn [15]*ltʿn . ʾaṯrt*	1 clause/3 constituents/3 units
VIII.	*ʾalp* [16]*kd . yqḥ . bḫmr*	1 clause/3 constituents/4 units
	[17]*rbt . ymsk . bmskh*	1 clause/3 constituents/3 units
IX.	[18]*qm . ybd . qyšr*	3 clauses/3 constituents/3 units
	[19]*mṣltm . bd . nʿm*	1 clause/2 constituents/3 units
X.	[20]*yšr . ǵzr . ṭb . ql*	1 clause/2 constituents/4 units
	[21]*ʿl . bʿl . bṣrrt ṣpn*	0 clause/2 constituents/3 units
IX.	*ytmr . bʿl* [23]*bnth*	1 clause/3 constituents/3 units
	yʿn . pdry [24]*bt . ʾar .*	1 clause/2 constituents/4 units

O'Connor's system of line division is based on syntactic constraints which are expressed in terms of three levels of syntactic analysis, the word, the phrase, and the clause. O'Connor's definitions of these three levels are as follows:

---

[54] Reference above in Introduction, note 2. O'Connor's most original contribution to the study of Hebrew poetry is his perception of a system of syntactic constraints which would have given inside and outside limits to the number of syntactic elements which may occur in a line of Hebrew poetry. I have not considered O'Connor's study of "tropes" (semantic parallelism) because of their limitations both as compared with other analyses of semantic parallelism (e.g., Geller's and Kugel's, to cite opposite extremes) and as compared with a systematic study of distributions of parallelism. See reference to Kugel in Introduction, note 2, my review of O'Connor cited in Ch. I, note 7, and Ch. III, note 4, below.

[55] The definitions of "clause," "constituent," and "unit" are given in the comments below.

a *unit* consists of an individual verb or substantive, along with dependent particles
a *constituent* is a verbal or nominal phrase, along with dependent particles
a *clause* is a) a verbal clause, of which the verb is the predicator; b) a nominal clause, with no expressed predicator[56]

These syntactic levels operate under constraints which O'Connor defines as follows:

on *clause predicators*: no line contains more than three[57]
on *constituents*: no line contains fewer than one or more than four
on *units*: no line contains fewer than two or more than five
on *units of constituents*: no more than four units in a constituent . . .
on *constituents of clauses*: no line of three clause predicators contains any dependent nominal phrases . . .
on *integrity of lines*: if a line contains one or more clause predicators, it contains only nominal phrases dependent on them[58]

Comparing the constraints which emerged from O'Connor's sample with the syntactic analysis of *ʿnt* I according to O'Connor's system given above, gives the following results:

no line contains more than three *clause predicators*
no line contains fewer than one or more than four *constituents*
two lines (§ IIb and § IVb) contain fewer than two but no line contains more than five *units*
no *constituent* contains more than four *units*
the one line which contains three *clause predicators* (§ IXa) does not contain a *dependent nominal phrase*
no line with one or more *clause predicators* contains a *nominal phrase not dependent* on it/them

The clear negative result of this analysis is that §§ II, IV, which have already shown up as difficult in both Collins' and Geller's systems, are the ones which violate O'Connor's constraint on units. The division of lines given here was, as indicated above, reached by a combination of quantitative, philological, and macro-structural considerations. A larger corpus of Ugaritic poetry would have to be analyzed by O'Connor's method before we would be able to decide whether the method is valid and requires a re-analysis of my §§ II and IV more directly on the model of § IX or if O'Connor's constraints have been too rigidly defined. It must be said, however, that with the exception of these two highly debatable instances, O'Connor's constraints describe very well this par-

---

[56] O'Connor, p. 68.
[57] Note that O'Connor's "line" is my "half-line."
[58] O'Connor, p. 87.

ticular sample cut and one is therefore tempted to say that they are generally valid ones. Even if they do not correctly describe all Ugaritic lines (if, in the present case, §§ II and IV should prove to be correctly analyzed as I have done), one may hold that the descriptive system is a valid one and that such aberrations as my §§ II and IV may be considered as normal occasional aberrations produced by the poet for one rhetorical reason or another. O'Connor may well, therefore, have put his finger on the "metrical" limits within which the Ugaritic and Hebrew poets generally worked.

Having said this, however, it must also be said that these are simply inside and outside limits, with a great deal of quantitative and syntactic variation allowed within these limits. We do not, therefore, have a "meter" in the narrow sense of the term,[59] nor even much beyond what we knew before O'Connor, viz., that the ancient Ugaritic and Hebrew poets tended to express themselves by means of terser phrases in poetry than in prose. (Moreover, the comparison itself between poetry and prose according to O'Connor's categories remains to be done—the same is true, of course, of the other systems of analysis studied here.)

A further remark: O'Connor tends to look upon his syntactic constraints as not operating in a parallel fashion. That is, his analysis by syntactic constraints was done by half-lines only (i.e., my "half-line"—his "line"). However much I may disagree with the analysis of tropes by half-lines,[60] the wisdom of O'Connor's approach at the level of syntactic constraints is borne out by the present analysis, for no parallelistic pattern, other than a relatively frequent but always partial likeness between two half-lines only, *à la* Stuart,[61] emerged from *ʿnt* I. This is as one would expect, however, for the most cursory grammatical analysis shows various deletions and compensations which lead to syntactic disparities between the two half-lines of a bicolon and between half-lines in other distributions. On the other hand, the analysis by half-lines according to syntactic entities can show up none of the details of lexical or even syn-

---

[59] See my article in *Ugarit in Retrospect* cited above in Ch. I, note 7. O'Connor would certainly agree with this assessment since he spent the first part of his book demolishing the notion that Hebrew poetry is characterized by meter. His syntactic constraints may, however, be considered to constitute a form of "meter" in a sense analogous to that in which parallelism can be called a form of "meter" (Landy, *JSOT* 28 [1984] 75).

[60] See my review of O'Connor cited in Ch. I, note 7.

[61] Douglas K. Stuart, *Studies in Early Hebrew Meter* (Harvard Semitic Monographs Series, vol. 13; Chico, CA: Scholars Press, 1976). Stuart's metrical system (syllable counting with emendation) was discussed at length in my article in *Ugarit in Restrospect* (see above Ch. I, note 7).

tactic variation on other levels which do show up in Geller's very detailed system, or even in Collins' less detailed system. Thus certain truly syntactic features, such as enjambment, must be analyzed as tropes according to O'Connor's system and his tropes end up being, therefore, a combination of semantic and syntactic features.

Whatever the parallelistic value of O'Connor's syntactic categories may be,[62] a good portion of the book is devoted to something closer to standard parallelistic analysis, which O'Connor attempts to re-form by means of new terminology and by (in my estimation) a very artificial trinitarian organization of the phenomena.[63] His analysis of "deletion-compensation," in spite of furnishing a more complete discussion of "gapping" (Geller's "deletion") than is to be found in Geller, is nonetheless deficient in that he does not study the balancing phenomenon of "compensation," i.e., does not explicitly link the quasi-metrical data of his syntactic analysis with the rhetorical structure of tropes.[64] (I hope to have shown below that "deletion-compensation" can be analyzed without resorting to meter, at least in the narrowest sense of the term.)

What to my mind is new, and very important, in O'Connor's study of tropes, is their arrangement within and across poetic cola (his "linear" and "supralinear" distributions). Though others have referred to various extra-colonic features,[65] O'Connor was the first to organize these distributions systematically. I do believe that my system of "half-line," "regular," "near," and "distant" categories (developed independently in spring of 1980[66]) is a more useful analytical tool because it is stated strictly in terms of parallelistic units[67] and because it includes distant structures of a non-repetitive nature,[68] but this does not keep me from ascribing full credit to O'Connor for moving in the direction of the macro-structural analysis that I am advocating so strongly here.

---

[62] On this aspect of O'Connor's work, see J. Wansbrough's studies: "Hebrew Verse: Scansion and Parallax," *BSOAS* 45 (1982) 5-13 and "Hebrew Verse: Apostrophe and Epanalepsis," *BSOAS* 45 (1982) 425-33.

[63] See my review (cited above, Ch. I, note 7).

[64] On p. 401, for example, O'Connor discusses the constituent structure of a gapped line (3 // 2) but does not bring in the possibility of a balancing of units, as in *ᶜnt* I §§ III (overbalanced!) and V.

[65] References above, Ch. I, note 13.

[66] Reference above, Introduction, note 1.

[67] See my review of O'Connor, *JNES* 42 (1983) 301.

[68] O'Connor's "burden" is a distant parallelistic structure, but it consists of distant repetition of larger units and does not include elements of minor repetition as well as semantic and grammatical elements such as may be found in, e.g., *ᶜnt* I, §§ II, IV, and IX. For a more complete discussion of O'Connor's macrostructures, see my review.

1.5 *Parallelism of Minor Elements*

	Distribution:	*Half-line*		*Regular*		*Near*		*Distant*		
I.	*ʿbd . ʾalʾiyn* ^{3}*bʿl*									
	sʾid . zbl . bʿl ^{4}*ʾarṣ*									
II.	*qm . yṯʿr*									
	^{5}*w . yšlḥmnh*					-h		w-	-nh[69]	
III.	^{6}*ybrd . ṯd . lpnwh*			l-		-h			-h	
	^{7}*bḥrb . mlḥt* ^{8}*qṣ . mrʾi .*			b-						b-
IV.	*ndd* ^{9}*yʿšr .*									
	wyšqynh					-h		w-	-nh	
V.	^{10}*ytn . ks . bdh*			b-	-h	-h			-h	b-
	^{11}*krpn . bklʾat . ydh*			b-	-h	-h			-h	b-
VI.	^{12}*bk rb . ʿẓm . rʾi*									
	dn^{13}*mt . šmm .*									
VII.	*ks . qdš* ^{14}*ltphnh . ʾaṯt .*			l-		-h			-nh	
	krpn ^{15}*ltʿn . ʾaṯrt .*			l-						
VIII.	*ʾalp* ^{16}*kd . yqḥ . bḫmr*			b-		-b				b-
	^{17}*rbt . ymsk . bmskh*			b-		-b	-h		-h	b-
IX.	^{18}*qm . ybd . wyšr*							w-		
	^{19}*mṣltm . bd . nʿm*					-b				b-
X.	^{20}*yšr . ǵzr . ṭb . ql*									
	^{21}*ʿl . bʿl . bṣrrt* ^{22}*ṣpn*	ʿl	b-			-b				b-
XI.	*ytmr . bʿl* ^{23}*bnth .*								-h	
	yʿn . pdry ^{24}*bt . ʾar*									

1.5.1 *Parallelism of Minor Elements: Comments*

It was Dahood who made the greatest contributions to outlining the parallelism of various particles, for in his collection of parallel pairs which occur in both Ugaritic and Hebrew[70] he noted prepositions, conjunctions, adverbs, etc., which occur in both repetitive and regular parallelism. Because of the short phonetic duration of these particles (as compared with the usually longer nouns and verbs) and because of their frequency of appearance coupled with a relatively slight semantic load, the contribution made to the poetic structure by the particles is relatively less than that offered by the principal words, those which are phonetically longer and semantically distinctive enough to make an impression on the

[69] The two forms of the suffix, *-h* and *-nh*, are treated as different forms in the "near" and "distant" columns because the *-nh* form does not occur in near parallelism; thus only the pronominal portion of the energic + pronoun combination is listed in the "near" column.

[70] *RSP* I (1972) 71-382; *RSP* II (1975) 1-39; *RSP* III (1981) 1-206.

listener's mind. This is especially true of distant parallelism, where the parallelistic load could hardly be borne by particles alone.

This said, we would nonetheless be remiss to overlook the contributions made by the particles, minor though they be. The main types of parallelism represented are repetitive and/or grammatical: repetitive for the reasons given in the preceding paragraph, grammatical because the parallelism is usually that of particles which belong to the same grammatical class, e.g., preposition // preposition, rather than preposition // conjunction.[71]

Of repetitive parallelism of minor elements, several are present in *ʿnt* I: one prepositional (*b*), one pronominal (*-h*/*-nh*), one adverbial (*l*, § VII), and one conjunctival (*w*). The *b* // *b* . . . *b* // *b* parallelism in §§ V and VIII may form a macro-structure in that one pair is part of the bicolon which begins the six-line unit describing the cup (syntactically discrete because of the continuous syntax of the three bicola) whereas the second pair is in the bicolon which closes off the drinking section.

The pronominal parallelism consists of the third masculine singular suffix on nouns and on the energic form of the verb (*-nh*). The string of suffixes all referring to *bʿl* serves to bind together the four bicola in §§ II-V, the 'serving' section. In § V the structure of minor elements (as well as of major ones) is especially strong, with the "regular" repetitive parallelism of *b* and *-h* along with that of *-d-* // *yd-*. This suffixing of like pronouns also leads to a sound parallelism, the type known as 'weak rhyme' in poetic systems which include rhyme in a language with frequently repeated final morphemes.

The repetitive adverbial parallelism (*l*, § VII) is one that is frequently attested.[72] It is only one of many possible structures based on possible synonymy and antonymy provided by main terms modified by negative particles ('good' // 'good' = 'good' // 'not bad' ≠ 'good' // 'bad' = 'good' // 'not good', etc.). In this particular instance, there is strict synonymy of both of the two verbs and of the particles.

Besides these repetitive parallelisms, there are two non-repetitive parallelisms, both prepositional, one "regular" (*l* // *b*, § III) and one within a half-line (*ʿl* . . . *b*, § X). Though as prepositions they are of the same grammatical class, in both instances the prepositions play different

---

[71] Dahood's attempts to isolate discrete semantic properties in repetitive parallelistic structures of minor elements (e.g., *b* // *b* "from // from" as opposed to "in // in," et cetera: *RSP* I [1974] 133-36) must be examined critically rather than adopted wholesale because several of these distinctions are features of syntax, verb-preposition patterning, or simply of English translation. At least the latter category must not be ascribed to the ancient poet's subtlety! Even more dubious are alleged instances of different semantic properties within a given poetic unit (e.g., *b* // *b* "from // in, into": *RSP* III [1981] 40).

[72] See Dahood, *RSP* I (1972) 242.

syntactic roles: in the first case the *l* is local while the *b* is instrumental, while in the second case the *ʿl* indicates something approaching the indirect object of the verb *yšr* (indicating the honoree of the song rather than the position of the singer), while the *b* is local. More research is necessary to determine the distribution of similar and dissimilar syntactic functions in the various distributions of parallelism.

Finally, there is one clear case of distant parallelism of a particle, though the parallelism of the particle stands out more because of the repetition of the larger structure in which it is found than because of the particle itself. The thrice-repeated sequence of three verbs which marks the major junctures of *ʿnt* I has in all three instances the conjunction *w* before the third verb (and in no case anywhere else in the sequence or in the column, for that matter). Moreover, in the first two sequences the third verb is transitive with an expressed direct object; in both cases the object is expressed as a 3 masc. sing. pronominal suffix attached to the energic form of the verb.[73]

1.6 *Positional Parallelism*

The concept of positional parallelism is one which has a limited usefulness and it is certainly not one which can lead to an independent notational system such as those which serve to depict semantic or grammatical parallelism. Indeed, I found it most useful, before the publication of Collins' and Geller's systems of analysis, when I needed a concept to express the relationship between terms which were grammatically parallel but semantically dissimilar.

The clearest case of the usefulness of the concept in *ʿnt* I has already been discussed in detail from the semantic perspective, viz., *yqḥ* // *ymsk* (§ VIII—see above at *Semantic Parallelism: Geller's Categories*). In this pairing the semantic parallelism has to be termed poor, since the verbs have little in common, are not elsewhere attested in parallel, and serve, in any case, to depict a sequence of actions (i.e., the relationship is on the order of Geller's "list" parallelism). On the other hand, the two verbs are locked into positional parallelism by the surrounding semantic parallelisms (*ʾlp* // *rbt*; *ḫmr* // *msk*) and by the syntactic structure (OVM // OVM). I argued above that it was this tight structure which permitted the looseness of the semantic parallelism.

In other instances, the term "position" might better be replaced by "slot" and one slips over into the sphere of grammatical parallelism. In

---

[73] Note that even if the poetic division is adopted which makes of §§ II and IV the first line of a tricolon, the structure with *w*- and -*nh* still stands out clearly.

§ III, for example, the modifier slot is filled by two prepositional phrases (*lpnwh // bḥrb mlḥt*). Here the positional parallelism would have to be termed chiastic (if the concept retains any validity when allowed to be switched into any but the basic positions 1-2-3 // 1-2-3). Grammatical parallelism identifies both phrases as modifier clauses made up of prepositional phrases consisting of preposition plus noun phrase(s). It is the semantics of the prepositional phrases and the syntax of the line, however, which show the morphological likeness to hide a functional difference (local vs. instrumental). This particular identification of slots is very much akin to Collins' level of notation, according to which the respective phrases would be identified as modifiers, with no deeper analysis carried out. Indeed, it can be said that a system such as Collin's which goes no deeper than noting V, S, O, and M is a sort of notational system for four major "slots," and is a sort of positional parallelism conceived in terms of syntactic slot rather than of physical position.

In the parallelism of minor elements in *ᶜnt* I, one may be positionally distributed: the 3 m.s. pronominal suffixes which refer to *bᶜl* are always affixed to words in final position in the poetic line, whereas, in the one case of another antecedent, the suffixed word is not in final position (*tphnh* in line 14, referring to the cup).

There are two other aspects of the parallelism of *ᶜnt* I which may be partially elucidated by the concept of positional parallelism. The first is the thrice-repeated three-verb structure which is so important in the formation of this portion of the text. Here the positional parallelism must be analyzed as distant, for there are no slots, positional, semantic, or grammatical, which may be observed to correspond to the three-verb structure, either as such or as variants thereof, outside of §§ II, IV, and IX. (This situation changes with respect to the first two, of course, if they are analyzed as first segments of tricola.) When the three sections are set side-by-side, however, each positional slot is filled in like fashion: V + V + *w* + V. Further grammatical analysis only proves fruitful in regard to the third verb of the sequence, which is transitive verb + object . . . transitive verb + object . . . intransitive verb. Though one is somewhat surprised by the three-verb sequence on first encounter, when it becomes clear that this is a repeated structure, with virtually the same grammatical elements repeated each time in the same order/position, one realizes that the structure is not a momentary lapse into "bad" parallelism on the part of the poet, but a purposeful structure which only becomes clear when analyzed as distant parallelism, with some elements responding to analysis as repetitive parallelism, others as semantic parallelism, and the structure itself as a combination of grammatical and positional parallelism.

The second instance alluded to above is the poetic division of § IX. This section has already been analyzed above in "Semantic Parallelism: Geller's Categories." The parallelism of this bicolon is problematic from all points of view: it follows none of the three major types of parallelism (repetitive, semantic, or grammatical) nor does it respond to analysis by positions or slots within the line. If, however, "positional parallelism" is expanded to include macrostructures, then § IX must be analyzed as a bicolon because of the position of *mṣltm bd nᶜm* between two clearly defined structures: the three-verb structure of §§ II, IV, and IX along with the fourth verb which regularly begins the following poetic unit, here *yšr* in line 20 the parallelistic force of which is emphasized by being repetitive with the third verb of the third three-verb structure in § IX (*yšr*, line 18). It may well be this tight locking into the macrostructure which allows the parallelism of § IX to relax into sequential description.

1.7.1 *Phonetic Parallelism*: *Repetition of Consonants*[74] (see foldout at the end of the book)

1.7.1.1 *Phonetic Parallelism: Repetition of Consonants: Remarks*

In the case of the Ugaritic consonants, we are dealing more with graphemes than with phonemes, for the actual pronunciation is uncertain and we have little knowledge of phonetic mergers of which a previous phoneme has been preserved graphically or of allophonic variations in the pronunciation of a given sign. In the case of vowels, with the exception of the three *ʾaleph*s, we have only occasional *matres lectiones* and even these are disputed. Thus in a phonetic analysis of a Ugaritic text, the consonants, for which we have at least the graphic evidence, must be kept rigorously separate from the vowels. The analysis of the consonants may, therefore, be carried forward in a more or less traditional fashion. As for the vowels, it is extremely speculative to carry out a phonetic analysis on the basis of a reconstructed text. This becomes obvious when one considers the verb, where a given "imperfect" form may have as its final vowel *-u*, *-a*, or Ø, while "enclitic" *mem* may be vocalized as *-ma*, *mi*, or as *-um*. Many, indeed virtually all, forms are doubtful because, in general, they are vocalized on a comparative Semitic basis and the Ugaritic form of a given word may have differed from whatever comparative evidence has been given precedence in the analysis of that word.

A further point must be made about my analysis: I have attempted no psychological interpretation based on the human perception of the various phonemes.[75] Though such an analysis may be valid, I am not

[75] For a summary of research from the perspectives of both accoustics and literary criticism, see R. Jakobson and L. R. Waugh, *The Sound Shape of Language*, Bloomington, IN: Indiana University Press, 1979.

qualified to carry it out and abstain from attempting to do so. For whatever psycho-acoustic reason, though, it is clear that there are groupings of consonants into clearly discernible patterns. These I have noted descriptively and add some specific remarks below.

Alliteration in the strict sense of the term (repetition of consonants in initial and/or accented syllables[76]) does not appear to be a structural device of Ugaritic poetry. There certainly is repetition of consonants, but without a clear distribution. Margalit has given the following rules for recognizing consonantal distribution:[77]

1) "By alliteration is meant the repetition of one or more consonants (= DOMINANT LETTERS) within a specific framework (verse-line, verse, or strophe), either with a minimal frequency of 1:8, or in immediately contiguous words, but not necessarily of initial consonants (= PARONOMASIA).

2) 'Partial alliteration' refers to the repetition of phonetically close but distinct consonants ... in the above ... circumstances.

3) An alliterative 'sequence' involves the repetition of two or more consonants in identical or inverted order, either within the individual word boundaries or transcending them.

4) 'Linkage' (via alliteration) denotes the phenomenon whereby verse lines (stichoi) of distinct verses (bicola, tricola etc.) are linked together by participating in a common alliterative pattern, whether in terms of shared 'dominant letters' or 'sequences'."

Though these points are suggestive,[78] a larger sample than the one chosen here, as well as specific attention to Margalit's rules, are necessary to prove or disprove their validity. I would make a terminological point, however, with regard to Margalit's use of the term 'alliteration',[79] viz., that he does not use it in the commonly accepted

---

[76] *OED*, definitions 1 and 2.

[77] *UF* 11 (1979) 538; restated in slightly different terms in *Matter* (reference above, Ch. I, note 10) 220-21. In particular the ratio of "1:8" in rule 1 is changed in the later formulation to " ... with a frequency significantly higher than [that of] the other, non-alliterating consonants; or than can be accounted for by mere random probability." Though the rule is now stated in statistical terms, no attempt is made to define the dividing line between a frequency representing "mere random probability" and a non-random frequency.

[78] By including "partial alliteration" of different sibilants in my chart, an "alliterative linkage" of sibilants would have been produced. The "sequences" in my chart are, however, simply physical sequences of the same consonants; these sequences do constitute "linkages."(His term would include both "near" parallelism and "sequences" in my chart.) I avoid the term "linkage" because my organization of the repetitions differs in scope and in form from Margalit's and because I am unwilling, at this point, to declare in favor of whatever degree of intentionality may be implied in the word "linkage."

[79] *Mutatis mutandis*, this point is similar to the one I made regarding Margalit's use of the term 'meter': whether or not his facts are right, the technique described is not 'meter' as narrowly defined (article in *Ugarit in Restrospect* cited in Ch. I, note 7).

poetic sense.[80] He even goes so far as to include in his examples consonants taken from pronominal suffixes, a position usually reserved for the occurrence of rhyme (and/or assonance of vowels). Because of the "physical" limitations of the Ugaritic texts (i.e., lack of vowels), Margalit's exclusive attention to consonants is certainly justifiable, but it should not be termed a study of "alliteration." For the purposes of this portion of the present experimental, descriptive analysis, I have noted all repetitions of consonants in half-line, regular, and near distributions.

§ I. Apparently in order to reinforce the divine title and name *ʾalʾiyn bᶜl* there is a profusion of /ʾ/, /b/, /ᶜ/, and /l/ in this bicolon.[81] The only other letter repeated is /d/, which binds together the verbs which open each line. These repetitions leave very few unparalleled consonants (only /y/ and /n/ in the first half-line and /s/, /z/, /r/, and /ṣ/ in the second half-line, with three of these four being sibilants; all but the sibilants have near parallels with § II). All forms of phonetic parallelism are, of course, included in the repetitive parallel *bᶜl* // *bᶜl* because of both occurrences being in the same case (object case as analyzed here: *baᶜla* // *baᶜla*).

§ II. The parallelism here is very tenuous: only one /y/ in each half-line (and /y/ is a morpheme of great frequency in verb formations) and one /m/ in each half-line, near the outer extremes of each. The unit is, however, tied in with both the preceding and following bicola by near parallels. Indeed, there are sufficient near parallels with § III to constitute an argument for §§ II and III forming a tricolon (but see below on § IV).

§ III. This bicolon is characterized by regular parallelism of letters repeated frequently through the column (/b/, /r/, /d/, and /l/) and by half-line parallelism. The latter is weakened, however, if §§ II and III are scanned as a bicolon (/ḥ/ and /m/ occur als in § II).

§ IV. As with § II, though less so, the internal parallelism here is weak. Note also, however, that the near parallelism with the following bicolon is not so strong as was the case between §§ II and III, making less of a phonetic argument for §§ IV and V being a tricolon than was the case above.

§ V. Here begins a phonetic sequence that continues strongly through § VIII (i.e., the entire "cup" section). The principal repetitions are of the occlusives /k/ and /q/, but the liquids /r/ and /l/ also occur with some frequency, especially /r/, which is present in all four bicola. The words being reinforced are those which designate the wine vessels, *ks*, *krpn*, *bk*,

---

[80] See above, Ch. I, notes 76 and 79, and, for Hebrew poetry, O. S. Rankin, "Alliteration in Hebrew Poetry," *JTS* 31 (1930) 285-91.

[81] Individual letters are enclosed in slashes only to prevent them from getting lost in the text; no indication of phonetic nature is intended.

and *kd*, and comparing this list with the sequences shows that /d/ and /b/ are also repetitive features of the "cup" section. Indeed, the only consonants of these four nouns which are not included in extended patterns are /s/ and /p/—and even these "weaknesses" are partially palliated by the sibilant repetition in *ks qdš* (line 13—with near repetition of the /š/ with *šmm* earlier in the line), by the near parallelism of /s/ in §§ VII and VIII, by the regular and near parallelism of /p/ in §§ VII and VIII, and by the repetitive parallelism of *ks* . . . *ks* and of *krpn* . . . *krpn* in §§ V and VII. It appears clear to me that in the case of §§ V-VIII we have an extended phonetic sequence with a definite semantic reference point (wine vessels) which contributes its part, alongside the repetitive, semantic and grammatical parallels and structures, to bind the extended unit together.

§ IX Because of their different semantic and grammatical characteristics, the phonetic parallelism (and "sequence," in Margalit's sense of the term) of *bd* // *bd* would not be noted except in a specifically phonetic inquiry.

1.7.1.2 *Distributions of Phonetic Parallelism (Consonants)*

Because of the limited repertory of consonants, because of their brevity (as compared with most lexical items), and because of the limited retainability of single elements of such a repertory, it did not appear useful to chart distant phonetic parallelism. (Distant parallels are only noted when a sequence of regular and near parallels occurs elsewhere in the column, and then in parentheses—see /h/, /ʾ/, /b/, and /ᶜ/.) On the other hand, because of the proximity of at least the adjacent members of adjacent cola, charting of near phonetic parallelism did appear useful and indeed the chart of near parallels compared with that of sequences shows the building-up of a phonetic structure. The most striking instances, already discussed above, are perhaps /r/, /k/, and /q/—striking because they are not (at least here in the case of /k/) grammatical morphemes and because they contribute to a semantic structure. When /b/, /d/, and /n/ are added (the first of which occurs only two times out of seven as a grammatical morpheme, the second once out of five, but /n/ is a non-root letter five times out of six §§ V-VIII) we have all the consonants in the four words for wine vessels excepts /s/ and /p/. Though there is a certain amount of repetition of sibilants in the column and in the "cup" section, there is no extended structure of a single one. Other letters which occur in sequences go to make up the divine title and name *ʾalʾiyn bᶜl*, two of which, /b/ and /n/, are also part of the "cup" structure. Three of these letters also occur as grammatical/lexical morphemes (/b/ as a preposition, /l/ as preposition and adverb, any /y/ as a pronominal element).

Moreover, several of these letters do not occur in sequence after the occurrence of the title + name itself in § I (see chart of sequences, where /ʾ/, /b/, and /ʿ/ are seen to occur as sequences but beginning as such only in §§ V and VI). I am thus not prepared to say that *ʾalʾiyn bʿl* triggered a repetitive phonetic structure beyond the microstructure of § I. Such a decision could only be made on the basis of a frequency count of consonants from a larger sample.[82]

1.7.2 *Phonetic Parallelism: Repetition of Vowels*[83]

<table>
<tr><th></th><th></th><th>Like Vowel in Accented Syllable[84]</th><th>Like Vowel in Final Syllable</th><th>Like Pattern of Vowels in Two Syllables With Like Consonant(s)</th></tr>
<tr><td>I.</td><td>ʿábada ʾalʾiyā́na báʿla</td><td>ʿa-, -yā-, ba-</td><td>-da, -na, -la</td><td>baʿla</td></tr>
<tr><td></td><td>sáʾida zabū́la báʿla ʾárṣi</td><td>sa-, ba-, ʾa</td><td>-da, -la, -la</td><td>baʿla</td></tr>
<tr><td>II.</td><td>qā́ma tá<u>t</u>ʿuru</td><td>qā-, ya<u>t</u>-</td><td>-ru</td><td></td></tr>
<tr><td></td><td>wayašalḥimánnahu</td><td>-man-</td><td>-hu</td><td></td></tr>
<tr><td>III.</td><td>yábrudu <u>t</u>ádda lêpanī́hu</td><td>yab-, <u>t</u>a- | -nī-</td><td>-du, -hu | -da |</td><td></td></tr>
<tr><td></td><td>biḥárbi malū́ḥati qíṣṣa marī́ʾi</td><td>-ḥar- | qi-, -rī-</td><td>| -ṣa- | bi, -ti, -ʾi</td><td></td></tr>
<tr><td>IV.</td><td>nádada yáʿšuru</td><td>na-, yaʿ-</td><td>-ru</td><td></td></tr>
<tr><td></td><td>wayašaqqiyánnahu</td><td>-yan-</td><td>-hu</td><td></td></tr>
<tr><td>V.</td><td>yáttinu kā́sa bádihu</td><td>yat-, kā, ba-</td><td>-nu, -hu | -sa</td><td>(-dihu)</td></tr>
<tr><td></td><td>kárpana bikílʾatê yadḗhu</td><td>kar-</td><td>-hu | -na</td><td>(-dêhu)</td></tr>
<tr><td>VI.</td><td>bíka rábba ʿáẓuma rúʾí</td><td>rab-, ʿa- | bi-</td><td>-ka, -ba, ma | -ʾí</td><td>-uma</td></tr>
<tr><td></td><td>dānumā́ti šamī́ma</td><td>-mā- | -mī́-</td><td>-ma | -ti</td><td>-umā-</td></tr>
<tr><td>VII.</td><td>kā́sa qúdši lātiphā́nnahu ʾá<u>tt</u>atu</td><td>kā-, -hân-, ʾa<u>t</u>- |</td><td>-sa | -hu, -tu</td><td>-atu (ʾa<u>tt</u>atu)</td></tr>
<tr><td></td><td>kárpana lātaʿī́nu ʾa<u>t</u>íratu</td><td>kar- | -ʿī-, -<u>t</u>i-</td><td>-na | -nu, -tu</td><td>-atu (ʾa<u>t</u>[ir]atu)</td></tr>
<tr><td>VIII.</td><td>ʾálpa káddi yíqqaḥu biẖámri</td><td>ʾal-, kad-, ẖam-</td><td>-pa | -di, -ri | -ḥu</td><td></td></tr>
<tr><td></td><td>rabbā́ta yámsuku bimáskihu</td><td>-bā-, yam-, -mas-</td><td>-ta | | -ku, -hu</td><td></td></tr>
<tr><td>IX.</td><td>qā́ma yabúddu wayašī́ru</td><td>qā | -šī</td><td>-ma | -du, -ru</td><td>-āma</td></tr>
<tr><td></td><td>maṣiltâma bádê naʿī́mi</td><td>-tâ-, ba- | -ʿī-</td><td>-ma |</td><td>-âma</td></tr>
<tr><td>X.</td><td>yašī́ru ǵázru ṭā́bu qā́li</td><td>-šī- | ǵa-, ṭa-, qā-</td><td>-ru, -ru, -bu | -li</td><td>(-āli)</td></tr>
<tr><td></td><td>ʿálê báʿli biṣarī́rati ṣapā́ni</td><td>-rī- | ʿa-, ba-, -pā-</td><td>| -li, -ti, -ni</td><td>(-a[ʿ]li)</td></tr>
<tr><td>XI.</td><td>yítamiru bāʿlu binā́tihu</td><td>yi- | ba, -na-</td><td>-ru, -lu, -hu |</td><td></td></tr>
<tr><td></td><td>yaʿī́na pidraya bítta ʾā́ri</td><td>-ʿī-, pid-, bit- | ʾā-</td><td>-nu | -ya, -ta</td><td></td></tr>
</table>

[82] A quick check of a section of comparable length in *ʿnt* II (lines 2-21) shows fairly close similarities with *ʿnt* I for three key letters in the latter column:

	ʿnt I	*ʿnt* II
r:	$\frac{21}{225} = 9.33\%$	$\frac{20}{284} = 7.02\%$
ʿ:	$\frac{11}{225} = 4.44\%$	$\frac{12}{284} = 2.23\%$
k:	$\frac{8}{225} = 3.55\%$	$\frac{13}{284} = 4.58\%$

The relatively higher frequence of /k/ in *ʿnt* II may be owing to the key word *kp* in lines 9-13. A larger sample needs to be analyzed, however, and a statistical criterion for significantly higher rate of occurrence needs to be determined.

[83] The reconstructed accent is as hypothetical as the vowels. Here the basic rules for accent placement in Arabic are assumed and an accent is indicated even on words "in construct."

[84] "Like vowel" means that I have considered the long and short grades of a vowel as one element in this listing.

1.7.2.1 *Phonetic Parallelism: Repeated vs. Non-Repeated Vowels*

	Accented Syllables	*Final Syllables*
I.	$\frac{6}{7}$ = a/ā; $\frac{1}{7}$ = ū	$\frac{6}{7}$ = a; $\frac{1}{7}$ = i
II.	$\frac{3}{3}$ = a/ā	$\frac{2}{3}$ = u; $\frac{1}{3}$ = a
III.	$\frac{3}{7}$ = a; $\frac{3}{7}$ = i/ī; $\frac{1}{7}$ = ū	$\frac{2}{7}$ = u; $\frac{2}{7}$ = a; $\frac{3}{7}$ = i
IV.	$\frac{3}{3}$ = a/ā	$\frac{2}{3}$ = u; $\frac{1}{3}$ = a
V.	$\frac{4}{6}$ = a/ā; $\frac{1}{6}$ = i; $\frac{1}{6}$ = ê	$\frac{3}{6}$ = u; $\frac{2}{6}$ = a; $\frac{1}{6}$ = ê
VI.	$\frac{3}{6}$ = a/ā; $\frac{2}{6}$ = i/ī; $\frac{1}{6}$ = u	$\frac{4}{6}$ = a; $\frac{2}{6}$ = i/î
VII.	$\frac{4}{7}$ = a/ā/â; $\frac{2}{7}$ = i/ī; $\frac{1}{7}$ = u	$\frac{4}{7}$ = u; $\frac{2}{7}$ = a; $\frac{1}{7}$ = i
VIII.	$\frac{6}{7}$ = a/ā; $\frac{1}{7}$ = i	$\frac{2}{7}$ = a; $\frac{2}{7}$ = i; $\frac{3}{7}$ = u
IX.	$\frac{3}{6}$ = a/ā/â; $\frac{2}{6}$ = ī; $\frac{1}{6}$ = u	$\frac{2}{6}$ = a; $\frac{2}{6}$ = u; $\frac{1}{6}$ = ê; $\frac{1}{6}$ = i
X.	$\frac{6}{8}$ = a/ā; $\frac{2}{8}$ = ī	$\frac{4}{8}$ = i; $\frac{3}{8}$ = u; $\frac{1}{8}$ = ê
XI.	$\frac{4}{7}$ = i/ī/î; $\frac{3}{7}$ = a/ā	$\frac{4}{7}$ = u; $\frac{2}{7}$ = a; $\frac{1}{7}$ = i
	8 = Non-parallel (14%)	9 = Non-parallel (16%)
	59 = Parallel	58 = Parallel

1.7.2.2 *Phonetic Parallelism: Repetition of Vowels: Remarks*

These charts show a high degree of repetition of vowels, but the repetition occurs in patterns that do not vary a great deal: *a*-vowels appear most frequently within words and such vowels form the primary parallelism in all but one case of the parallelism of accented vowels (§ XI; even there the number of *a*-vowels is close behind!). On the other hand, the use of *-u*-vowels to mark the nominative case and the indicative mood makes that vowel the most common in endings, increased in this text by the repetition of the 3m.s. suffix *-hu*. In final syllables *a*-vowels are less frequent because the accusative case is less frequent in this text than the nominative and the "subjunctive" (*-a*) mood does not appear at all; *i*-vowels as well because the genitive case is not as frequent as the nominative and there is no *i*-marked verbal mood.

Five of the eleven poetic units considered here show repetition of the vowel of the final syllable of the half-line, and three show a fuller form of repetition at the end (§ V *-hu* // *-hu*; § VII *-atu* // *-atu*; § X *-āli* // *āni*). Moreover, there is a good deal of half-line repetition of final elements (e.g., § I *-da* // *-da*). True rhyme, defined for English prosody as likeness of last accented vowel and of all following vowels and consonants (*OED*), only appears in complete repetitive parallelism, where, of course, all the forms of parallelism come together.

Because of the small number of variables in the vocalic system (reconstructed as consisting of eight qualities and quantities), the charting of near and distant parallelism does not appear to be a worthwhile pursuit. Indeed this small number of variables and the morphosyntactic patterns noted above make one wonder just how important the role of vocalic patterning was in Ugaritic poetic structure.

1.8 *Length Compensation*

	Equivalent Elements			*Deleted Elements*		*Compensatory Elements*			*Total*
I.	*ʿabada*		+			*ʿalʿiyāna baʿla*			
	saʾida					*zabūla baʿla ʾarṣi*			
	1/3/6		+			1+1/4+2/10+5			3/9/21 =
	1/3/6					1+1+1/3+2+2/7+5+5			4/10/23
II.	*yaṯʿuru*		+	*qāma*					
	wayašalḥimannahu								
	1/3/6		+	1/2/5					2/5/11 =
	1/7/16								1/7/16
III.				*yabrudu*	+	*ṯadda*	+	*lêpanīhu*	
						qiṣṣa marīʾi		*biḥarbi malūḥati*	
				1/3/7		1+2+5	+	1/4/9	3/9/21 =
						1+1/2+3/5+7		1+1/3+4/7+9	4/12/28
IV.	*yaʿšuru*		+	*nadada*					
	wayašaqqiyannahu								
	1/3/7		+	1/3/6					2/6/13 =
	1/7/16								1/7/16
V.	*kāsa*		+	*yatinu*	+	*badihu*			
	karpana					*bikilʾatê yadêhu*			
	1/2/5		+	1/3/6	+	1/3/6			3/8/16 =
	1/3/7					1+1/4+3/10+7			3/10/24
VI.	*bīka*		+	*rabba ʿaẓuma ruʾí*					
	dānumāti				+	*šamêma*			
	1/2/5		+	1+1+1/2+3+2/5+6+5	+				4/9/21 =
	1/4/10					1/3/7			2/7/17
VII.	*lātiphânnahu*	*ʾaṯṯatu*	+			*kāsa qudši*			
	lātaʿīnu	*ʾaṯiratu*				*karpana*			
	1/5/14	1/3/7				1+1/2+2/5+5			4/12/31 =
	1/4/10	1/4/8				1/3/7			3/11/25
VIII.	*yiqqaḥu*	*biḫamri*	+			*ʾalpa kaddi*			
	yamsuku	*bimaskihu*				*rabbata*			
	1/3/7	1/3/7	+			1+1/2+2/5+5			4/10/24 =
	1/3/7	1/4/9				1/3/7			3/10/23
IX.				*qāma yabuddu wayašīru*	+	*maṣaltâma badê naʿīmi*			3/9/20 =
				1+1+1/2+3+4/4+7+9	+	1+1+1/4+2+3/10+5+7			3/9/22
				yasīru ǵazru ṭābu qāli	+	*ʿalê baʿli biẓīrati ṣapāni*			4/9/22 =
				1+1+1+1/3+3+3+3/7+5+5+5	+	1+1+1+1/2+2+5+3/5+5+11+7			4/12/28
XI.	*yîtamiru*		+	*baʿlu*	+	*binātihu*			
	yaʿīnu					*pidraya bitta ʾāri*			
	1/4/9		+	1/2/5	+	1/4/9			3/10/23 =
	1/3/7					1+1+1/3+2+2/7+5+5			4/10/24

1.8.1 *Length Compensation: Remarks*

It is only Geller who has devised a system of notation which is intended specifically to note compensation features. This is done at two levels: the more explicitly noted (by the use of the term "compensation") is in cases of deletion, where the compensation is given as part of the "comparison" rubric. The other innovational notation of compensation is in Geller's system of noting the parallelism of compounds (discussed extensively above in the note to § I in the section on Geller's system). These two innovations are to be warmly applauded for they mark a definite advance in the explicitation of a phenomenon which has, of course, been noted randomly over the years[85] but which has not received consistent attention.

Several remarks need to be made with regard to this phenomenon before passing on to notes on the particular text at hand. First, three criticisms need to be made of Geller's system, not intended to detract from the excellent progress he has made but with the purpose of making clear the need for another step. The first criticism has already been made with regard to § I: Geller's system tries to note too much with too few signs. While the compensatory nature of the phenomenon labeled "deletion + compensation" is absolutely clear, that of the compound phrases is beset by the extreme brevity and partial ambiguity of that system. Second, the essential identity of the two areas of compensation is lost sight of, owing to the separate notational systems employed for the two. Finally, perhaps because Geller has already crowded so much information into one notational system, it includes only the two major areas mentioned. Granted that this where the major compensatory features are found, and further granted that the other compensatory features mentioned below are partially visible from most notations of quantitative parallelism ('meter'); nonetheless it appears valid to propose that a minute analysis of the Northwest Semitic poetic system such as the one being proposed here should include a complete notation of the compensatory system. This Geller's notation is unable to do because it is already too charged to bear a further burden which consists of pointing out the finest nuances of balancing and which would, because of its highly nuanced nature, be lost in the already dense thicket of Geller's sigla.

The other major area of preliminary comment is in the nature of a conclusion: glancing over the various balancing phenomena in *ᶜnt* I, it

[85] Cf. C. H. Gordon, *Ugaritic Grammar* (Analecta Orientalia 20; Rome: Pontifical Biblical Institute, 1940) § 12.11; idem, *Ugaritic Handbook* (Analecta Orientalia 25; Rome: Pontifical Biblical Institute, 1947) § 13.107; idem, *Ugaritic Manual* (Analecta Orientalia 35; Rome: Pontifical Biblical Institute, 1955) § 13.107; *UT* (1965) § 13.116.

becomes clear that the compensatory features are not intended to produce absolute quantitative uniformity, i.e., that the purpose is not metrical in the narrowest sense of the term.[86] They may be fitted into a metrical system which would be based partially on stress considerations, e.g., Margalit's "word-meter" system,[87] but they cannot fit into any purely quantitative metrical system.[88] These compensatory features are clearly used, however, as balancing devices ("ballast variants" in Gordon's terminology[89]) and they result in approximate comparability of length of line.[90] Moreover, there appears to be no pattern in the distribution of various approximations to equality, that is, deletion-compensation does not lead to closer approximation than does compounding not associated with deletion, while non-parallel lines, from which deletion-compensation of individual words and compounding of a semantic nature are excluded by definition, may show what might be called "positional compensation" leading to a very close approximation of quantitative comparability (e.g., § IX, see discussion below).

§ I. I have considered the object phrases in their entirety as compensatory elements, because of the compounded nature of the two phrases (words: 2 // 3). It should be pointed out, however, that in another sense *ʾalʾiyn* is parallel to *zbl*, while *bᶜl* // *bᶜl* is, of course, repetitive. Thus the word *ʾarṣ* is in a sense deleted from the first half-line. Note that this analysis of compensatory features is purely descriptive: we can perceive no metrical,

---

86 See my article in *Ugarit in Restrospect* cited in Ch. I, note 7 as well as the other "anti-metrical" studies also cited in Ch. I, note 7.

87 Ibid., and *AfO* 28 (1981-1982) 267-70.

88 Margalit's system, even in its most pristine form as devised by its author, does not qualify as metrical in the narrow sense of the word; and when various philological criticisms are applied to individual passages the system becomes even more questionable. See my remarks on both aspects of the question in the studies cited in the two previous notes.

89 References in Ch. I, note 85. Kugel (*Idea* [1981] 46—complete reference above, Introduction, note 2) is correct in criticizing Gordon for not making a greater effort at determining the rhetorical purpose of the "ballast" addition and to some extent Geller is open to the same criticism. In the present study, I have followed Geller in studying the phenomenon primarily as a quantitative one rather than as a rhetorical one. A complete literary commentary would have to include rhetorical considerations. Indeed, a separate study of the rhetorical aspects of deletion-compensation is needed: why does the poet sometimes delete, sometimes not, and what is the purpose of the various degrees of deletion (one word, two words, or "synthetic" parallelism, where the entire first half-line is "deleted" with respect to the second [§§ IX and X of *ᶜnt* I are noted as such in this chart, though an alternative analysis of § IX is possible—see Ch. I, note 19, above; no examples in Proverbs 2])? Should both semantic and grammatical parallelism be required for elements to be considered equivalent (as I have done in representing § VI as containing deletion-compensation but § IX as not doing so) or is semantic parallelism sufficient (i.e., *ybd wyšr* could be noted as parallel to *mṣltm* in § IX and hence they could be equivalent elements, with the other elements in both half-lines as "deleted")?

90 See brief discussion with references above in Ch. I, note 7.

rhythmic, or simply quantitative reason why 3/9/21 // 4/10/23 should be superior to 3/9/21 // 3/8/19 (i.e., the quantitative analysis without *ʾarṣ* in the second half-line). Indeed, the compound phrase *ʾalʾiyn bᶜl* // *zbl bᶜl ʾarṣ* is clearly a frozen one, since all attestations of *bᶜl ʾarṣ* listed in Whitaker's concordance (p. 141) occur in this parallelistic structure, and it is probably beyond our means to determine from our present perspective to what extent, if any, compensatory considerations entered into the canonization of these parallel phrases. (We may note in passing that in Margalit's "word-meter" system there is no "metrical" problem in this bicolon, since both *bᶜl* and *bᶜl arṣ* would be considered single "verse-units".)

§ II. It appears to me beyond doubt that there is compensation in the second half-line of the bicola in §§ II and IV: if these lines have been correctly identified as bicola, rather than as third-lines within tricola, then the pattern of short + long // long in these bicola (as compared with short + short + short in the first half-line of § IX) is inescapable. In other words, the two short words of the first half-line are paralleled by one long word in the second half-line—the length of the word in the second half-line compensates for its singleness. The concept of compensation is valid semantically, as well, in this case: if, as seems probable, *yṯᶜr* is more closely parallel semantically to *yšlḥmnh* than to *qm* (and *yᶜšr* is closer to *yšqynh* than to *ndd* in § IV), then it is the semantic parallel to *qm* (*ndd*) which is "deleted" in the second half-line and *wyšlḥmn* (and *wyšqynh*) may be interpreted as compensating for that deletion (i.e., A [short] + B [short] // B [long] = A [short] + B [short] // A [short] + B [short]). Instead of judging by the grammatical parallelism for the analysis of deletion-compensation in this line (i.e., the three-verb structure could be taken as totally compensatory), I have analyzed according to the semantic structure just discussed and *qm* is considered to be "deleted" from the second half-line. In any case, the longer verb in the second half-line of both §§ II and IV has "overcompensated" for the two shorter verbs in the first half-line.

§ III. According to the grammatical analysis adopted here (*qṣ* = noun), the deletion with double compensation is clear and the compensations have, once again, been "overcompensatory".

§ IV. See note on § II.

§ V. The deletion is again clear here and the compensation is again double, though here of two types: one of equivalent elements one of which is longer than the other (*karpana* than *kāsa*), the other being explicit lexical compensation by compounding (*badihu* // *bikilʾatê yadêhu*).

§ VI. The only form of parallelism in this bicolon is the semantic (part-whole) parallelism of *bk* and *nmt*. If this means that the other elements are deleted, then *rb ᶜẓm rʾi* is given as deleted (according to Geller's norms an element cannot be deleted from the first half-line) and *šmm* is the compensatory element. If such an analysis of how deletion-compensation works is correct, and I have my doubts, the "compensating" element does little of the actual compensation, much of which is furnished by *dnmt*.

§ VII. The most obvious element of the compensatory structure here is the compounding in the parallelism *ks qdš* // *krpn*. The compensatory features of the "equivalent elements" (i.e., those without lexical compensation by compounding) are arranged chiastically (see chart at the head of this section) and the result is not quantitative equivalence). Though the ratio of short // long in this bicolon is short + short + long + short // long + short + long—and thus the line might be expected to balance out because there are more words in the first half-line but they are shorter—the fact is that there is a quantitative imbalance in favor of the first half-line. The origin of the imbalance might be expressed thus: *karpana* cannot overcome the combined length of *kāsa qudši*, while the one syllable difference between *ʾaṯiratu* and *ʾaṯṯatu* is not enough to counterbalance the two-syllable deficit which has accumulated at this point. The difference, at least as expressed in syllables, is not great, however (though the difference in the "vocable-count" is greater). It is clear, in any case, that the imbalance in number of words in the first half-line has not been allowed to create a serious imbalance in the overall comparability of length of line. If a stricter metrical goal had been in view, *ltphnh* and/or *ltᶜn* could have been altered to provide a more precise quantitative fit—e.g., *tᶜn* could have been in the energic with a pronominal suffix, which would have provided "better" parallelism, both grammatical and quantitative). The many examples of imprecise quantitative results of deletion-compensation leave little doubt that quantitative precision was not an objective of the Ugaritic poetic system.

§ VIII. This bicolon furnishes the clearest example from the poem under discussion of quantitative regularity resulting from compensation. The four words in the first half-line are balanced by three in the second which provide the additional quantities necessary for an equal number of syllables and a virtually equal number of vocable-counts. This result is of special interest when compared with the preceding bicolon, for the major compensatory feature here is precisely the same as in the preceding bicolon (*ks qdš* // *krpn* there, *ʾalp kd* // *rbt* here); nevertheless, the quantitative result is different. Thus the criteria for constructing poetic units did not include quantitative precision.

§ IX. Because of the complicated intermingling of elements and because of the lack of grammatical parallelism between the two half-lines, I have not tried to indicate deletion-compensation in a form comparable to that ot §§ II and IV. In the latter sections, the first verb was semantically different from the second and third, as here, but there the second and third verbs were in "regular" semantic parallelism (at least when, as here, analyzed as part of a bicolon). In § IX *mṣltm* is in some sense semantically parallel to *ybd wyšr*, but the lack of grammatical parallelism makes me doubt that those three words could be listed as "equivalent" elements. However the deletion-compensation works, it has produced a nicely balanced line from the quantitative perspective.

§ X. Again grammatical parallelism is missing, but this time the quantitative aspect is also imbalanced.

§ XI. The deletion-compensation here is clear: subject omitted in second half-line, object expanded. The quantitative balance as expressed in syllables and in the vocable-count is virtually perfect.

1.9. *Distribution of Parallelisms (Repetitive, Sematic, Minor Elements, Grammatical, Positional)*[91]

A. Half-line Parallelism[92]
   1) *rb* + *ᶜẓm* (§ VI) (synonym)[93]
   2) *ymsk* + *mskh* (§ VIII) (repetition)
   3) *ybd* + *yšr* (§ IX) (synonym)[94]
   4) *ᶜl* + *b* (§ X) (list)

B. "Regular" Parallelism
   1) *ᶜbd* // *sʾid* (§ I) (synonym)
   2) *ʾalʾiyn* // *zbl* (§ I) (synonym)
   3) *bᶜl* // *bᶜl* (§ I) (repetition)
   4) *yṯᶜr* // *yšlḥmnh* (§ II) (synonym/list)
   5) *ṯd* // *qṣ mrʾi* (§ III) (whole-part)
   6) *l* // *b* (§ III) (grammatical, positional: chiastic)

---

[91] "Grammatical" and "positional" parallelism are mentioned in this chart only when semantic parallelism is weak.

[92] See Watson's *SEL* 1 article (full reference above in Ch. I, note 13).

[93] The terms in parentheses follow Geller's categories of semantic parallelism already utilized above at "Semantic Parallelism: Geller's Categories" and elsewhere.

[94] Several terms that I have listed as "synonyms" should perhaps be classified as members of a "list" (it is frequently difficult to decide when words are truly synonymous or only members of a class—indeed, I have indicated both in several instances below). In near and distant distributions it is easier to see a "list" operating, for there are often several members of the semantic group to make up the "list." See further below, Ch. III, note 4.

7) *pnwh* // *ḥrb mlḥ* (§ III) (grammatical, positional: chiastic)
8) *yˁšr* // *yšqynh* (§ IV) (synonym/list)
9) *ks* // *krpn* (§ V) (synonym/list)
10) *b* // *b* (§ V) (repetition)
11) *-d-* // *klˀat yd-* (§ V) (part-whole, repetition)
12) *-h* // *-h* (§ V) (repetition)
13) *bk* // *nmt* (§ VI) (part-whole)
14) *ks* // *krpn* (§ VII) (synonym/list)
15) *l* // *l* (§ VII) (repetition)
16) *tphnh* // *tˁn* (§ VII) (synonym [whole-part?])
17) *ˀaṯt* // *ˀaṯrt* (§ VII) (whole-part, proper name)
18) *ˀalp* // *rbt* (§ VIII) (number)
19) *yqḥ* // *ymsk* (§ VIII) (grammatical, positional)
20) *b* // *b* (§ VIII) (repetition)
21) *ḫmr* // *mskh* (§ VIII) (part-whole)
22) *ybd* + *yšr* // *mṣltm* (§ IX) (whole-part?)
23) *ytmr* // *yˁn* (§ XI) (synonym/list)
24) *bnth* // *pdry bt ˀar* (§ XI) (whole-part, proper name, epithet)

C. Near Parallelism

1) *ˁbd* // *sˀid . . . yṯˁr* // *yslḥmnh* (§§ I, II) (list)
2) *-h . . . -h . . . -h . . . -h* // *-h*; *-h . . . -h* (§§ II, III, IV, V, VII, VIII) (repetition)
3) *yˁšr* // *yšqynh . . . ytn ks* (§§ IV, V) (list)
4) *rˀi . . . tphn* // *tˁn* (§§ VI, VIII) (list)
5) *ks* // *krpn . . . bk . . . ks* // *krpn . . . kd* (§§ V-VIII) (list)
6) *ybd* + *yšr . . . yšr* (§§ IX, X) (synonym, repetition)
7) *nˁm . . . ṭb* (§§ IX, X) (synonym)
8) *bˁl . . . bˁl* (§§ X, XI) (repetition)
9) *b* // *b . . . b . . . b* (§§ VIII-X) (repetition)

D. Distant Parallelism

1) *bˁl* // *bˁl*; *bˁl . . . bˁl* (§§ I, X, XI) (repetition)
2) *qm*; *ndd*; *qm* (§§ II, IV, IX) (synonym)
3) *ṯˁr* // *yšlḥmnh*; *yˁšr* // *yšqynh . . . ytn ks* (§§ II, IV, V) (list)
4) *w*; *w*; *w* (§§ II, IV, IX) (repetition)
5) *-h . . . -h . . . -h . . . -h* // *-h*; *-h . . . -h -h* (§§ II, III, IV, V, VII, VIII, XI) (repetition)
6) *ks* // *krpn . . . bk . . . ks* // *krpn . . . kd* (§§ V-VIII) (list)
7) *-d-* // *yd-*; *-d* (§§ V, IX) (repetition)
8) *ytn*; *lqḥ* (§§ V, VIII) (antonym)
9) *rˀi . . . tphn* // *tˁn*; *ytmr* // *yˁn* (§§ VI, VII, XI) (list)
10) *b*; *b* // *b*; *b* // *b . . . b . . . b* (§§ III, V, VIII, IX, X) (repetition)

1.9.1 *Distributions of Parallelisms: Remarks*

Two notations of parallelism which extends beyond a single poetic unit (here all bicola) have appeared in this study: both repetitive and semantic parallelism were noted in all forms of relationship. Notational devices were relatively simple: for repetitive parallelism alone it is enough to note the root.[95] For a system meant to note both repetitive and semantic parallelism at once it was found useful to apply numbers in sequence to each successive word, repeating the number in cases of repetitive parallelism (a superscript number may be used to note the number of occurrences of the repetition) and using a primed form of the number for semantic parallelism—which is simply an extension of using primed letters to note parallelism within a poetic unit. The system of primed numbers is not highly communicative, however, for it does not permit any distinction between the various forms of parallelism (as delineated by Geller, for example) nor does it permit any distinction between various degrees of semantic proximity of parallel members. Nevertheless, even with these limitations, the system of using numbers is an effective one to note distant parallelism, for any time a number smaller than the next expected number appears one realizes that some form of parallelism is occurring. The two main types of parallelism, repetitive and semantic, are distinguished easily by the two forms of notation (superscript vs. priming) and the number of occurrences is immediately visible, making it easy to glance back and note the previous examples of any given parallelism.

The system of noting semantic parallelism over the extent of a long text by primed numbers does become cumbersome, while the meaningfulness of the notation probably decreases in inverse proportion to the length of the text, for the following reason. Though semantic parallelism is not the strongest recall device in distant parallelism (repetitive parallelism being stronger), various chains of semantic parallelisms are formed, with different nuances developing at one point or another of the sequence and in various semantic relationships with previous elements of the chain. These multiple bifurcations make any single notation of semantic parallelism over a long work an oversimplification. This said, however, it must be added that the attempt to determine the chains of parallelism is an excellent exercise for the exegete, for the various shifts in meaning emerge clearly from the attempt to outline the parallelism. Therefore, either such a chart (a more readily accessible form of notation would render the chart even more useful) or a prose version thereof, or both,

---

[95] See above, Ch. I, note 12.

should be part of an exegesis of the formal structure of an ancient Northwest Semitic poem.[96]

In the preceding lists of forms of parallelism (repetitive, semantic, minor elements—for grammatical and phoenetic parallelism, see below, this section) it was found useful to note parallelism as occurring in four distributions: 1) half-line (within a stich); 2) "regular" (between the members of a distich or a larger single unit); 3) near (between elements of contiguous poetic units); 4) distant (between elements of non-contiguous units).

Half-line parallelism has received the most attention in the works of Dahood.[97] From the small sample furnished by *ʿnt* I, it appears that half-line parallelism functions as a strengthening device for poetic units otherwise lacking cohesion. Cases 1, 3, and 4 in the preceding chart all occur in lines which do not exhibit strong "regular" parallelism. Moreover, case 3 is a variant form of the bicolon containing the three-verb sequence, which in its two previous occurrences was complete with the three verbs. Finally, case 2 seems to function as a means of strengthening the loose semantic parallelism *yqḥ* // *ymsk*. In anticipation of the discussion of near parallelism, it may be noted that all three of the bicola in this sample text which do not contain strong "regular" parallelism are marked by both half-line (cases 1, 3, and 4) and near parallelism (cases 4, 6, 7, and 8). Though a more extensive sample is needed, we may at least take as a working hypothesis that lack of "regular" parallelism[98] will frequently be compensated for in the form of other distributions of parallelism.

In purely numerical terms, there can be no doubt that "regular" parallelism, that between elements located in different half-lines of an

---

[96] See Ch. I, note 15 for the reference to my other attempt at this form of notation (Ps. 89).

[97] In *RSP* I, II, and III (1972, 1975, 1981). The greatest problem with Dahood's examples of "juxtaposition" and "collocation" is the mixture of prose and poetic sources (see my review of *RSP* I in *JNES* 36 [1977] 65-68, esp. pp. 66-67). See also now Watson's important article on "internal parallelism" (ref. above, Ch. I, note 13).

[98] Given the camparatively large number of occurrences of all types of parallelism in "regular" distribution in the sample text, it appears legitimate to go on considering parallels between the members of a line to be the regular distribution of parallelism and to express the other distributions of parallelism in terms of comparison with this regular distribution. (I do not refer here to *parallelismus membrorum* as the basic form of parallelism because that term is so closely linked with a particular type of parallelism, viz., semantic.) If, as has been claimed (e.g., Landy, *JSOT* 28 [1984] 75—see above, Ch. I, note 59), parallelism is the Ugaritic-Hebrew equivalent of meter, and if it be granted that the analysis of the two sample texts in this work shows that the primary organization of parallelism is between the members of the line, then that distribution of parallelism may be considered the "regular" one—in statistical terms if in no others. For a recent defense of the bicolon or tricolon as the "basic period" of Hebrew poetry, see E. C. Webster, "Strophic Patterns in Job 3-28," *JSOT* 26 (1983) 33-60, and "Strophic Patterns in Job 29-42," *JSOT* 30 (1984) 95-109.

individual poetic unit, is indeed the most regular form of parallelism. Nevertheless, one of the main criticisms which can be leveled against the traditional study of parallelism, and even against the more modern analytical and notational systems, is that they limit themselves to regular parallelism.[99] That this distribution of parallelism is clear and of frequent occurrence accounts fully for the emphasis on its study; but this is not a reason for the neglect of the other distributions. This said, we may go on to the other distributions, for "regular" parallelism has already dominated this analysis as it has so many before it.

Near parallelism has the clear function of binding weakly cohesive units into their context and of binding together sequences of bicola into larger rhetorical units. The first of these functions was discussed above in the section on half-line parallelism (cases 4 through 9). The second function emerges from an examination of the chart. Especially clear is the sequence of the words for vessels (case 5). This macrostructural function is closely linked with the similar function of distant parallelism, for near parallelism may set up a series of links between the elements of the distant parallelism (cf. especially case 5). It is of interest that all of the examples but one of near parallelism in this sample text group semantic and grammatical parallelism. The exception is *rʾi*, an abstract noun, parallel with finite verbal forms (case 4). Note also the different syntactic functions of the two adjectives *nʿm* and *ṭb* (case 7), the first a substantive, the second an attributive adjective. Near parallelism also exhibits other features of parallelism discussed here: phonetic (case 5), minor elements (cases 2 and 9), and positional (case 2—all examples of *-h* which refer to *bʿl* are in final position, while the one *-h* with an antecedent other than *bʿl* is in the middle of the line: *ltphnh*[100]). This situation is somewhat different from that of distant parallelism.

Distant parallelism provides macrostructural links of various kinds. When joined with the other distributions, especially near parallelism, it constitutes a part of long chains of parallel elements. When it is not linked with near parallelism, there definitely appears, on the basis of the present sample, to be a gradation of strength in the types of parallelism used. Repetitive parallelism is the strongest and it may be used to bind together units small (e.g., half-line: *ymsk bmskh*, § VIII) and large (e.g., distant: *qm*; *qm*, §§ II, IX). Semantic parallelism is the next strongest device and is most useful in relatively smaller units, ranging from the half

---

[99] Of the recent authors discussed here, only O'Connor has liberated himself consistently from the bicolonic limitation. For the differences between his levels of analysis and mine, see my review cited above in Ch. I, note 7.

[100] This example may have phonetic dissimilarity as well if *ks* is feminine in gender: *lā tiphânnaha*.

line (e.g., *rb ᶜẓm*, § VI) to four bicola (*ks* to *kd*, §§ V-VIII, in a chain of near parallelisms and linked with repetitive parallelism). Repetitive parallelism can apparently bind together units more disparate in content than can semantic parallelism: *qm* binds together the entire feast, while *ks-kd* binds the "cup" + "drink" sequences. Grammatical parallelism is weaker than the two preceding types, apparently only useful as a distant device when accompanying repetitive and /or semantic parallelism (e.g., *qm*; *ndd*; *qm*, §§ II, IV, IX). Finally comes phonetic parallelism, which, like grammatical parallelism, is probably limited to relatively small units and would not have been perceived over greater distances without the aid of other devices (i.e., if, in column II, there is another series of occlusives such as we have in §§ V-VIII of col. I, it would probably not be perceived as parallel to col. I unless the subject of the section were there also cups). The only really plausible example of distant phonetic parallelism unaided by near parallelism in *ᶜnt* I is *yṯᶜr*; *yᶜšr* (§§ II, IV), where the actual parallelism is assured by position, semantics, and grammar.

CHAPTER TWO

THE PARALLELISTIC STRUCTURE OF PROVERBS 2

2.00

	Text[1]	*Vocalization*
1.	*bny ʾm-tqḥ ʾmry*	*b^{e}nī^{y} ʾim-tiqqaḥ ʾămāray*
	wmṣwty tṣpn ʾtk	*ûmiṣwō^{w}tay tiṣpōn ʾittāk*
2.	*lhqšyb lḥkmh ʾznk*	*l^{e}haqšī^{y}b laḥokmā^{h} ʾoznekā*
	tṭh lbk ltbwnh	*taṭṭe^{h} libb^{e}kā latt^{e}bū^{w}nā^{h}*
3.	*ky ʾm lbynh tqrʾ*	*kī^{y} ʾim labbī^{y}nā^{h} tiqrāʾ*
	ltbwnh ttn qwlk	*latt^{e}bū^{w}nā^{h} tittēn qō^{w}lekā*
4.	*ʾm tbqšnh kksp*	*ʾim-t^{e}baqšennā^{h} kakkāsep*
	wkmṭmwnym tḥpśnh	*w^{e}kammaṭmō^{w}nī^{y}m taḥp^{e}śennā^{h}*
5.	*ʾz tbyn yrʾt yhwh*	*ʾāz tābī^{y}n yirʾat yahweh*
	wdʿt ʾlhym tmṣʾ	*w^{e}daʿat ʾĕlōhī^{y}m timṣāʾ*
6.	*ky yhwh ytn ḥkmh*	*kī^{y}-yahweh yittēn ḥokmā^{h}*
	mpyw dʿt wtbwnh	*mippī^{y}w daʿat ût^{e}bū^{w}nā^{h}*
7.	*wṣpn lyšrym twšyh*	*w^{e}ṣāpan* (K!) *layšārī^{y}m tū^{w}šiyyā^{h}*
	mgn lhlky tm	*māgēn l^{e}hōl^{e}kē^{y} tōm*
8.	*lnṣr ʾrḥwt mšpṭ*	*linṣōr ʾorḥō^{w}t mišpāṭ*
	wdrk ḥsydw yšmr	*w^{e}derek ḥăsī^{y}dō^{w}* (K!) *yišmōr*
9.	*ʾz tbyn ṣdq wmšpṭ*	*ʾāz tābī^{y}n ṣedeq ûmišpāṭ*
	wmyšrym kl-mʿgl-ṭwb	*ûmē^{y}šārī^{y}m kol-maʿgal-ṭō^{w}b*
10.	*ky-tbwʾ ḥkmh blbk*	*kī^{y}-tābō^{w}ʾ ḥokmā^{h} b^{e}libbekā*
	wdʿt lnpšk ynʿm	*w^{e}daʿat l^{e}napš^{e}kā yinʿām*
11.	*mzmh tšmr ʿlyk*	*m^{e}zimmā^{h} tišmōr ʿāle^{y}kā*
	tbwnh tnṣrk	*t^{e}bū^{w}nā^{h} tinṣ^{e}rekkā^{h}*
12.	*lhṣylk mdrk rʿ*	*l^{e}haṣṣī^{y}l^{e}kā midderek rāʿ*
	mʾyš mdbr thpkwt	*mēʾī^{y}š m^{e}dabbēr tahpūkō^{w}t*
13.	*hʿzbym ʾrḥwt yšr*	*haʿōz^{e}bī^{y}m ʾorḥō^{w}t yōšer*
	llkt bdrky ḥšk	*lāleket bedarkē^{y} ḥōšek*
14.	*hśmḥym lʿśwt rʿ*	*haśś^{e}mēḥī^{y}m laʿăśō^{w}t rāʿ*
	ygylw bthpkwt rʿ	*yāgī^{y}lū^{w} b^{e}tahpūkō^{w}t rāʿ*

[1] In order to provide uniformity with the Ugaritic text in part I, the Hebrew text is here given in transliteration. The same form of the vocalized text is used below in the analyses of phonetic parallelism and for that reason I have clearly distinguished *matres lectionis* from sounding consonants by putting the former in superscript. Note that the vocalized text is in two instances based on the *Ketiv* (vss. 7, 8).

15.	*ʾšr ʾrḥtyhm ʿqšym*	*ʾăšer ʾorḥōtēʸhem ʿiqqᵉšīʸm*
	wnlwzym bmʿglwtm	*ûnᵉlōʷzīʸm bᵉmaʿgᵉlōʷtām*
16.	*lhṣylk mʾšh zrh*	*lᵉhaṣṣīʸlᵉkā mēʾiššāʰ zārāʰ*
	mnkryh ʾmryh hḥlyqh	*minnokriyyāʰ ʾămāreʸhā heḥĕlīʸqāʰ*
17.	*hʿzbt ʾlwp nʿwryh*	*haʿōzebet ʾallūʷp nᵉʿūʷreʸhā*
	wʾt-bryt ʾlhyh škḥh	*wᵉʾet-bᵉrīʸt ʾĕlōheʸhā šākēḥāʰ*
18.	*ky šḥh ʾl-mwt byth*	*kīʸ šāḥāʰ ʾel-māwet bēʸtāh*
	wʾl-rpʾym mʿgltyh	*wᵉʾel-rᵉpāʾīʸm maʿgᵉlōteʸhā*
19.	*kl-bʾyh lʾ yšwbwn*	*kol-bāʾeʸhā lōʾ yᵉšūʷbūʷn*
	wlʾ-yśygw ʾrḥwt ḥyym	*wᵉlōʾ-yaśśīʸgūʷ ʾorḥōʷt ḥayyīʸm*
20.	*lmʿn tlk bdrk ṭwbym*	*lᵉmaʿan tēlēk bᵉderek ṭōʷbīʸm*
	wʾrḥwt ṣdyqym tšmr	*wᵉʾorḥōʷt ṣaddīʸqīʸm tišmōr*
21.	*ky-yšrym yšknw-ʾrṣ*	*kīʸ-yᵉšārīʸm yiškᵉnūʷ ʾāreṣ*
	wtmymym ywtrw bh	*ûtᵉmīʸmīʸm yiwwātᵉrūʷ bāh*
22.	*wršʿym mʾrṣ ykrtw*	*ûrᵉšāʿīʸm mēʾereṣ yikkātērūʷ*
	wbwgdym ysḥw mmnh	*ûbōʷgᵉdīʸm yissᵉḥūʷ mimmennāʰ*

2.01 *Translation*

1. My son, if you accept my sayings,
   Store up my commandments,
2. By bending your ear to wisdom,
   Inclining your mind to discernment;
3. If indeed you call out to understanding,
   Shout aloud to discernment;
4. If you seek it like silver,
   Search for it as for treasure;
5. Then you will understand the fear of YHWH,
   you will find out the knowledge of God.
6. When YHWH gives wisdom,
   From his mouth, knowledge and discernment;
7. Stores up cleverness for the upright,
   A shield for those who conduct themselves perfectly,
8. Guarding the ways of justice
   Watching the way of his devotee;
9. Then you will understand rightness and justice,
   Uprightness (and) every good track.
10. When wisdom enters your mind (lit.: "heart"),
    Knowledge is a pleasure to your senses (lit.: "gullet"),
11. Foresight will watch over you,
    Discernment will guard you;

12. Saving you from the evil way,
    From anyone speaking perversion,
13. (From) those who abandon straight paths
    So as to go on ways of darkness,
14. Who rejoice in the doing of evil,
    Delight in evil perversion,
15. Whose paths are crooked,
    Who are devious in their tracks;
16. Saving you from the strange woman,
    From the foreign woman whose sayings are smooth,
17. Who has abandoned her master of younger days,
    Forgot the covenant of her God;
18. For her house inclines to Death,
    To the Shades her track;
19. None who goes into her shall ever return,
    Ever touch the paths of life.
20. Thus you shall walk the way of the good,
    Keep to the paths of the righteous.
21. For the upright will dwell in the land
    And the blameless will remain in it;
22. While the wicked will be cut off from the land
    And the treacherous will be uprooted from it.

2.02 *Sense Units*

How a son may acquire Wisdom

Exhortation to Wisdom

1. *bny ʾm-tqḥ ʾmry*
   wmṣwty tṣpn ʾtk
2. *lhqšyb lḥkmh ʾznk*
   tṭh lbk ltbwnh
3. *ky ʾm lbynh tqrʾ*
   ltbwnh ttn qwlk
4. *ʾm tbqšnh kksp*
   wkmṭmwnym tḥpśnh
5. *ʾz tbyn yrʾt yhwh*
   wdʿt ʾlhym tmṣʾ

YHWH Giver of Wisdom

6. *ky yhwh ytn ḥkmh*
   mpyw dʿt wtbwnh
7. *wṣpn lyšrym twšyh*
   mgn lhlky tm
8. *lnṣr ʾrḥwt mšpṭ*
   wdrk ḥsydw yšmr
9. *ʾz tbyn ṣdq wmšpṭ*
   wmyšrym kl-mʿgl-ṭwb

Wisdom enters

10. *ky-tbwʾ ḥkmh blbk*
    wdʿt lnpšk ynʿm
11. *mzmh tšmr ʿlyk*
    tbwnh tnṣrk

Effects of Wisdom

Wisdom protects from the evil man

12. *lhṣylk mdrk rʿ*
mʾyš mdbr thpkwt
13. *hʿzbym ʾrḥwt yšr*
llkt bdrky ḥšk
14. *hśmḥym lʿśwt rʿ*
ygylw bthpkwt rʿ
15. *ʾšr ʾrḥtyhm ʿqšym*
wnlwzym bmʿglwtm

Wisdom protects from the evil woman

16. *lhṣylk mʾšh zrh*
mnkryh ʾmryh hḥlyqh
17. *hʿzbt ʾlwp nʿwryh*
wʾt-bryt ʾlhyh škḥh
18. *ky šḥh ʾl-mwt byth*
wʾl-rpʾym mʿgltyh
19. *kl-bʾyh lʾ yšwbwn*
wlʾ-yśygw ʾrḥwt ḥyym

Conclusion in form of promise and warning

Summary for the son

20. *lmʿn tlk bdrk ṭwbym*
wʾrḥwt ṣdyqym tšmr

Contrasted fate of good and evil

21. *ky-yšrym yšknw-ʾrṣ*
wtmymym ywtrw bh
22. *wršʿym mʾrṣ ykrtw*
wbwgdym ysḥw mmnh

2.1 *Quantitative Analysis*

	Word Count	Syllable Count	Consonant Count	"Vocable" Count	"Verse-units"
1.	4 // 3	8 // 8	12 // 13	23 // 25[2]	3 // 3
2.	3 // 3	9 // 9	15 // 12	25 // 25	3 // 3
3.	4 // 3	7 // 9	13 // 13	22 // 26	3 // 3
4.	3 // 2	8 // 9	12 // 15	23 // 26	2 // 2
5.	4 // 3	7 // 8	14 // 13	23 // 22	3 // 3[3]
6.	4 // 3	7 // 8	13 // 13	22 // 22	3 // 3
7.	3 // 3	9 // 7	15 // 10	27 // 21	3 // 3
8.	3 // 3	6 // 8	13 // 13	21 // 22	3 // 3
9.	4 // 4	8 // 8	14 // 16	25 // 25	3 // 3
10.	4 // 3	9 // 9	14 // 13	26 // 24	3 // 3
11.	3 // 2	8 // 7	12 // 10	24 // 19	3 // 2
12.	3 // 3	9 // 8	12 // 14	25 // 26	3 // 3
13.	3 // 3	8 // 8	14 // 12	24 // 22	3 // 3
14.	3 // 3	8 // 8	13 // 14	24 // 25	3 // 3
15.	3 // 2	9 // 9	15 // 15	26 // 25	2 // 2
16.	3 // 3	10 // 12	13 // 17	28 // 33	3 // 3
17.	3 // 4	10 // 11	15 // 16	28 // 31	3 // 3
18.	5 // 3	8 // 10	14 // 15	24 // 28	3 // 3
19.	4 // 4	8 // 9	14 // 17	24 // 28	3 // 3[4]
20.	4 // 3	10 // 8	16 // 16	28 // 26	3 // 3
21.	4 // 3	9 // 9	15 // 14	26 // 26	3 // 2
22.	3 // 3	11 // 10	15 // 15	31 // 27	3 // 3

[2] Long vowel + *mater lectionis* is given two counts rather than three, i.e., the syllable is counted as open and long (CV:) rather than as closed and long (CV:C).

[3] Construct chains in Margalit's system vary in "verse-unit" count. I am assuming that the proclitic *w-* + noun + noun will here count as two verse-units.

[4] I am assuming that in order to avoid a 2 // 3 bicolon, Margalit would give to *lōʾ* a full count.

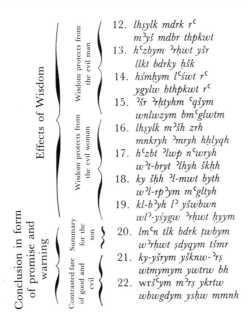

2.2 *Parallelism: Repetive Parallelism*[5]

1) *-y* (vs. 1tris)
2) *ʾm* (vss. 1, 3, 4)
3) *ʾmr* (*ʾmry*: vs. 1; *ʾmryh*: vs. 16)
4) *w-* (vss. 1, 4, 5, 6, 7, 8, 9bis, 10, 15, 17, 18, 19, 20, 21, 22bis)
5) *ṣpn* (*tṣpn*: vs. 1; *ṣpn*: vs. 7)
6) *l-* (vss. 2tris, 3bis, 7bis, 8, 10, 12, 13, 14, 16, 20)
7) *ḥkmh* (vss. 2, 6, 10)
8) *-k* (vss. 2bis, 3, 10bis, 11bis, 12, 16)
9) *lb* (*lbk*: vss. 2, 10)
10) *bn* (*tbwnh*: vss. 2, 3, 6, 11; *bynh*: vs. 3; *tbyn*: vss. 5, 9)
11) *ky* (vss. 3, 6, 10, 18, 21)
12) *ntn* (*ttn*: vs. 3; *ytn*: vs. 6)
13) -(*n*)*h* (*-nh*: vs. 4bis; *-h*: vss. 16, 17bis, 18bis, 19, 21, 22)
14) *k-* (vs. 4bis)
15) *ʾz* (vss. 5, 9)
16) *yhwh* (vss. 5, 6)
17) *dʿt* (vss. 5, 6, 10)
18) *ʾlh* (*ʾlhym*: vs. 5; *ʾlhyh*: vs. 17)
19) *m*(*n*)- (vss. 6, 12bis, 16bis, 22bis)
20) *-w* (vss. 6, 8)
21) *yšr* (*yšrym*: vss. 7, 21; *myšrym*: vs. 19; *yšr*: vs. 13)
22) *hlk* (*hlky*: vs. 7; *lkt*: vs. 13; *tlk*: vs. 20)
23) *tm* (*tm*: vs. 7; *tmymym* vs. 21)
24) *nṣr* (*nṣr*: vs. 8; *tnṣr*: vs. 11)
25) *ʾrḥ* (*ʾrḥwt*: vss. 8, 13, 19, 20; *ʾrḥtyhm*: vs. 15)
26) *špṭ* (*mšpṭ*: vss. 8, 9)
27) *drk* (*drk*: vss. 8, 12, 20; *drky*: vs. 13)
28) *šmr* (*yšmr*: vs. 8; *tšmr*: vss. 11, 20)
29) *ṣdq* (*ṣdq*: vs. 9; *ṣdyqym*: vs. 20)
30) *kl* (vss. 9, 19)
31) *mʿgl* (*mʿgl*: vs. 9; *mʿglwtm*: vs. 15; *mʿgltyh*: vs. 18)
32) *ṭb* (*ṭwb*: vs. 9; *ṭwbym*: vs. 20)
33) *bʾ* (*tbwʾ*: vs. 10; *bʾyh*: vs. 19)
34) *b-* (vss. 10, 13, 14, 15, 20, 21)
35) *nṣl* (*hṣyl*: vss. 12, 16)
36) *rʿ* (vss. 12, 14bis)
37) *thpkwt* (vss. 12, 14)
38) *h-* (vss. 13, 14, 17)

[5] Space does not permit a chart facing the text as was given for *ʿnt* I at this point; a simple list is given, therefore, in order of first appearance.

39) *ʿzb* (*ʿzbym*: vs. 13; *ʿzbt*: vs. 17)
40) -(*h*)*m* (-*hm*, -*m*: vs. 15)
41) *ʾl* (vs. 18bis)
42) *lʾ* (vs. 19bis)
43) *ʾrṣ* (vss. 21, 22)

2.2.1 *Repetitive Parallelism: Distribution*

A. Half-line
1) -*y* + -*y* (vs. 1)
2) -*l* + *l*- (vs. 2)

B. Regular[6]
1) -*y* + -*y* // -*y* (vs. 1)
2) *l*- + *l*- // *l*- (vs. 2); *l*- // *l*- (vss. 3, 7)
3) -*k* // -*k* (vss. 2, 10, 11)
4) *bynh* // *tbwnh* (vs. 3)
5) *k*- // *k*- (vs. 4)
6) -*nh* // -*nh* (vs. 4); -*h* // -*h* (vss. 17, 18)
7) *w*- // *w*- (vss. 9, 22)
8) -*k* // -*k* (vss. 10, 11)
9) *m*(*n*)- (vss. 12, 16, 22)
10) *rʿ* // *rʿ* (vs. 14)
11) -*hm* // -*m* (vs. 15)
12) *ʾl* // *ʾl* (vs. 18)
13) *lʾ* // *lʾ* (vs. 19)

C. Near
1) *l*- + *l*- // *l*- . . . *l*- // *l*- (vss. 2, 3); *l*- . . . *l*- (vss. 7, 8); *l*- . . . *l*- . . . *l*- (vss. 12, 13, 14)
2) -*k* // -*k* . . . -*k* (vss. 2, 3); -*k* // -*k* . . . -*k* // -*k* . . . -*k* (vss. 10, 11, 12)
3) *ʾm* . . . *ʾm* (vss. 3, 4)
4) *tbwnh* . . . *bynh* // *tbwnh* (vss. 2, 3); *tbyn* . . . *tbwnh* (vss. 5, 6)
5) *w*- . . . *w*- . . . *w*- . . . *w*- . . . *w*- . . . *w*- // *w*- . . . *w*- (vss. 4, 5, 6, 7, 8, 9, 10); *w*- . . . *w*- . . . *w*- . . . *w*- . . . *w*- . . . *w*- // *w*- (vss. 17, 18, 19, 20, 21, 22)
6) *yhwh* . . . *yhwh* (vss. 5, 6)

---

[6] Repetitive parallelism in "regular" distribution is almost exclusively limited to minor elements. The only exceptions are *bynh* // *tbwnh* (#4, vs. 3), which are different forms of a same root and do not even qualify as "repetitive" for O'Connor (see above, Ch. I, note 12), and *rʿ* // *rʿ* (#10, vs. 14), which is provided some variation by the combination of repetitive, semantic, and grammatical parallelism in the collocation of *thpkwt* to *rʿ* in the second half-line.

7) *dʿt . . . dʿt* (vss. 5, 6)
8) *mšpṭ . . . mšpṭ* (vss. 8, 9)
9) *drk . . . drky* (vss. 12, 13)
10) *ʾrḥwt . . . ʾrḥwt* (vss. 19, 20)
11) *b- . . . b- . . . b-* (vss. 13, 14, 15); *b- . . . b-* (vss. 20, 21)
12) *-h . . . -h // -h . . . -h // -h . . . -h* (vss. 16, 17, 18, 19); *-h . . . -h* (vss. 21, 22)
13) *h- . . . h-* (vss. 13, 14)
14) *ʾrṣ . . . ʾrṣ* (vss. 21, 22)

D. Distant[7]

1) *ʾm . . . ʾm . . . ʾm* (vss. 1, 3, 4)
2) *ʾmr* (*ʾmry . . . ʾmry*: vss. 1, 16)
3) *w- . . . w- . . . w- . . . w- . . . w- . . . w- . . . w- // w- . . . w- . . . w- . . . w- . . . w- . . . w- . . . w- . . . w- . . . w- // w-* (vss. 1, 4, 5, 6, 7, 8, 9, 10, 15, 17, 18, 19, 20, 21, 22)
4) *ṣpn* (*tṣpn . . . ṣpn*: vss. 1, 7)
5) *l- + l- // l- . . . l- // l- . . . l- . . . l- . . . l- . . . l- . . . l- . . . l- . . . l- . . . l-* (vss. 2, 3, 7, 8, 10, 12, 13, 14, 16, 20)[8]
6) *ḥkm* (*ḥkmh . . . ḥkmh . . . ḥkmh*: vss. 2, 6, 10)
7) *-k // -k . . . -k . . . -k // -k . . . -k // -k . . . -k . . . -k* (vss. 2, 3, 10, 11, 12, 16)
8) *lb* (*lbk . . . lbk*: vss. 2, 10)
9) *bn* (*tbwnh . . . bynh // tbwnh . . . tbyn . . . tbwnh . . . tbyn . . . tbwnh*: vss. 2, 3, 5, 6, 9, 11)
10) *ky . . . ky . . . ky . . . ky . . . ky* (vss. 3, 6, 10, 18, 21)
11) *ytn* (*ttn . . . ytn*: vss. 3, 6)
12) *-nh // -nh . . . -h . . . -h // -h . . . -h // -h . . . -h . . . -h . . . -h* (vss. 4, 16, 17, 18, 19, 21, 22)
13) *ʾz . . . ʾz* (vss. 5, 9)
14) *ydʿ* (*dʿt . . . dʿt . . . dʿt*: vss. 5, 6, 10)
15) *ʾlh* (*ʾlhym . . . ʾlhyh*: vss. 5, 17)
16) *m(n)- . . . m(n)- // m(n)- . . . m(n)- // m(n)- . . . m(n)- // m(n)-* (vss. 6, 12, 16, 22)
17) *-w . . . -w* (vss. 6, 8)
18) *yšr* (*yšrym . . . myšrym . . . yšr . . . yšrym*: vss. 7, 9, 13, 21)
19) *hlk* (*hlky . . . lkt . . . tlk*: vss. 7, 13, 20)

---

[7] All but eight of the repetitive parallelisms listed sequentially in the previous chart appear in distant structures. The eight are: ##1 (*-y*), 14 (*k-*), 16 (*yhwh*), 26 (*špṭ*), 40 (*-(h)m*), 41 (*ʾl*), 42 (*lʾ*), 43 (*ʾrṣ*).

[8] Cf. the chiastically arranged compound distant structure *b- // l- . . . l- // b-* (vss. 10, 14)

20) *tm* (*tm* . . . *tmymym*: vss. 7, 21)
21) *nṣr* (*nṣr* . . . *tnṣr*: vss. 8, 11)
22) *ʾrḥ* (*ʾrḥwt* . . . *ʾrḥwt* . . . *ʾrḥtyhm* . . . *ʾrḥwt* . . . *ʾrḥwt*: vss. 8, 13, 15, 19, 20)
23) *drk* (*drk* . . . *drk* . . . *drky* . . . *drk*: vss. 8, 12, 13, 20)
24) *šmr* (*yšmr* . . . *tšmr* . . . *tšmr*: vss. 8, 11, 20)
25) *ṣdq* (*ṣdq* . . . *ṣdyqym*: vss. 9, 20)
26) *kl* . . . *kl* (vss. 9, 19)
27) *ʿgl* (*mʿgl* . . . *mʿglwtm* . . . *mʿgltyh*: vss. 9, 15, 18)
28) *ṭb* (*ṭwb* . . . *ṭwbym*: vss. 9, 20)
29) *bʾ* (*tbwʾ* . . . *bʾyh*: vss. 10, 19)
30) *b-* . . . *b-* . . . *b-* . . . *b-* . . . *b-* . . . *b-* (vss. 10, 13, 14, 15, 20, 21)
31) *nṣl* (*hṣylk* . . . *hṣylk*: vss. 12, 16)
32) *rʿ* (*rʿ* . . . *rʿ* // *rʿ*: vss. 12, 14)
33) *hpk* (*thpkwt* . . . *thpkwt*: vss. 12, 14)
34) *h-* . . . *h-* . . . *h-* (vss. 13, 14, 17)
35) *ʿzb* (*hʿzbym* . . . *hʿzbt*: vss. 13, 17)

E. Combinations
1) *-y* (half-line, regular)
2) *ʾm* (near, distant)
3) *w-* (regular, near, distant)
4) *l-* (half-line, regular, near, distant)
5) *-k* (regular, near, distant)
6) *bn* (regular, near, distant)
7) *-(n)h* (regular, near, distant)
8) *dʿt* (near, distant)
9) *m(n)-* (regular, distant)
10) *ʾrḥ* (near, distant)
11) *drk* (near, distant)
12) *b-* (near, distant)
13) *rʿ* (regular, distant)
14) *h-* (near, distant)

2.2.2 *Repetitive Parallelism: Grammatical Relationships*

A. Complete Repetition[9]
1) *-y* (see also at B)
2) *ʾm*

[9] For full indications of attestations, see "Parallelism: Repetitive Parallelism." In arriving at the classification "Complete Repetition," pausal differences are not taken into account. Similar forms in different immediate environments are also listed at B, e.g., same suffix on nouns of different number, same forms with different proclitics.

3) *w-* (see also at B)
4) *l-* (linking vowel not taken into account)
5) *ḥkmh* (see also at B)
6) *-k* (see also at B)
7) *lb(k)* (see also at B)
8) *tbwnh* (see also at B, C)
tbyn (see also at C)
9) *ky*
10) *-nh* (see also at B)
-h (see also at B)
11) *k-*
12) *ʾz*
13) *yhwh*
14) *dʿt* (see also at B)
15) *m(n)-* (see also at B)
16) *yšrym* (see also at B)
17) *ʾrḥwt* (see also at B)
18) *mšpṭ* (see also at B)
19) *drk* (see also at B)
20) *tšmr* (see also at B)
21) *kl*
22) *b-*
23) *(l)hṣyl(k)*
24) *rʿ*
25) *thpkwt* (see also at B)
26) *h-*
27) *ʾl* (see also at B)
28) *lʾ* (see also at B)
29) *ʾrṣ* (see also at B)

B. Same Base
1) *-y* (on singular and plural nouns; see also at A)
2) *ʾmry*, *ʾmryh* (different suffixes)
3) *w-* (two forms of conjunction)
4) *ḥkmh* (proclitic variation; see also at A)
5) *-k* (on singular and plural nouns; see also at A)
6) *lb(k)* (proclitic variation; see also at A)
7) *tbwnh* (proclitic variation; see also at A)
8) *ttn*, *ytn* (difference of person)
9) *-(n)h* (as suffix on energic and non-energic verbal forms; on singular and plural nouns; see also at A)
10) *ʾlhym*, *ʾlhyh* (suffix variation)

11) *dᶜt* (proclitic variation; see also at A)
12) *m(n)-*, *m(n)mn(h)* (simple vs. reduplicated form, with suffix; see also at A)
13) *-w* (on singular and plural nouns)
14) *yšrym* (proclitic variation; see also at A)
15) *ʾrḥwt*, *ʾrḥtyhm* (suffix variation; see also at A)
16) *mšpṭ* (proclitic variation; see also at A)
17) *drk*, *drky* (difference of number; proclitic variation; see also at A)
18) *yšmr*, *tšmr* (difference of person)
19) *mᶜgl*, *mᶜglwtm*, *mᶜgltyh* (different numbers and suffixes)
20) *ṭwb*, *ṭwbym* (difference of number; probably difference of abstract vs. concrete substantive)
21) *thpkwt* (proclitic variation; see also at A)
22) *(h)ᶜzbym*, *(h)ᶜzbt* (different genders and numbers)
23) *-hm*, *-m* (elision of *-h-*)
24) *ʾl* (proclitic variation; see also at A)
25) *lʾ* (proclitic variation; see also at A)
26) *ʾrṣ* (proclitic variation; see also at A)

C. Different Base

1) *tṣpn*, *ṣpn* (imperfect vs. perfect)
2) *tbwnh*, *bynh*, *tbyn* (two different nominal forms and a verbal one)
3) *yšrym*, *myšrym*, *yšr* (three nominal forms)
4) *hlk*, *lkt*, *tlk* (three verbal forms)
5) *tm*, *tmymym* (two nominal forms)
6) *nṣr*, *tnṣr* (infinitive vs. imperfect)
7) *tbwʾ*, *bʾyh* (two verbal forms)
8) *ṣdq*, *ṣdyqym* (two nominal forms)

2.3 *Parallelism: Semantic Parallelism*[10]

1.	*bny ʾm-tqḥ ʾmry*	*a b c*	$1 \quad 2^1 + 3 \quad 4\ \mathrm{I}^1$
	wmṣwty tṣpn ʾtk	*c′ d a′*	$5^1 + 4\ \mathrm{II}^1 \quad 6\ \mathrm{I}^1 \quad 7$
2.	*lhqšyb lḥkmh ʾznk*	*a b c*	$8^1 + 9^1 \quad 8^2 + 10\ \mathrm{I}^1 \quad 11\ \mathrm{I}$
	tṭh lbk ltbwnh	*a′ c′ b′*	$9\ \mathrm{II} \quad 11\ \mathrm{II}^1 \quad 8^3 + 10\ \mathrm{II}^1$
3.	*ky-ʾm lbynh tqrʾ*	$a^2\ b\ c$	$12^1 + 2^2 \quad 8^4 + 10\ \mathrm{II}^2$
	ltbwnh ttn qwlk	$b\ c'^2\ (= x + y)$	$8^5 + 10\ \mathrm{II}^3 \quad 14^1 + 11\ \mathrm{III}\ (= 13\ \mathrm{II})$

---

[10] Because of the greater number of minor elements in Proverbs 2, the analysis of the text with and without minor elements has been abandoned and each lexical item is numbered sequentially. See above, Ch. I, note 15.

4.	*ʾm-tbqšnh kksp*	*a b*	$2^{3} + 15$ I $16^{1} + 6$ II
	wkmṭmwnym tḥpśnh	*b′ a′*	$5^{2} + 16^{2} + 6$ III 15 II
5.	*ʾz tbyn yrʾt yhwh*	*a a′ b*	$17^{1} + 10$ II^{4} 10 IV 18 I^{1}
	wdʿt ʾlhym tmṣʾ	*a″ b′ c*	$5^{3} + 10$ III^{1} 18 II^{1} 19
6.	*ky-yhwh ytn ḥkmh*	*a b c*	$12^{2} + 18$ I^{2} 14^{2} 10 I^{2}
	mpyw dʿt wtbwnh	*a′ c′ c″*	$20^{1} + 11$ IV 10 III^{2} $5^{4} + 10$ II^{5}
7.	*wṣpn lyšrym twšyh*	*a b c*	$5^{5} + 6$ I^{2} $8^{6} + 21$ I^{1} 10 V
	mgn lhlky tm	$d\ b'^{2}$	22 $8^{7} + 23$ I^{1} + 21 II^{1}
8.	*lnṣr ʾrḥwt mšpṭ*	*a b c*	$8^{8} + 24$ I^{1} 25 I^{1} 21 III^{1}
	wdrk ḥsydw yšmr	*b′ c′ a′*	$5^{6} + 25$ II^{1} 21 IV 24 II^{1}
9.	*ʾz tbyn ṣdq wmšpṭ*	*a b b′*	$17^{2} + 10$ II^{6} 21 V^{1} $5^{7} + 21$ III^{2}
	wmyšrym kl-mʿgl-ṭwb	$b''\ b'''^{2}$	$5^{8} + 21$ I^{2} $26^{1} + 25$ III^{1} + 21 VI^{1}
10.	*ky-tbwʾ ḥkmh blbk*	*a b c*	$12^{3} + 23$ II^{1} 10 I^{3} $27^{1} + 11$ II^{2}
	wdʿt lnpšk ynʿm	*b′ c′ d*	$5^{9} + 10$ III^{3} $8^{9} + 11$ V 21 VII
11.	*mzmh tšmr ʿlyk*	*a b c*	10 VI 24 II^{2} 28
	tbwnh tnṣrkh	*a′ b′*	10 II^{7} 24 I^{2}
12.	*lhṣylk mdrk rʿ*	*a b c*	$8^{10} + 24$ III^{1} $20^{2} + 25$ II^{2} 29 I^{1}
	mʾyš mdbr thpkwt	*d e c′*	$20^{3} + 30$ I 4 III 29 II^{1}
13.	*hʿzbym ʾrḥwt yšr*	*a b c*	31 I^{1} 25 I^{2} 21 I^{3}
	llkt bdrky-ḥšk	*d b′ e*	$8^{11} + 23$ I^{2} $27^{2} + 25$ II^{3} 32
14.	*hśmḥym lʿśwt rʿ*	*a b c*	33 I $8^{12} + 34$ 29 I^{2}
	ygylw bthpkwt rʿ	*a′ c′ c*	33 II $27^{3} + 29$ II^{2} 29 I^{3}
15.	*ʾšr ʾrḥtyhm ʿqšym*	*a b c*	35 25 I^{3} 29 III
	wnlwzym bmʿglwtm	*c′ b′*	$5^{10} + 29$ IV $27^{4} + 25$ III^{2}
16.	*lhṣylk mʾšh zrh*	$a\ b^{2}\ (= x + y)$	$8^{13} + 24$ III^{2} $20^{4} + 30$ II 36 I
	mnkryh ʾmryh hḥlyqh	$b'\ (= y')\ c\ d$	$20^{5} + 36$ II 4 I^{2} 37
17.	*hʿzbt ʾlwp nʿwryh*	*a b c*	31 I^{2} 38 39
	wʾt-bryt ʾlhyh škḥh	*d e a′*	$5^{11} + 40 + 41$ 18 II^{2} 31 II
18.	*ky šḥh ʾl-mwt byth*	*a b c*	$12^{4} + 42$ $43^{1} + 44$ I 45
	wʾl-rpʾym mʿgltyh	*b′ d*	$5^{12} + 43^{2} + 44$ II 25 III^{3}
19.	*kl-bʾyh lʾ yšwbwn*	*a b*	$26^{2} + 23$ II^{2} $46^{1} + 47$
	wlʾ-yśygw ʾrḥwt ḥyym	*c d e*	$5^{13} + 46^{2} + 48$ 25 I^{4} 49
20.	*lmʿn tlk bdrk ṭwbym*	*a b c*	$8^{14}+50$ 23 I^{3} $27^{5}+25$ II^{4} 21 V^{2}
	wʾrḥwt ṣdyqym tšmr	*b′ c′ d*	$5^{14}+25$ I^{5} 21 V^{2} 24 I^{3}
21.	*ky-yšrym yšknw-ʾrṣ*	*a b c*	$12^{5} + 21$ I^{4} 51 I 52
	wtmymym ywtrw bh	*a′ b′ c′*	$5^{15} + 21$ II^{2} 51 II 27^{6}
22.	*wršʿym mʾrṣ yktrw*	*a b c*	$5^{16} + 29$ V $20^{6} + 52^{2}$ 53 I
	wbwgdym ysḥw mmnh	*a′ c′ b′*	$5^{17} + 29$ VI 53 II 20^{7}

2.3.1 *List of Words as Semantic Parallels*[11]

1 *BN: bny* (vs. 1)

2 *ʾm* (vss. 1^{1}, 2^{3}, 4^{3})

3 *LQḤ: tqḥ* (vs. 1)

4 I *ʾMR: ʾmry* (vs. 1^{1})
ʾmryh (vs. 16^{2})
II *ṢWH: mṣwty* (vs. 1)
III *DBR: mdbr* (vs. 12)

5 *w-* (vss. 1^{1}, 4^{2}, 5^{3}, 6^{4}, 7^{5}, 8^{6}, $9^{7,8}$, 10^{9}, 15^{10}, 17^{11}, 18^{12}, 19^{13}, 20^{14}, 21^{15}, $22^{16,17}$)

6 I *ṢPN: tṣpn* (vs. 1^{1})
ṣpn (vs. 7^{2})
II *KSP* (vs. 4)
III *ṬMN: mṭmwnym* (vs. 4)

7 *ʾt: ʾtk* (vs. 1)

8 *l-* (vss. $2^{1,2,3}$, $3^{4,5}$, $7^{6,7}$, 8^{8}, 10^{9}, 12^{10}, 13^{11}, 14^{12}, 16^{13}, 20^{14})

9 I *QŠB: hqšyb* (vs. 2)
II *NṬH: tṭh* (vs. 2)

10 I *ḤKM: ḥkmh* (vss. 2^{1}, 6^{2}, 10^{3})
II *BN: tbwnh* (vss. 2^{1}, 3^{3}, 6^{5}, 11^{7})
bynh (vs. 3^{2})
tbyn (vss. 5^{4}, 9^{6})
III *YDʿ: dʿt* (vss. 5^{1}, 6^{2}, 10^{3})
IV *YRʾ: yrʾt* (vs. 5)
V *YŠH: twšyh* (vs. 7)
VI *ZMM: mzmh* (vs. 11)

11 I *ʾZN: ʾznk* (vs. 2)
II *LBB: lbk* (vss. 2^{1}, 10^{2})
III *QWL: qwlk* (vs. 3)
IV *PH: pyw* (vs. 6)
V *NPŠ: npšk* (vs. 10)

12 *ky* (vss. 3^{1}, 6^{2}, 10^{3}, 18^{4}, 21^{5})

13 I *QRʾ: tqrʾ* (vs. 3)
II *NTN QWL: ttn qwlk* (vs. 3)

14 *NTN: ttn* (vs. 3^{1})
ytn (vs. 6^{2})

15 I *BQŠ: tbqšnh* (vs. 4)
II *ḤPŚ: tḥpśnh* (vs. 4)

16 *k-* (vs. $4^{1,2}$)

17 *ʾz* (vss. 5^{1}, 9^{2})

---

[11] See Ch. II, note 10 and Ch. I, note 15.

18 I *yhwh* (vss. 5^{1}, 6^{2})
II *ʾLH*: *ʾlhym* (vs. 5^{1})
ʾlhyh (vs. 17^{2})
19 *MṢ*: *tmṣʾ* (vs. 5)
20 *m(n)*- (vss. 6^{1}, $20^{2,3}$, $16^{4,5}$, $22^{6,7}$)
21 I *YŠR*: *yšrym* (vss. 7^{1}, 21^{4})
myšrym (vs. 9^{2})
yšr (vs. 13^{3})
II *TMM*: *tm* (vs. 7^{1})
tmymym (vs. 21^{2})
III *ŠPṬ*: *mšpṭ* (vss. 8^{1}, 9^{2})
IV *ḤSD*: *ḥsydw* (vs. 8)
V *ṢDQ*: *ṣdq* (vs. 9^{1})
ṣdyqym (vs. 20^{2})
VI *ṬB*: *ṭwb* (vs. 9^{1})
ṭwbym (vs. 20^{2})
VII *NʿM*: *ynʿm* (vs. 10)
22 *GNN*: *mgn* (vs. 7)
23 I *HLK*: *hlky* (vs. 7^{1})
lkt (vs. 13^{2})
tlk (vs. 20^{3})
24 I *NṢR*: *nṣr* (vs. 8^{1})
tnṣrkh (vs. 11^{2})
II *ŠMR*: *yšmr* (vs. 8^{1})
tšmr (vss. 11^{2}, 20^{3})
III *NṢL*: *hṣylk* (vss. 12^{1}, 16^{2})
25 I *ʾRḤ*: *ʾrḥwt* (vss. 8^{1}, 13^{2}, 19^{4}, 20^{5})
ʾrḥtyhm (vs. 15^{3})
II *DRK*: *drk* (vss. 8^{1}, 12^{2}, 20^{4})
drky (vs. 13^{3})
III *ʿGL*: *mʿgl* (vs. 9^{1})
mʿglwtm (vs. 15^{2})
mʿgltyh (vs. 18^{3})
26 *kl* (vss. 9^{1}, 19^{2})
27 *b*- (vss. 10^{1}, 13^{2}, 14^{3}, 15^{4}, 20^{5}, 21^{6})
28 *ʿl*: *ʿlyk* (vs. 11)
29 I *Rʿʿ*: *rʿ* (vss. 12^{1}, $14^{2,3}$)
II *HPK*: *thpkwt* (vss. 12^{1}, 14^{2})
III *ʿQŠ*: *ʿqšym* (vs. 15)
IV *LWZ*: *nwzlym* (vs. 15)
V *RŠʿ*: *ršʿym* (vs. 22)
VI *BGD*: *bwgdym* (vs. 22)

30 I *ʾyš* (vs. 12)
II *ʾšh* (vs. 16)
31 I *ʿZB: hʿzbym* (vs. 13[1])
hʿzbt (vs. 17[2])
II *ŠKḤ: škḥh* (vs. 17)
32 *ḤŠK* (vs. 13)
33 I *ŚMḤ: hśmḥym* (vs. 14)
II *GL: ygylw* (vs. 14)
34 *ʿŚH: ʿśwt* (vs. 14)
35 *ʾšr* (vs. 15)
36 I *ZR: zrh* (vs. 16)
II *NKR: nkryh* (vs. 16)
37 *ḤLQ: hḥlyqh* (vs. 16)
38 *ʾLP: ʾlwp* (vs. 17)
39 *NʿR: nʿwryh* (vs. 17)
40 *ʾt* (vs. 17)
41 *BRH: bryt* (vs. 17)
42 *ŠḤ: šḥh* (vs. 18)
43 *ʾl* (vs. 18[1,2])
44 I *MT: mwt* (vs. 18)
II *RPʾ: rpʾym* (vs. 18)
45 *BT: byth* (vs. 18)
46 *lʾ* (vs. 19[1,2])
47 *ŠB: yšwbwn* (vs. 19)
48 *NŚG: yśgw* (vs. 19)
49 *ḤYH: ḥyym* (vs. 19)
50 *ʿNH: mʿn* (vs. 20)
51 I *ŠKN: yšknw* (vs. 21)
II *YTR: ywtrw* (vs. 21)
52 *ʾRṢ* (vss. 21[1], 22[2])
53 I *KRT: ykrtw* (vs. 22)
II *NSḤ: ysḥw* (vs. 22)

2.3.1.0 *Semantic Parallelism: Notes*

1. The grammatical and positional parallelism *lqḥ // ṣpn* illustrates the need for a concordance of Hebrew parallelisms; one might be more tempted to classify the pair as semantically parallel if it were attested elsewhere. In the present instance, the semantic parallelism can only be termed "sequential," that is, first one takes, then stores. This loose semantic parallelism is locked into place by the grammatical and positional parallelism (each verb occupies the central slot in its half-line). Because the semantic parallelism is loose and because I know of no

evidence for *lqḥ* // *ṣpn* being a traditional pair, I have not classified them in this purely semantic analysis as parallel terms. *bny* and *ʾtk*, on the other hand, are given like letters, a // a′, because they are "functionally" parallel, that is, they refer to the same person.

2. *hqšb* and *nṭh* are classified as parallel because of their general semantic similarity and because of the similarity of object (*ʾzn* // *lb*).

3. Though *qrʾ* and *ntn* are not in themselves a good semantic parallel; *qrʾ* and *ntn ql* are equivalent and are given as semantic parallels in the verse parallelism (c // c′ ²). Note, however, that in the macrostructure of the chapter, *ntn ql* is the grammatical as well as semantic parallel of *hqšb ʾzn* and of *nṭh lb*.

4. For the macrostructure, note the semantic parallelism of *mṭmwn* with *ṣpn* (vs. 1) and hence of *ksp* with *ṣpn*.

5. *bn* and *ydʿ* are semantically related and are thus classified as a semantic parallelism, in spite of the lack of grammatical parallelism. On the other hand, the grammatically parallel pair *tbyn* // *tmṣʾ* makes a poor semantic pair. This shows up especially in the macrostructure of the chapter, where *mṣʾ* fits in poorly with the other members of the "wisdom" group (no. 10). In this verse, therefore, it is the grammatical parallelism, the parallelism of the objects of the two verbs, and the positional parallelism (chiastic) which bear the structural burden.

6. Note that there is but one new number in the macrostructural notation of this verse and only one new parallel term (*mpyw*: 20^1 + 11 IV). Semantically speaking, then, the verse is almost entirely repetitive of ideas already introduced. The parallelism of the new terms *mpyw* is double: the body part 'mouth' is in distant parallelism with the other parts of the body in vss. 2, 3, and 10 and in regular parallelism with *yhwh*. The regular parallelism is itself double: whole // part (*yhwh* // his own mouth) and noun // pronoun (*yhwh* // his). The parallelism is what I have termed "functional," that is, in this case, referring to the same person by means of terms not otherwise semantically comparable.

7. In this verse, the semantic structure takes a new turn, with only one repetitive parallel of a major term (*ṣpn* going back to vs. 1) and only one clear semantic parallel with preceding terms (*twšyh*, a new word in the series of desirable wisdom attributes). With the introduction of *yšrym* and *hlky tm*, the new theme is to be that of *yhwh*'s faithful. The passage is thus from primarily wisdom terminology to moral terminology. This is especially clear in vs. 9, where *ʾz tbyn* of vs. 5 is repeated, but this time with objects which denote conduct rather than comprehension. As

regards the semantic-grammatical structure, *twšyh* and *mgn* are not classed as semantic parallels ('intelligence' vs. 'shield'), though they are grammatical parallels and "functional" semantic ones (i.e., according to the grammar and rhetoric of the verse, 'intelligence' *is* a 'shield').

8. The charting of the chapter structure becomes difficult here with the mixture of terms referring to animate and inanimate entities in the community of the faithful. I have taken such terms (vs. 7 *yšrym // hlky tm*, vs. 8 *mšpṭ // ḥsydw*, vs. 9 *ṣdq w mšpṭ // myšrym*) as semantic parallelisms, but the grammatical disparities cause some hesitation.

9. Note that both elements of the phrase *ʾz tbyn* are repeated from vs. 5. For the application of this phrase to a new set of categories, see note on vs. 7.

10. This is another verse that brings together previous elements (only one new number, 27, a minor element; three new parallel terms, 23 II[1], 11 V, 21 VII). The purpose of these multiple repetitive and semantic parallels with preceding verses seems to be to reunite the wisdom and moral elements that were separated in vss. 7-9. The intricate references to previous motifs (note especially *tbwʾ* and *hlky*, vs. 7) seem to be intended to stress the indissolubility of the two areas. Especially remarkable are the parallels with vs. 2 (where the wisdom terminology begins) and with vs. 6 (the previous summary verse—vss. 6 and 10 both begin with *ky*).

11. The forms of repetition here stress again the statements of vss. 6-8 to the effect that *yhwh* has appointed the various categories of wisdom as a protection. Some variety is introduced, however, into the lexical components: *mzmh* is a new synonym of *ḥkmh*; *ʿlyk* is a new reference to the addressee, the first such "metrically" independent reference since vs. 1 (note the "functional" parallelism of *ʿlyk* and the *-k* of *tnṣrkh*).

12. Three items of interest here, the first concerning the verse, the second and third the structure of the chapter: 1) The semantic and grammatical force of the minor element *m(n)*- is sufficient to carry the structure of the verse without semantic parallelism of the words modified (*drk* vs. *ʾyš mdbr*); 2) The distant semantic parallelism of *(m)dbr* and *ʾmr(y)* (vs. 1) seems to indicate a conscious opposition of the father's words with those of the one who would lead the son astray. In this context, note the repetitive parallelism of *ʾmr* (semantically parallel also, of course, with *dbr*) for the woman who would lead the son astray (vs. 16); 3) *rʿ* and *ṭwb* + *nʿm* (vss. 9, 10) are antonymic parallels but have been given separate numbers in the chapter analysis because *rʿ* is followed by its own synonyms—it would be awkward to have the same number apply to the

synonyms of both *ṭwb* and *rʿ*, though one would like to be able to show the antonymic parallelism of *ṭwb* and *rʿ* by some device in the notation of the semantic structure of the chapter as a whole.

13. The precise antecedent of *hʿzbym* is uncertain, for the obvious referent, *ʾyš* in the preceding verse, in morphologically singular. Either the plurality of *ʿzbym* is entended to take up a collective notion of *ʾyš* or else *rʿ* is animate ('evil man') rather than inanimate, which would provide two referents for *ʿzbym*. Note that *yōšer* and *ḥōšek* are in grammatical, positional, and partial phonetic parallelism, but that the semantic parallelism of the two terms is only a rather weak antonymic one ('straightness' vs. 'darkness'—as moral metaphors, of course, they are perfectly good antonyms).

14. The semantic structure of vss. 13-14 is antonymic. *yšr* and *rʿ* are antonymic and the attitude of the adversaries is kept consistently negative by using a verb of rejection with the positive noun (*ʿzb* + *yšr*) and one of acceptance with the negative noun (*śmḥ* + *rʿ*). *rʿ* // *rʿ* contains the only instance of regular complete repetitive parallelism of major elements in Prov. 2. That consideration renders at least plausible the old suggestion to replace the second *rʿ* with *ršʿ*.

15. The use of *ʾšr* points up even more clearly the obvious fact that the definite article functions as a relative pronoun with the participles in vss. 13, 14. *ʾšr* is used in a syntactic structure which does not permit the use of the definite article. The definite article only occurs in this chapter in the previous two verses and in vs. 17 and only with the relative function.

16. The repetitive and semantic parallels with vs. 12 show that this verse is intended to begin a new section parallel to vss. 12-15, here dealing with feminine evils: *lhṣylk* = *lhṣylk*, *m*(*n*)- repeated twice in both verses, *ʾšh* synonym/antonym of *ʾyš* (depending on one's point of view), *ʾmr* synonym of *dbr* (an explicit recall of the father's words in vs. 1, as pointed out above, note to vs. 12). The parallels continue in the following verses with the repetitive parallelism of *ʿzb* and *ʾrḥ*. This particular combination of repetitive and semantic parallelisms seems to be one of the principal organizing features of the chapter, in spite of the fact that the two recall phrases are hidden away in relative clauses in the second half-line of the respective verses. The wish to contrast the "male" and "female" sources of evil with the father's words is thus effected explicitly but discreetly.

17. If the prosaic *ʾt* is correct (the second half-line is quantitatively longer than the first half-line and the *ʾt* could thus be dispensed with on all accounts), its function may be to point up the grammatical parallelism,

structurally necessary because of the lack of semantic parallelism. Indeed, grammatical and semantic parallelisms are arranged chiastically in this verse: the semantically aligned pair *hʿzbt* // *škḥh* is grammatically dissimilar, while the "b" and "c" terms are semantically dissimilar but grammatically similar, in both morphology and syntax.

The repetition of *ʾlhym* (in vs. 5, *ʾlhym* was the giver of wisdom attributes), coupled with a new term which is antonymic of wisdom (*škḥ*), stresses both structurally and lexically the "strange" woman's deleterious effect on wisdom.

18. *ky* here has a function different from the one it had in vss. 6 and 10, where it introduced summary verses. Here it introduces the strongest statement of the sub-section on the "strange" woman. This strong lexical marker of conclusion was perhaps felt to be necessary because of the few parallelistic links with previous statements. Only *mʿgl* shows up to remind the listener that the woman's deathly ways are being compared with the evil ways of the evil man (vs. 15) and, of course, with the good ways of the good man (vs. 9). This "path" motif is repeated in the next verse and again in vs. 20 as a transition to the conclusion to the chapter in vss. 21, 22.

The internal parallelism of vs. 18 is mixed: semantically weak in *byth* // *mʿgltyh* (but strengthened by the repetition of the pronominal suffix, by the positional parallelism, by the repetitive and semantic parallelism of *mʿgl* in the chapter as a whole, and by the "functional" parallelism of the two terms: at least one of the paths leads to the door of her house!), semantically strong in *ʾl-mwt* // *ʾl-rpʾym* (the phrases are repetitive by the preposition, positionally parallel after the "deletion" of the verb, and semantically similar since the *rpʾym* are the shades of the dead).

19. Though there are several forms of parallelism in this verse, there is no real internal semantic parallelism, other than the repetitive parallelism of the minor element *lʾ*. This element, along with grammatical and positional parallelism, permits the lack of semantic parallelism in *yšwbwn* // *yśygw*. Note the two antonymic parallelisms, one interior to this verse (*bʾ*, *šb*), one in near parallelism with the preceding verse (*ḥyh*, *mt*). The verse is held in the semantic structure of the chapter by the semantic and repetitive parallels of *bʾ* and *ʾrḥwt*.

20. *tlk* and *tšmr* are grammatically parallel, and their objects are semantically parallel, but the two verbs are not.

The fact that there are no new terms in this verse (other than the minor element *mʿn*) seems to indicate a summary verse. In fact vs. 20 is a transitional verse between the "strange" woman section and the conclusion.

It is introduced by means of a purpose clause (*lmʿn*); this type of clause was previously used to introduce the second verse of a section (vss. 2, 7, 12) or the first verse of a sub-section (vs. 16, recalling vs. 12). Here the function of the purpose clause seems to be a similar one for the entire chapter: it both summarizes the previous unit (in its repetition of terms) and serves as the "second" bicolon of the chapter seen as a unit, with this bicolon introducing a new section, here the conclusion. Thus the structure of each section is:

Statement (vss. 1, 7, 11)
  purpose clause (vss. 2, 8, 12+16)
  body (vss. 3-5, 9, 13-15+17-19)
  conclusion (vss. 6, 10, 20)

The chapter has a similar structure:

Statement (vs. 1)
  purpose clause (vs. 20)
  body = conclusion (vss. 21, 22)

Thus the backbone of the chapter might be seen as its purpose clauses, in that each depends on the first statement of vs. 1 as well as on the new statements of vss. 7 and 11:[12]

Statement (vs. 1)
  purpose clause 1 (vs. 2)
  ,, ,, 2 (vs. 8)
  ,, ,, 3 (vs. 12)
  ,, ,, 4 (vs. 16)
  ,, ,, 5 (vs. 20)
  conclusion (vss. 21, 22)

21. The chapter conclusion differs from the two section conclusions by including a significant new vocabulary: two new verbs, the noun *ʾrṣ*, and its substitutes the pronominal forms of *b*- and *m*(*n*)-.

The structure of vss. 1-19 is recapitulated in vss. 21 and 22 in that vs. 21 mirrors vss. 1-11 by dealing with the good effects of wisdom (stated in moral terms as in vss. 7-9), while vs. 22 reflects vss. 12-19 by dealing with the punishment of those who refuse wisdom (again stated in moral terms). As regards the structure of the chapter, it is of interest that the terms used to describe the wise were previously used in the statement in vs. 7 which preceded the second section (*yšrym* = *yšrym*, *tmymym* = *hlky tm*), while the terms for the wicked in vs. 22 are new (*ršʿym*, *bwgdym*), though they are, of course, semantically parallel to previously used terms (especially to *r*ʿ). There is also an important new term in vss. 21 and 22

[12] Vss. 7 and 11 are identified as new statements, as stated above in the notes to the verses, by their new vocabulary and by the fact that they follow summary verses.

which serves as an important link in their structures, viz. *ʾrṣ*, for it is the pivot around which the reward/punishment structure turns—the wise receive it, the evil are cut off from it. This pivot term is also highlighted in both verses by being alone: it is paralleled only by a pronominal form of the prepositions *b*- and *m*(*n*)-, rather than by a different noun.

22. Besides the new (but semantically unparalleled) terms for the wicked which were discussed in the preceding note, there are also two new verbs in this verse, as there were in vs. 21.

2.3.2 *Semantic Parallelism: Distribution*

A. Half-line

1) *dʿt* + *tbwnh* (vs. 5)
2) *tbyn* + *yrʾt* (vs. 5)
3) *ṣdq* + *mšpṭ* // *myšrym* + (*kl-mʿgl-*)*ṭwb* (vs. 9)
4) *thpkwt* + *rʿ* (vs. 14)
5) *bʾyh* + *yšwbwn* (antonymic; vs. 19)

B. Regular[13]

1) *ʾmry* // *mṣwty* (vs. 1)
2) *hqšyb* // *tṭh* (*nṭh*) (vs. 2)
3) *ḥkmh* // *tbwnh* (vss. 2, 6)
4) *ʾznk* // *lbk* (vs. 2)
5) *tqrʾ* // *ttn* (*ntn*) *qwlk* (vs. 3)
6) *tbqšnh* // *tḥpśnh* (vs. 4)
7) *ksp* // *mṭmwnym* (vs. 4)
8) *tbyn* // *dʿt* (vs. 5)
9) *yrʾt* // *dʿt* (vs. 5)
10) *yhwh* // *ʾlhym* (vs. 5)
11) *ḥkmh* // *dʿt* (vss. 6, 10)
12) *yšrym* // *hlky tm* (vs. 7); *yšrym* // *tmymym* (vs. 21)
13) *nṣr* // *yšmr* (vs. 8); *tšmr* // *tnṣr* (vs. 11)
14) *ʾrḥwt* // *drk*(*y*) (vss. 8, 13); *drk* // *ʾrḥwt* (vs. 20)
15) *mšpṭ* // *ḥsydw* (vs. 8)
16) *ṣdq* + *mšpṭ* // *myšrym* + (*kl-mʿgl-*)*ṭwb* (vs. 9; cf. vs. 20, #29, below)
17) *lbk* // *npšk* (vs. 10)

---

[13] Functional parallels, e.g., references to same person by noun and pronoun (*bny* // *ʾtk*, vs. 1) or by name and term for a part of the body (*yhwh* // *pyw*, vs. 6) or references to two different entities as metaphorically identical (*twšyh* // *mgn*, vs. 7) are not included here. On the other hand, antonymic parallels, such as *yšr* // *ḥšk* (vs. 13), are included.

18) *mzmh* // *tbwnh* (vs. 11)
19) *rʿ* // *thpkwt* (vs. 12); *rʿ* // *thpkwt* + *rʿ* (vs. 14)
20) *yšr* // *ḥšk* (antonymic; vs. 13)
21) *hśmḥym* // *ygylw* (vs. 14)
22) *ʾrḥtyhm* // *mʿglwtm* (vs. 15)
23) *ʿqšym* // *nlwzym* (vs. 15)
24) *zrh* // *nkryh* (vs. 16)
25) *hʿzbt* // *škḥh* (vs. 17)
26) *mwt* // *rpʾym* (vs. 18)
27) *byth* // *mʿgltyh* (vs. 18)[14]
28) *yšwbwn* // *yśygw* (antonymic; vs. 19)
29) *ṭwbym* // *ṣdyqym* (vs. 20)
30) *yšknw* // *ywtrw* (vs. 21)
31) *ršʿym* // *bwgdym* (vs. 22)
32) *ykrtw* // *ysḥw* (vs. 22)

C. Near

1) *ḥkmh* . . . *tbwnh* (vss. 2, 3)
2) *ʾznk* // *lbk* . . . *qwlk* (vss. 2, 3)
3) *tbyn* + *yrʾt* // *dʿt* . . . *ḥkmh* // *dʿt* + *tbwnh* . . . *twšyh* (vss. 5-7)
4) *yhwh* // *ʾlhym* . . . *yhwh* // *mpyw* (vss. 5, 6)
5) *yšrym* // *hlky tm* . . . *mšpṭ* // *ḥsydw* . . . *ṣdq* + *mšpṭ* // *myšrym* + (*kl-mʿgl-*)*ṭwb* (vss. 7-9)
6) *ʾrḥwt* // *drk* . . . *mʿgl* (vss. 8, 9)
7) *tbyn* . . . *ḥkmh* // *dʿt* . . . *mzmh* // *tbwnh* (vss. 9-11)
8) *ṭwb* . . . *ynʿm* (vss. 9, 10)
9) *tšmr* . . . *tnṣrkh* . . . *hṣylk* (vss. 11, 12)
10) *rʿ* // *thpkwt* . . . *yšr* // *ḥšk* . . . *rʿ* // *thpkwt rʿ* (list + antonymic; vss. 12-14)
11) *drk* . . . *ʾrḥwt* // *drky* (vss. 12, 13)
12) *rʿ* // *thpkwt rʿ* . . . *ʿqšym* // *nlwzym* (vss. 14, 15)
13) *mwt* // *ḥyym* (antonymic; vss. 18, 19)
14) *bʾyh* . . . *tlk* (*hlk*) (vss. 19, 20)
15) *ṭwbym* // *ṣdyqym* . . . *yšrym* // *tmymym* . . . *ršʿym* // *bwgdym* (list + antonymic; vss. 20-22)
16) *yšknw* // *ywtrw* . . . *ykrtw* // *ysḥw* (antonymic; vss. 21, 22)

D. Distant

1) *ʾmry* . . . *mdbr* . . . *ʾmryh* (vss. 1, 12, 16)
2) *ṣpn* . . . *ksp* // *mṭmwnym* (vss. 1, 4)

---

[14] *byth* and *mʿgltyh* form a simple "list" parallelism if one of the senses of the second term is that of the "path(s)" that lead to the woman's house. See further below, especially Ch. III, note 1.

3) *ḥkmh* // *tbwnh* . . . *bynh* // *tbwnh* . . . *tbyn* + *yrʾt* // *dʿt* . . . *ḥkmh* // *dʿt* + *tbwnh* . . . *twšyh* . . . *tbyn* . . . *ḥkmh* // *dʿt* . . . *mzmh* // *tbwnh* (vss. 2, 3, 5, 6, 7, 9, 10, 11)
4) *ʾznk* // *lbk* . . . *qwlk* . . . *mpyw* . . . *lbk* // *npšk* (vss. 2, 3, 6, 10)
5) *yhwh* // *ʾlhym* . . . *yhwh* . . . *ʾlhyh* (vss. 5, 6, 17)
6) *yšrym* // *hlky tm* . . . *mšpṭ* // *ḥsydw* . . . *ṣdq* + *mšpṭ* // *myšrym* + (*kl-mʿgl-*) *ṭwb* . . . *ṭwbym* // *ṣdyqym* . . . *yšrym* // *tmymym* (vss. 7, 8, 9, 20, 21; cf. list of antonyms, #10, below)
7) *hlky* . . . *tbwʾ* . . . *lkt* . . . *bʾyh* + *yšwbw* // *yśygw* . . . *tlk* (vss. 7, 10, 13, 19, 20)
8) *nṣr* // *yšmr* . . . *tnṣrkh* // *tšmr* . . . *hṣylk* . . . *hṣylk* . . . *tšmr* (vss. 8, 11, 12, 16, 20)
9) *ʾrḥwt* // *drk* . . . *mʿgl* . . . *drk* . . . *ʾrḥwt* // *drky* . . . *ʾrḥtyhm* // *mʿglwtm* . . . *mʿgltyh* . . . *drk* // *ʾrḥwt* (vss. 8, 9, 12, 13, 15, 18, 20)
10) *rʿ* // *thpkwt* . . . *rʿ* // *thpkwt* + *rʿ* . . . *ʿqšym* // *nlwzym* . . . *ršʿym* // *bwgdym* (vss. 12, 14, 15, 22)
11) *ʾyš* . . . *ʾšh* (vss. 12, 16)
12) *hʿzbym* . . . *hʿzbt* // *škḥh* (13, 17)

E. Combinations[15]

1) *ḥkm*, *bn* (regular, near, distant)
2) *ḥkm*, *ydʿ* (regular, near, distant)
3) *ydʿ*, *bn* (half-line, regular, near)
4) *yhwh*, *ʾlhym* (regular, near, distant)
5) *yšr*, *tm* (regular, distant)
6) *nṣr*, *šmr* (regular, distant)
7) *ʾrḥwt*, *drk* (regular, near, distant)
8) *drk*, *mʿgl* (near, distant)
9) *ʾrḥwt*, *mʿgl* (regular, near, distant)
10) *ṣdq*, *mšpṭ* (half-line, distant)
11) *mšpṭ*, *yšr* (regular, near, distant)
12) *ṣdq*, *yšr* (regular, distant)
13) *yšr*, *ṭb* (half-line, near, distant)
14) *ṣdq*, *ṭb* (regular, distant)
15) *mšpṭ*, *ṭb* (regular, near, distant)
16) *rʿ*, *thpkwt* (half-line, regular, distant)
17) *bʾ*, *hlk* (near, distant)
18) *šmr*, *nṣr*, *hṣyl* (near, distant)

[15] All the possible distributions for words which appear but once are not listed, e.g., *ynʿm* is not listed as in near and distant parallelism with *ṭwb*.

2.3.3 *Semantic Parallelism: Semantic Relationships*[16]

A. Synonymous

1) *bny* // *ʾtk* (pronoun; vs. 1)
2) *ʾmry* // *mṣwty* (vs. 1)
3) *hqšyb* // *tṭh* (vs. 2)
4) *ḥkmh* // *tbwnh* (vss. 2, 6)
5) *ʾznk* // *lbk* (vs. 2)
6) *tqrʾ* // *ttn qwlk* (vs. 3)
7) *tbqšnh* // *tḥpśnh* (vs. 4)
8) *ksp* // *mṭmwnym* (vs. 4)
9) *tbyn* + *yrʾt* // *dʿt* (vs. 5)
10) *yhwh* // *ʾlhym* (vs. 5)
11) *yhwh* // *mpyw* (whole-part; pronoun; vs. 6)
12) *ḥkmh* // *dʿt* + *tbwnh* (vs. 6; cf. nos. 4, 18)
13) *yšrym* // *hlky tm* (vs. 7); *yšrym* // *tmymym* (vs. 21)
14) *nṣr* // *yšmr* (vs. 8); *tšmr* // *tnṣrkh* (vs. 11)
15) *ʾrḥwt* // *drk(y)* (vss. 8, 13); *drk* // *ʾrḥwt* (vs. 20)
16) *mšpṭ* // *ḥsydw* (vs. 8)
17) *ṣdq* + *mšpṭ* // *myšrym* + *(kl-mʿgl-)ṭwb* (vs. 9)
18) *ḥkmh* // *dʿt* (vs. 10; cf. nos. 4, 12)
19) *lbk* // *npšk* (vs. 10)
20) *mzmh* // *tbwnh* (vs. 11)
21) *rʿ* // *thpkwt* (vs. 12); *rʿ* // *thpkwt* + *rʿ* (vs. 14)
22) *hśmḥm* // *ygylw* (vs. 14)
23) *ʾrḥtyhm* // *mʿglwtm* (vs. 15)
24) *ʿqšym* // *nlwzym* (vs. 15)
25) (*ʾšh*) *zrh* // *nkryh* (vs. 16)

---

[16] See Ch. I, note 19 for the purpose and organization of this chart and the following. There are four major differences between the two sample texts that emerge from these two charts: (1) There is one bicolon in the Ugaritic text which has neither grammatical nor semantic parallelism (§ X—and two others which show no grammatical parallelism and only weak semantic parallelism: §§ VI and IX). In Proverbs 2, on the other hand, there is no line which is totally lacking in grammatical or semantic parallelism (and individual examples of "positional" parallels, without grammatical or semantic likeness, only number two in that text). (2) Synonymous parallelism without grammatical likeness is relatively more frequent in Proverbs 2 (seven cases as opposed to two in *ʿnt* I), though the semantic parallelisms in *ʿnt* I are weaker than those listed below in section E while the relevant bicola in the Ugaritic text are not characterized by the other strong parallelistic devices found in their counterparts in Proverbs 2. (3) Antonymic lexical parallelism is missing in *ʿnt* I, while there are two examples in Proverbs 2. (4) There are, absolutely and comparatively, many more semantic parallelisms in Proverbs 2 that include major grammatical dissimilarity (section C of the chart of grammatical relationships: nineteen in Proverbs 2, only two in *ʿnt* I). Numbers of "same" and "similar" forms are not so markedly different.

26) *hʿzbt* // *škḥh* (vs. 17)
27) *mwt* // *rpʾym* (vs. 18)
28) *ṭwbym* // *ṣdyqym* (vs. 20)
29) *yšknw* // *ywtrw* (vs. 21)
30) *ʾrṣ* // *bh* (vs. 21); *ʾrṣ* // *mmnh* (vs. 22) (pronoun)
31) *ršʿym* // *bwgdym* (vs. 22)
32) *ykrtw* // *ysḥw* (vs. 22)

B. Antonymic
1) *yšr* // *ḥšk* (vs. 13)
2) *yšwbwn* // *yśygw* (vs. 19)

C. Grammatical but not Semantic[17]
1) *tqḥ* // *tṣpn* (vs. 1)
2) *tbyn* // *tmṣʾ* (vs. 5)
3) *twšyh* // *mgn* (vs. 7)
4) *tbwʾ* // *ynʿm* (vs. 10)
5) *mdrk* // *mʾyš mdbr* (vs. 12)
6) *ʾlwp* // *bryt* (vs. 17)
7) *nʿwryh* // *ʾlhyh* (vs. 17)
8) *byth* // *mʿgltyh* (vs. 18)[18]
9) *ṭlk* // *tšmr* (vs. 20)

D. Neither Grammatical nor Synonymous
1) *hʿzbym* // *llkt* (vs. 13)
2) *lʿśwt* // *bthpkwt* (vs. 14)[19]

E. Synonymous but not Grammatical
1) *bny* // *ʾtk* (vs. 1; = A 1)
2) *tbyn* // *dʿt* (vs. 5; = A 9)
3) *yhwh* // *mpyw* (vs. 6; = A 11)
4) *yšrym* // *hlky tm* (vs. 7; = A 13)[20]
5) *hśmḥym* // *ygylw* (vs. 14; = A 22)
6) *hʿzbt* // *škḥh* (vs. 17; = A 26)
7) *ʾrṣ* // *bh*; *ʾrṣ* // *mmnh* (vss. 21, 22; = A 30)

---

[17] For a division according to grammatical similarity and dissimilarity, see next chart.

[18] See above at "Semantic Parallelism: Notes" and Ch. II, note 14 and Ch. III, note 1.

[19] The major constituents are grammatically parallel (M // M = prepositional phrases), but the nouns themselves are not (verbal noun, singular // common noun, plural). The weak grammatical microparallelism is partially offset by the parallelism of the major constituents and by phonetic parallelism ($-\bar{o}^{w}t$ // $-\bar{o}^{w}t$).

[20] This example is included because of the grammatical dissimilarity between *yšrym*, which is a common adjective, plural absolute, and the compound phrase *hlky tm*, made up of a verbal adjective, plural construct + common noun, singular.

2.3.4 *Semantic Parallelism: Grammatical Relationships*

A. Same Grammatical Form[21]

1) *tqḥ* // *tṣpn* (semantically dissimilar; vs. 1)
2) *ʾmry* // *mṣwty* (vs. 1)
3) *ḥkmh* // *tbwnh* (vss. 2, 6)
4) *ʾznk* // *lbk* (vs. 2)
5) *tbqšnh* // *tḥpśnh* (vs. 4)
6) *tbyn* // *tmṣʾ* (semantically dissimilar; vs. 5)
7) *yrʾt* // *dʿt* (vs. 5)
8) *ḥkmh* // *dʿt* + *tbwnh* (vs. 6); *ḥkmh* // *d*ṯ (vs. 10)
9) *twšyh* // *mgn* (semantically dissimilar; vs. 7)
10) *lbk* // *npšk* (vs. 10)
11) *mzmh* // *tbwnh* (vs. 11)
12) *mdrk* // *mʾyš* (semantically dissimilar; vs. 12; cf. C 10)
13) *yšr* // *ḥšk* (antonymic; vs. 13)
14) *ʾrḥtyhm* // *mʿglwtm* (vs. 15)
15) *mʾšh* (*zrh*) // *mnkryh* (vs. 16; cf. C 15)
16) *ʾlwp* // *bryt* (semantically dissimilar; vs. 17)
17) *nʿwryh* // *ʾlhyh* (semantically dissimilar; vs. 17)
18) *tlk* // *tšmr* (semantically dissimilar; vs. 20)
19) *ṭwbym* // *ṣdyqym* (vs. 20)
20) *yšrym* // *tmymym* (vs. 21)

B. Similar Grammatical Form

1) *ksp* // *mṭmwnym* (singular // plural; vs. 4)
2) *yhwh* // *ʾlhym* (singular // plural; vs. 5)
3) *ʾrḥwt* // *drk* (plural vs. singular, feminine // masculine vs. 8; cf. vs. 20, reversed order, and vs. 13, both plural)
4) *ṣdq* + *mšpṭ* // *myšrym* + (*kl-mʿgl-*)*ṭwb* (singular // plural; vs. 9)
5) *tbwʾ* // *ynʿm* (semantically dissimilar; feminine // masculine; vs. 10)
6) *rʿ* // *thpkwt* (singular // plural, masculine // feminine; vs. 12); cf. *thpkwt* + *rʿ* // *rʿ* (vs. 14)
7) *mwt* // *rpʾym* (singular // plural; vs. 18)
8) *byth* // *mʿgltyh* (semantically dissimilar; singular // plural; masculine // feminine types; vs. 18)
9) *yšwbwn* // *yśygw* (antonymic; energic // indicative; vs. 19)
10) *yšknw* // *ywtrw* (Qal // Niphal; vs. 21)
11) *yktrw* // *ysḥw* (Niphal // Qal; vs. 22)

[21] As in the previous chart and as in the corresponding ones for the Ugaritic text, only parallelisms in "regular" distribution are included (see Ch. I, note 19 and Ch. II, note 16).

C. Different Grammatical Form

1) *bny* // *ʾtk* (noun + pronoun // preposition + different pronoun; vs. 1)
2) *hqšyb* // *tṭh* (infinitive // finite form; vs. 2)
3) *tqrʾ* // *ttn qwlk* (verb // verb + noun; vs. 3)
4) *tbyn* // *dʿt* (verb // noun; vs. 5)
5) *yhwh* // *mpyw* (proper noun // common noun + pronoun; vs. 6)
6) *yšrym* // *hlky tm* (adjective // participle + noun; vs. 7)
7) *nṣr* // *yšmr* (infinitive // finite fom; vs. 8)
8) *mšpṭ* // *ḥsydw* (noun // noun + pronoun; vs. 8)
9) *tšmr ʿlyk* // *tnṣrkh* (verb + preposition + pronoun // verb + pronoun; vs. 11)
10) *mdrk rʿ* // *mʾyš mdbr thpkwt* (preposition + noun + adjective // preposition + noun + participle + noun; vs. 12; cf. A 12)
11) *hʿzbym* // *lkt* (participle // infinitive; semantically dissimilar; vs. 13)
12) *hśmhym* // *ygylw* (adjective // finite verb; vs. 14)
13) *ʿśwt* // *thpkwt* (infinitive // common noun; semantically dissimilar; vs. 14)
14) *ʿqšym* // *nlwzym* (adjective // participle; vs. 15)
15) *ʾšh zrh* // *nkryh* (noun + adjective // nisbe adjective; vs. 16)
16) *h'zbt* // *škḥh* (participle // finite verb; vs. 17)
17) *ʾrṣ* // *bh* (noun // preposition + pronoun; vs. 21)
18) *ršʿym* // *bwgdym* (adjective // participle; vs. 22)
19) *mʾrṣ* // *mmnh* (preposition + noun // preposition + pronoun; vs. 22)

2.3.4.0 *Semantic Parallelism: Arrangements*

A. Parallel alignment: A B C // A′ B′ C′

1. Complete: vs. 21
2. With deletion of major element
   a. a^2 *b c*
      b′ c'^2 (vs. 3)
   b. *a b c*
      a′ b′ (vs. 11)
3. With deletion and non-parallel elements
   a. *a* b^2
      b′ c d (vs. 16: *c* and *d* are expansions of *b*)
   b. *a b*
      c d e (vs. 19: $c \neq b$, *d* and *e* are completely non-paralleled)

4. With half-line parallelism
   a. *a a′ b*
      a″ b′ c (vs. 5)
   b. *a b b′*
      b″ b‴[2] (vs. 9)

5. With deletion and half-line parallelism
   a. *a b c*
      a′ c′ c″ (vs. 6)
   b. *a b c*
      a c′ c (vs. 14)

6. With deletion and grammatical but not semantic parallelism
   a. *a b c*
      d e c′ (vs. 12: $d = b$ grammatically; *e* has neither grammatical nor semantic parallel)
   b. *a b c*
      b′ d (vs. 18: $d = c$ grammatically)

7. With grammatical but not semantic parallelism
   a. *a b c*
      d e c′ (vs. 13 *a* and *d* both verbs, though different forms; $e \neq c$)

B. Chiastic Alignment: A B C // C′ B′ A′
   1. Complete: none
   2. With reduced number of elements
      a. *a b*
         b′ a′ (vs. 4)
   3. With grammatical but not semantic parallelism
      a. *a b c*
         c′ d a′ (vs. 1: $d = b$ grammatically)
   4. With deletion and grammatical but not semantic parallelism
      a. *a b c*
         d b′[2] (vs. 7)

C. Partially Chiastic Alignment: A B C // A′ B′ C′ and A B C // B′ C′ A′
   1. Chiasmus of second and third elements
      a. Complete: vs. 22
      b. With deletion: *a b c*
         c′ b′ (vs. 15)

   2. Chiasmus of first element only
      a. Complete: vs. 8

b. With grammatical but not semantic parallelism:
   i. *a b c*
      b′ c′ d (vss. 10, 20: *d* = *a* grammatically)
   ii. *a b c*
      d e a′ (vs. 17: *d* = *b*, *e* = *c* grammatically

D. Remarks
1. There is only one instance of the repetition of a given parallelistic pattern (vss. 10, 20).
2. The complete forms of a pattern are comparatively rare: three examples in twenty-two verses (vss. 8, 21, 22).
3. Note high number of chiastic alignments compared with Ugaritic example.
4. Chiasmus and deletion/compensation rarely occur together: two examples in twenty-two verses (vss. 7, 15—in the latter instance the deleted element is "metrically" important but semantically minor [*ʾšr*]).

2.3.5 *Semantic Parallelism: Geller's Categories*

1. *bny ʾm-tqḥ ʾmry*	*a b c*	Noun + verb + noun
wmṣwty tṣpn ʾtk	*c′ d a′*	Noun (A) + verb (C) + adverbial (preposition + pronoun: C)

The parallelism of *bny* and *ʾtk* is what I have termed "functional," in this case referring to the same person. The operative element in this equation, the pronouns which refer to the same person, are classified by Geller as a third-rank parallelism (C). The verbs are not attested as parallels and have little in common (C); one would like to have representations for each of these features (one designation for parallel pairs that are real-world parallels but which happen not to be attested as parallel pairs, another for parallel pairs which are semantically dissimilar).[22] *ʾmr* and *mṣwh* are a logical pair and are thus first-rank pair (A).

2. *lhqšyb lḥkmh ʾznk*	*a b c*	Verb + adverbial (preposition + noun) + noun
tṭh lbk ltbwnh	*a′ c′ b′*	Verb (A) + noun (A) + adverbial (preposition + noun: A)

All semantic relationships are primary and the variation in the verse is provided by chiasmus and by grammatical variation (infinitive // finite form).

[22] Cf. Ch. I, note 23, above.

3. *ky-ʾm lbynh tqrʾ*	a^2 *b c*	Compound particle + adverbial (preposition + noun) + verb
ltbwnh ttn qwlk	*b* c'^2 $(=x+y)$	Adverbial (preposition + noun: D) + verb + noun (A)

The compound particle is classified as a semantic and metrical element because of its length; when the particles are omitted in the second half-line that length is compensated for by the *semantic* compound *ttn qwlk. lbynh* and *ltbwnh* are classified as repetitive because derived from the same root (D). In spite of the grammatical difference, *ttn qwlk* is considered a compound phrase semantically parallel to the verb *tqrʾ* (A).

4. *ʾm-tbqšnh kksp*	*a b*	Verb + adverbial (preposition + noun)
wkmṭmwnym tḥpśnh	*b′ a′*	Adverbial (preposition + noun: A) + verb (A)

Both semantic relationships are primary; the variation in the verse is provided only by chiasmus and by the different particles (*ʾm* // *w-*).

5. *ʾz tbyn yrʾt yhwh*	*a a′ b*	Verb + compound nominal phrase
wdʿt ʾlhym tmṣʾ	*a″ b′ c*	Compound nominal phrase (A/A + verb (C)

Both elements of the compound phrases are first-rank parallel pairs, *yrʾt* // *dʿt* representing standard wisdom philosophy, *yhwh* being a proper name for the generic *ʾlhym* (or is the second also a proper name here?). The verbs are semantically dissimilar but are, of course, grammatically and positionally (chiastic) parallel. Geller's system has no way of expressing the piling-up of wisdom terms by means of the half-line non-grammatical parallelism of *tbyn* and *yrʾt*.

6. *ky-yhwh ytn ḥkmh*	*a b c*	Noun + verb + noun
mpyw dʿt wtbwnh	*a′ c′ c″*	Adverbial (preposition + noun + pronoun: C/[WP, PR]) + compound nominal phrase (/A)

Again in spite of the grammatical dissimilarity, *yhwh ytn* is classified as a compound equivalent to *mpyw* in the second half-line; the semantic rank "C" is owing to the functional equivalence being the pronoun, though there is also a whole-part relationship (*yhwh* // his mouth). The omission of an explicit verb in the second half-line is compensated for by a compound nominal phrase in primary semantic relationship to *ḥkmh* in the first half-line.

7. *wṣpn lyšrym twšyh*	*a b c*	Verb + adverbial (preposition + noun) + noun
mgn lhlky tm	*d b′*[2]	Noun (C) + compound adverbial (preposition + noun + substantive: /A [Met.])

The compound *hlky tm* is classified as a first-rank parallel (A) to *yšrym* because of the semantic proximity of *tm* to *yšr* (attested later in the chapter). The grammatical parallel *twšyh* // *mgn*, on the other hand, is purely circumstancial or functional in this context, metaphorical in nature (intelligence will serve as a shield). Hence the different notations in my standard notation (c // d) and the "C" ranking according to Geller's system.

8. *lnṣr ʾrḥwt mšpṭ*	*a b c*	Verb + compound nominal phrase
wdrk ḥsydw yšmr	*b′ c′ a′*	Compound nominal phrase (A/B [Concr.-Abstr.]) + verb (A)

The "B" ranking for *mšpṭ* // *ḥsydw* reflects in part the somewhat weak parallelism of the notions ("ruling" // "pious ones") but also the abstract versus concrete relationship of the two compound phrases ("paths of *justice*" // "way of his *pious ones*"). These references to paths and ways are not here classified as metaphorical in the same sense as in verse 9, where *mʿgl* is "understood" and is in parallel with purely abstract terms, for here the paths are guarded and protected.

9. *ʾz tbyn ṣdq wmšpṭ*	*a b b′*	Verb + compound nominal phrase
wmyšrym kl-mʿgl-ṭwb	*b″ b‴*	Compound nominal phrase (A/B [Met.])

mʿgl-ṭwb is classified as "B" because of the relative closeness of *mšpṭ* and *ṭwb* coupled with the real-world disparity of *mšpṭ* and *mʿgl*. The analysis of the compounds as such may be found below under "Grammatical Parallelism: Geller".

10. *ky-tbwʾ ḥkmh blbk*	*a b c*	Verb + noun + adverbial (preposition + noun)
wdʿt lnpšk ynʿm	*b′ c′ d*	Noun (A) + adverbial (preposition + noun: A) + verb (C)

The semantic dissimilarity of *tbwʾ* and *ynʿm* is compensated for by the semantic closeness of both elements of each of the subject + adverbial phrases and by the positional parallelism, i.e., the chiasmus that rejects *ynʿm* to the end of the verse, where it is heard only after the good semantic parallels just noted.

11. *mzmh tšmr ʿlyk*	*a b c*	Noun + verb + prepositional phrase
tbwnh tnṣrkh	*a′ b′*	Noun (A) + verb (A)

Geller's system does not illuminate the obvious grammatical dissimilarity of *tšmr ʿlyk* and *tnṣrk* which because of the semantic equivalence may be classified as a purposeful grammatical/lexical variation injected into an otherwise very uniform verse.

12. *lhṣylk mdrk rʿ*	*a b c*	Verb + compound adverbial (preposition + noun + adj.)
mʾyš mdbr thpkwt	*d e c′*	Compound adverbial (preposition + participle + noun) (C/A [Met.])

The "C" ranking indicates the semantic dissimilarity between *drk* and *ʾyš mdbr*, the "A" ranking the similarity between *rʿ* and *thpkwt*. For the analysis of the compounds, see below at "Grammatical Parallelism: Geller." The parallelism of *drk* and *ʾyš mdbr* is classified as metaphorical because *drk rʿ* appears to indicate a line of conduct rather than a literal "path" on which one would encounter evil.

13. *hʿzbym ʾrḥwt yšr*	*a b c*	Verb + compound nominal phrase
llkt bdrky-ḥšk	*d b′ e′*	Verb (C) + compound nominal phrase (A/C [list + ant.])

Variety is provided by the two different forms of verbal nouns, by the semantic dissimilarity of the two verbal nouns, and by the antonymic relationship between the two second members only of the two compound nominal phrases.

14. *hśmḥym lʿśwt rʿ*	*a b c*	Verb/adjective + verb + substantive
ygylw bthpkwt rʿ	*a′ c′ c*	Verb (A) + compound adverbial (preposition + noun + substantive: C/D)

Again the semantic dissimilarity of two syntactically similar forms (*lʿśwt // bthpkwt*—grammatically very different, though syntactically similar) is fixed into position between two good semantic parallels, including the one example of regular repetitive parallelism of non-minor elements in this chapter. Again, also, the primary verbal forms are of two major types (stative verbal adjective // finite form), though here, as opposed to vs. 13 and in conformity with vss. 2, 8, 17, and 20, the semantic parallelism is excellent.

15.	*ʾšr ʾrḥtyhm ʿqšym*	*a b c*	Relative pronoun + noun + adjective
	wnlwzym bmʿglwtm	*c′ b′*	Adjective (A) + adverbial (preposition + noun: A)

The semantic similarity of the major elements is here varied by the use of the lexical relative marker (as opposed to *h-*) and by syntactic dissimilarity (the two predicate adjectives having different subjects).

16.	*lhṣylk mʾšh zrh*	*a* b^2 $(=x+y)$	Verb + adverbial (preposition + noun) + adj.
	mnkryh ʾmryh hḥlyqh	*b′* $(=y')$ *c d*	Adverbial (preposition + substantive: A) + compound verbal phrase (noun + verb: /Ȼ [WP])

The semantic and syntactic dissimilarity between *lhṣylk* and *hḥlyqh* (the only real point of contact being that they are both Hiphil verbs) has led me to dissociate them at all levels of analysis. Thus the only semantic parallels are *mʾšh zrh* and *mnkryh*, though the "words" are tentatively identified as a "part" of the woman, the "whole."

17.	*hʿzbt ʾlwp nʿwryh*	*a b c*	Verb + compound nominal phrase
	wʾt-bryt ʾlhyh škḥh	*d e a′*	Compound nominal phrase (C/C) + verb (A)

The semantic dissimilarity of the compound phrases is hidden by their syntactic and morphological similarity and by the semantic closeness of the two verbal forms (again the verbal forms are morphologically dissimilar). Indeed, the syntactic and morphological similarities of the compound phrases is such that only a distinction between semantic and grammatical parallelism would lead one to ascribe them the different designations *b c // d e* in standard notation.

18.	*ky šḥh ʾl-mwt byth*	*a b c*	Verb + adverbial (preposition + noun) + noun
	wʾl-rpʾym mʿgltyh	*b′ d*	Adverbial (preposition + noun: A) + noun (B)

For the semantic parallelism of *byth* and *mʿgltyh*, see note above at "Semantic Parallelism: Notes"; here the letter "*d*" in the standard notation is meant to indicate the difference between houses and paths, while the "B" ranking in Geller's system is meant to indicate that, though not a standard pair, the two terms may function as a semantic pair in this verse, i.e., one of the paths leads to the woman's house and the use of the term *mʿgl* would not, therefore, be purely metaphorical.

19. *kl-bʾyh lʾ yšwbwn*	*a b*	Verb + verb
wlʾ-yśygw ʾrḥwt ḥyym	*c d e*	Verb (B [Ant.]) + compound nominal phrase (no parallelism)

Geller's system cannot note the piling up of verbs of motion, with *bʾyh*, a verbal noun/adjective, standing morphologically and syntactically outside of the unity formed by *lʾ yšwbwn* and *lʾ-yśygw*, whereas *bʾyh* and *yśygw* stand in semantic similarity over against *yšwbwn* in that both of those verbs denote arrival, as opposed to the "return" of *yšwbwn*. As elsewhere in my notation of this chapter, I have not indicated the antonyms *yšwbwn* and *yśygw* with the same letter, whereas the structure of the verse and the "list" character of the possible parallelism just discussed of *bʾyh* and *yśygw* have kept me from ascribing to these two words a same letter. The structure of the verse is not supplied solely, therefore, by the semantic, grammatical, and repetitive parallelism of *lʾ yšwbwn* and *lʾ-yśygw*, with *kl-bʾyh* and *ʾrḥwt ḥyym* standing in chiastic isolation, for *bʾyh* is linked semantically to the two main verbs.

20. *lmʿn tlk bdrk ṭwbym*	*a b c*	Verb + compound nominal phrase (noun + substantive)
wʾrḥwt ṣdyqym tšmr	*b′ c′ d*	Compound nominal phrase (noun + substantive: A/A) + verb (C)

On the analysis of *lmʿn* according to Geller's system, see note below to "Grammatical Parallelism: Geller" (I have analyzed the phrase as a particle, in spite of its quantitative importance, and have assumed that Geller would do the same). Once again, the separating out of the grammatical and semantic levels isolates *tlk* // *tšmr* as a grammatical but not semantic parallel. Note that Geller's system of analysis precludes a separate notation of the semantic parallelism of the elements of the compound phrases *drk ṭwbym* // *ʾrḥwt ṣdyqym*. This is a distinct disadvantage for each pair may have its own semantic relationship. In the present instance, while *drk* // *ʾrḥwt* might be termed a synonymous pair or members of a list, *ṭwbym* // *ṣdyqym* might be considered a synonymous pair or in whole // part relationship (if *ṭwb* be generic and *ṣdq* specific).

21.	*ky-yšrym yšknw-ʾrṣ*	*a b c*	Substantive + verb + noun
	wtmymym ywtrw bh	*a′ b′ c′*	Substantive (A) + verb (B) + adverbial (preposition + pronoun: C)

The verbs are classified as second rank proximity because of the relatively important semantic disparity between 'settling' and 'inheriting', with no intention of denying that they form an excellent "functional" parallelism here (one 'settles' after having 'inherited'). On the parallelism of noun with pronoun and the "C" ranking used by Geller, see on vs. 1.

22.	*wršʿym mʾrṣ yktrw*	*a b c*	Substantive + adverbial (preposition + noun) + verb
	wbwgdym ysḥw mmnh	*a′ c′ b′*	Substantive (B: WP) + verb (B) + adverbial (preposition + pronoun: C)

This verse has basically the same structure as vs. 21, except for the inversion of the 'earth' phrases. *ršʿym* and *bwgdym* are classified as a "whole-part" parallelism because the first is more generic than the second.

2.4.1 *Grammatical Parallelism: Collins*

1.	*bny ʾm-tqḥ ʾmry*	S V O	II C: i)6
	wmṣwty tṣpn ʾtk	O V (S)	

Two basic sentences of the same kind (= II) consisting of (optional) subject + verb + object (= C) wherein the subject is expressed normally (= i), in the specific order attested here (SVO // OVS = 6). This particular form, exhibiting complete chiasm, is unattested in Collins' sample from the prophetic books (pp. 109-110).[23]

2.	*lhqšyb lḥkmh ʾznk*	V M O	II D: ii)7
	tṭh lbk ltbwnh	V O M	

---

[23] If *ʾtk* is analyzed as a modifier phrase rather than as a subject phrase, i.e., strictly according to grammar rather than according to sense (*bny* = *ʾtk*), the line type SVO // OVM would be IV C/D iii (two different basic sentences of the types SVO [= C] and (S)VOM [= D], of which S is found only in the first half-line [= iii]). Collins lists sixteen examples of this general type on p. 119, but no example with the particular word order SVO // OVM.

Two basic sentences of the same kind (= II) consisting of (optional) subject + verb + object + modifier (= D), with subject omitted (= ii), in the specific order attested here (VMO // VOM = 7). This line-type occurs three times in Collins' sample (p. 117). The two main characteristics of the type II D: ii) in the prophetic books are found here: "a) to have initial V in the first hemistich, b) to have direct repetition of pattern in both hemistichs" (p. 122).

3. *ky-ʾm lbynh tqrʾ*	M M V	IV B/D: ii)2 variation
ltbwnh ttn qwlk	M V O	

On the basis of Collins' discussion of doubled elements (e.g., pp. 89-90, 108, 219-223) and of his analysis of *ky* plus another element in other sentences (e.g., p. 242), one must assume that he would consider *ky-ʾm* and *lbynh* as separate modifier phrases. This sentence is, therefore, a variant of the sentence-type IV B/D: ii)2: two different basic sentences (= IV) of the types (optional) subject + verb + modifier (= B) and (optional) subject + verb + object + modifier (= D), here with subject omitted (= ii), and in the specific order MV in the first half-line (= 2—there are not sufficient examples to merit complete break-down by both half-lines). Neither the specific order MV // MVO nor the variant type MMV // MVO is attested in Collins' sample (p. 174).

4. *ʾm-tbqšnh kksp*	V M	II B: ii)2
wkmṭmwnym tḥpśnh	M V	

Two basic sentences of the same kind (= II) of the type (optional) subject + verb + modifier (= B), here with the subject omitted (= ii), in the specific order VM // MV (= 2). This specific line-type is attested twelve times of a total of seventy attestations for the general line-type II B: ii) (p. 106). The ratio of only twelve to seventy reflects the fact that "the pattern of direct repetition is preferred to a chiastic one" (p. 107).

5. *ʾz tbyn yrʾt yhwh*	V O	II C: ii)2
wdʿt ʾlhym tmṣʾ	O V	

Two basic sentences of the same kind (= II) of the type (optional) subject + verb + object (= C), here with the subject omitted (= ii), in the specific order VO // OV. This specific line-type is attested twenty-eight times, of a total of eighty-three times for the general line-type II C: ii) (p. 114). In comparison with Collins' sample, this alignment with a frequently attested line-type appears to be owing to the verb-initial structure of the first half-line, which is frequent (70/83), and not to the chiastic structure, which is less frequent (31/83—the OV // VO order is the rarer, with only three examples).

6. *ky-yhwh ytn ḥkmh*	S V O	IV C/nominal
mpyw dᶜt wtbwnh	M (O)	

As noted above in "Semantic Parallelism: Notes" and in "Semantic Parallelism: Geller's Categories" *mpyw* takes the place of both the subject (*-w* = *yhwh*) and the verb (*mpy(w)* = *ytn*) of the first half-line. Thus, in a sense, this verse represents a variation of the line-type IV C/D: iii): two different basic sentences (= IV) of the types (optional) subject + verb + object and (optional) subject + verb + object + modifier (= D), with the subject actually present only in the first half-line (= iii). This would represent a deletion/compensation analysis as follows:

ky-yhwh ytn ḥkmh
(*yhwh ytn*) *mpyw dᶜt wtbwnh*

In actual surface structure, however, the actual line-type is IV C/nominal:

For *yhwh* gives wisdom,
From his mouth (are *or* come) knowledge and understanding.

In any case, the line represents a type not discussed by Collins (on IV C/D: iii), see p. 181; on nominal sentences, see pp. 215-218, where several type IV sentences are listed, but not IV C/nominal).

7. *wṣpn lyšrym twšyh*	V M O	III D: ii)2e
mgn lhlky tm	O M	

Two basic sentences of the same kind but with deletion (= III), of the type (optional) subject + verb + object + modifier (= D), here with subject omitted (= ii), with the specific order of the first half-line VMO (= 2) and of the second half-line OM (= e). Collins lists ten examples of this specific line-type (p. 154). Prov. 2:7 shows the "clear preference for initial V" (p. 157) which characterizes the general line-type III D: ii). It shows an element of relative infrequency, however, in the chiasmus of MO // OM (p. 157).

8. *lnṣr ʾrḥwt mšpṭ*	V O	II C: ii)2
wdrk ḥsydw yšmr	O V	

See on vs. 5, the only important variation from which is that the verb here is an infinitive rather than a finite form as in vs. 5. In both verses the object phrases are compound nominal phrases.

9. *ʾz tbyn ṣdq wmšpṭ*	V O	III C: ii)1
wmyšrym kl-mᶜgl-ṭwb	O	

Two basic sentences of the same kind but with deletion (= III), of the type (optional) subject + verb + object (= C), here with subject omitted (= ii), in the specific order VO // O (= 1). This is by far the most frequent sub-type of the line-type II C: ii) (24/29—p. 149). From some of Collins' examples (e.g., Isa. 48:5), it is clear that he would not take the "metrical" arrangement of the objects (here VOO // OO²) to indicate a variation—i.e., 2 // 2 and 3 // 3 lines may both be analyzed as VO // O.

10. *ky-tbwʾ ḥkmh blbk*	V S M	II B: i)14
wdʿt lnpšk ynʿm	S M V	

Two basic sentences of the same kind (II), of the type (optional) subject + verb + modifier (= B), here with the subject included (= i), in the specific order VSM // SMV (= 14). This specific line-type has ten examples in Collins' sample (p. 101). Prov. 2:10 has two of the three principal characteristics of the general line-type II B: i) "a) initial V in the first hemistich, b) initial NP¹ [= S] in the second hemistich; c) direct repetition of pattern" (p. 105) and this type thus qualifies as a "strong" line-form (ibid.). It is worth noting that the missing element is "direct repetition of pattern," here replaced by chiasmus.

11. *mzmh tšmr ʿlyk*	S V M	IV B/C variation: i)1
tbwnh tnṣrk	S V-O	

Two different basic sentences (= IV) of the types (optional) subject + verb + modifier (= B) and (optional) subject + verb + object (= C), with expressed subject (= i), in the specific order in the first half-line of SVM (= 1—there are not sufficient examples to merit complete breakdown according to both half-lines). In Collins' sample (p. 166) there are two examples of the order of Prov. 2:11, both of which also have the object suffixed to the verb (Isa. 50:9; 60:7—the modifier phrase in both verses also carries a pronoun with the same antecedent as that of the pronoun object on the verb, as in Prov. 2:11). The present verse shares the main characteristic of the general line-type IV:i), that of showing a preference for the sentence-type SVM (= B: p. 169).

12. *lhṣylk mdrk rʿ*	V M	III B: ii)1
mʾyš mdbr thpkwt	M	

Two basic sentences of the same type but with deletion (= III), of the type (optional) subject + verb + modifier (= B), here with subject omitted (= ii), in the specific order VM // M (= 1). This is a frequent line-type (37 examples, as opposed to seven examples of III B: ii)2 = MV // M: p. 140). To arrive at this formula, *mdbr* was analyzed as a further modifier of *ʾyš* and the nominal aspect of the participle was thus emphasized. If its verbal character is stressed, the order of principle elements is VM // MVO = IV B/D: ii)1. Collins (p. 172) lists three examples of this specific line-type (Isa. 10:28, 11:14, 53:12), in none of which is the verb of the second half-line in the form of a participle. I am not certain as to whether Collins would in the present instance prefer the analysis of the second half-line as a complex modifier phrase or would prefer to break it up into its component parts (cf. the similar problem with *ʿnt* I, § VII, discussed above). In the next verse, the participle certainly functions as a primary verbal component—though there the problem is with the infinitive in the second half-line (see note on vs. 13).

13. *hʿzbym ʾrḥwt yšr*	V O	IV C/B: ii)1
llkt bdrky-ḥšk	V M	

Two different basic sentences (= IV) of the types (optional) subject + verb + object (= C) and (optional) subject + verb + modifier (= B), here with the subject omitted (= ii), and with the specific order VO in the first half-line (= 1—Collins does not provide separate numbers for the break-down according to order of the second half-line). The specific word-order of Prov. 2:13 is relatively frequent, with nine cases listed (p. 173). The general line-type IV: ii) shows a preference for the sentence-type (S)VO (= C), which is found here in the first half-line (pp. 175-176). If *llkt* is analyzed according to its nominal aspect, it becomes a modifier phrase and the order of major constituents is then VO // M = I D: ii)1 (i.e., one basic sentence with verb + object + modifier, with subject omitted, in the specific order given here). This is a frequent line-type, with thirty-nine examples (pp. 83-84), and frequency is not, therefore, at issue in choosing between the two analyses and one must reach a decision as to which analysis best represents the syntax of the sentence in question. As the infinitive here could be replaced by a finite form, as in vs. 14, or by a participial form, as in the first half-line and in vss. 14 and 17, and as *llkt* is not a modifier of a major element in the second half-line, as was *mdbr* in vs. 12), it appears preferable that the verbal aspect of the infinitive should be emphasized here. Note that in vs. 14, on the other hand, the infinitive clause *lʿśwt* is paralleled by a nominal modifier phrase (*bthpkwt*).

14. *hśmḥym lᶜśwt rᶜ*	V M	II B: ii)1
ygylw bthpkwt rᶜ	V M	

Two basic sentences of the same kind (= II), of the type (optional) subject + verb + modifier (= B), here with subject omitted (= ii), in the specific order VM // VM (= 1). This is the most frequent sub-type of the general line-type II B: ii), with thirty-three of seventy examples (p. 106). Here the agreement of the verse from Proverbs with Collins' sampling from the prophets is owing to the lack of chiasmus (only nineteen of the seventy examples from the prophets show chiasmus).

If the verbal aspect of *lᶜśwt* is emphasized, the analysis is VVO // VM. All of Collins' examples of the variant form VVO have two finite verbal forms (p. 221), rather than finite + infinitive. The first analysis given here, which takes *lᶜśwt* as a modifier phrase, is thus based in part on the frequency of the line-type and in part on the parallelism of the verse (*bthpkwt* being a clear preposition + common noun adverbial phrase). This particular verse and procedure of analysis show up both the strength of Collins' system, in that it forces the exegete to do a grammatical analysis of each verse and thus brings out such syntactic-grammatical parallelisms as *lᶜśwt // bthpkwt*, and its weakness, in that its few major categories force the analyst to choose between two aspects of the nature of a given form, such as *lᶜśwt* in the present verse (and, for that matter, such as *hśmḥym* in the present verse, a stative verbal adjective).

15. *ʾšr ʾrḥtyhm ᶜqšym*	S P	Nominal IV
wnlwzym bmᶜglwtm	S M	

"P" here stands for 'predicate' (corresponding to the object of a verbal sentence). This nominal sentence would correspond to a verbal line-type IV C/B: i) (SVO // SVM). Strictly speaking, the sentence in vs. 15 is SSP // VM, for *ʾšr* represents the real subject of both half-lines, with *ʾrḥtyhm ᶜqšym* linked to this subject by the pronominal suffix, while *nlwzym* is a verbal adjective. Collins would probably, however, consider that such a collocation of subjects (*ʾšr* + *ʾrḥtyhm*) represents a compound subject—hence the "S" in my formula. One could, in any case, analyze the sentence as IV Nominal/B: iii), that is, as two different basic sentences (= IV), of which the first is nominal, with subject expressed (= iii), while the second is of the type (optional) subject, verb, modifier (= B). Once again the analysis depends on whether a non-finite verbal form (here the verbal adjective *nlwzym*) is to be analyzed nominally or verbally. I have placed the analysis as an adjectival form first because of the structure of the bicolon in which *nlwzym* is parallel to *ᶜqšym*, the latter a common adjective.

16. *lhṣylk m'šh zrh*	V M	III B: ii)1
mnkryh 'mryh hḥlyqh	M	

The formula for this verse is the same as that of vs. 12 and principal problem of analysis, that of a verb embedded in the second modifier clause, is the same, though here the problem is even more acute since the verb is a finite form. Thus the analysis of the surface forms would be VM // MOV = IV B/D: ii)1, similar to vs. 3. The problem of relativization was already seen in *ʿnt* I, § VII (see above on that text and on Prov. 2:12).

17. *hʿzbt 'lwp nʿwryh*	V O	II C: ii)2
w't-bryt 'lhyh škḥh	M	

The formula is the same as that of vss. 5 and 8 (see on vs. 5 for explanation). Note that the structure of this verse is different from that of its macrostructural parallel, vs. 13, though the similarities are great.

18. *ky šḥh 'l-mwt byth*	V M S	III B: i)4d
w'l-rp'ym mʿgltyh	M S	

Two basic sentences of the same type but with deletion (= III), of the type (optional) subject + verb + modifier (= B), with subject expressed (= i), with the order VMS in the first half-line (= 4) and MS in the second half-line (= d). There are no examples of this specific line-type in Collins' sample (p. 135). It is the second half-line that is rare, occurring only twice out of 160 examples of the general line-type III B: 1), both in the sub-type MVS // MS (see pp. 130, 137, 138). I see no good reason for the rarity of this rather simple form of verb deletion in Collins' sample. Nor does Collins' own reason seem very probing (pp. 138-139: MS must be preceded by the same order of the same elements in the first half-line), for it does not account for the absence of the form MS in the second half-line of verses of which the first half-line is VMS or MSV—though one can grant that the present example, in that it provides an instance of MS // MS patterning, does fit Collins' reasoning and does thus provide it with some support.

19. *kl-b'yh l' yšwbwn*	S V	IV A/C: iii)1
wl'-yśygw 'rḥwt ḥyym	V O	

Two different basic sentences (= IV), of the types (optional) subject + verb (= A) and (optional) subject + verb + object (= C), with the subject present only in the first half-line (= iii), in the specific order SV in the first half-line (= 1—a separate notation is not given for the second half-line). The precise order of Prov. 2:19 is attested three times in Collins' sample (p. 178). Collins offers no special characterization of the type IV iii).

20. *lmᶜn tlk bdrk ṭwbym*	V M	IV B/C: ii)1
wʾrḥwt ṣdyqym tšmr	O V	

Two different basic sentences (= IV), of the types (optional) subject + verb + modifier (= B) and (optional) subject + verb + object (= C), with subject omitted from both sentences (= ii), in the specific order VM in the first half-line (= 1—a separate notation is not given for the order of the second half-line). The specific order of Prov. 2:20 is attested four times in Collins' sample (p. 171). The sentence-type OV (= C) is the commonest type in the general type IV: ii) (p. 175).

21. *ky-yšrym yšknw-ʾrṣ*	S V O	II C: i)1
wtmymym ywtrw bh	S V O	

Two basic sentences of the same kind (= II), the sentence-type being (optional) subject + verb + object (= C), with the subject expressed (= 1), in the specific order SVO // SVO (= 1). This specific line-type is attested nine times in Collins' sample, the most frequently attested subtype of the general type II C: i) (nine of twenty-seven attestations, with thirty-six possible different orders: pp. 109-112). Collins' most interesting remark (p. 112, see also pp. 92-93) regarding this line-type points out the comparative rarity of this 'most perfect' expression of poetic parallelism. (The even more 'correct' form, in that it contains the normal prose word-order VSO // VSO, is even rarer, with only three examples: p. 110.)

22. *wršᶜym mʾrṣ yktrw*	S M V	II B: i)7
wbwgdym ysḥw mmnh	S V M	

Two basic sentences of the same kind (= II), the sentence-type being (optional) subject + verb + modifier (= B), with subject expressed (= i), in the specific order SMV // SVM (= 7). This line-type is only attested once in Collins' sample (Isa. 40:10: p. 100). The general line-type II B: i), with the V + M elements, is generally characterized by intransitive verbs and this feature obtains in Prov. 2:22, with its Niphal forms.

2.4.1.1 *Conclusions Regarding Collins' Notation of Grammatical Parallelism*

Regular line-types: vss. 2, 4, 5, 7, 8, 9, 10, 12, 13, 14, 16, 17, 19, 20, 21, 22

Variant line-types: vss. 3, 6, 11, 15

Unattested line-types: vss. 1, 18

The most surprising thing, perhaps, about this analysis of Prov. 2 by Collins' system is how much better the system works here than for his own corpus: only four verses show any variation whatever (= 18%), while only two (vss. 6, 15) are nominal (= 9%), and one of these has a regular type in the first half-line (vs. 6). Thus Prov. 2 is analyzable by Collins' system in from 96% to 82% of its verses (depending on degree of strictness of application of rules for regularity). This is not only in great contrast with the Ugaritic example (54% to 45%—see above, corresponding Ugaritic section) but with Collins' own sample as well (about 40%: p. 215). This appears to indicate that regular sequences of major grammatical elements was considered more desirable in wisdom poetry than in that of the prophets. Did regularity of syntax and of poetic structure reflect the ordered world-view of the wisdom poets?

All but two of the "regular" line-types of Prov. 2 are attested in Collins' sample and one of the variant types overlaps with a regular category (vs. 11, in which an object is expressed as a suffixed pronoun). Of the verses of Prov. 2 which fall into "regular" categories, the frequency of attestation of the specific line-types as compared with Collins' sample ranges from rare to most frequent; most of the verses of Prov. 2 do fall into well-attested, and not rare, categories. This agrees with the Ugaritic sample text, where all of the bicola analyzable by Collins' system fell into regular categories, including one of the variations (see above). The main factor which caused verses from Prov. 2 to fall into less well-attested categories was chiasmus (vss. 4, 5, 7, 8, 10, 17). This is in sharp contrast with the Ugaritic sample, in which chiasmus was a negligible factor.

Of the two syntactic features which caused the greatest difficulty in the analysis of the Ugaritic text, viz., relativization and enjambment, the first was a problem in Proverbs 2 (vss. 12, 15, 16), though not as great a problem as in the Ugaritic text. This is true because in *ʿnt* I, § VII, relativization and enjambment combine, whereas in Prov. 2 enjambment is not a factor. (It is not a factor in that it does not affect the analysis by Collins' system. It is a major factor in the macrostructure of the text, as the various infinitives and *h*-relativizers show.)

A new problem arose in the analysis of Prov. 2 which was not a factor in *ʿnt* I: the analysis of forms having verbal as well as nominal functions (infinitives and verbal adjectives). The structure of the various verses seemed to call for analysis now as nouns, now as verbs, now as modifiers (*l-* + infinitive). This problem requires further study in the context of Collins' system. At the very least, however, it can be said that this system, by forcing a decision on each of the forms in question, has revealed that the variation of verbal forms (finite, infinite, and verbal adjectives of all categories—transitive, stative, of verbs of movement, and of derived stems) is one of the principal features of the structure of Prov. 2.

2.4.2 *Grammatical Parallelism: Geller*

1. *bny ʾm-tqḥ ʾmry*
   wmṣwty tṣpn ʾtk

   Grammatical Structure: 1-s! ptcl a 2-s
   & 2-2 a 3(prep-)s
   Transformation: none
   Addition: none
   Reconstructed sentence: *bny ʾm-tqḥ ʾmry*
   (*ʾm*) *tṣpn mṣwty ʾtk*
   Comparison: 1-s! : 3(prep-)s :: C (PR)
   ptcl a : a :: C
   2-s : & 2-s :: A (List)
   Result:
   Formula: C C A
   Deletion-compensation: none
   Semantic parallelism: PR; List
   Transformation: none

In the notation of the grammatical structure, 1-s.! = subject (1), with pronominal suffix (-s), in the vocative (!), ptcl = particle, a = transitive verb, & = coordinating conjunction, 2-s = direct object (2) with pronominal suffix (-s).

Reconstructed sentence: Geller "reconstructs" all sentences, including those which have no transformations or additions (the only exception is non-parallel sentences). In the present case, the word *ʾm* would not in Geller's system be "added" into the second half-line because it is not metrically significant. It would, however, be noted in the reconstructed sentence as modifying both verbs. In Geller's notation, the *ʾm* would be written between the two half-lines; I have added it to the second half-line in parentheses (as in *ʿnt* I, § III).[24]

[24] In the following notes I have not given a reconstructed sentence (or verse—see above, Ch. I, note 43) if the reconstruction would consist only of a reordering of elements (as, e.g., in Deut. 32:23, pp. 125-26 in Geller) or of no change at all (as, e.g., in Gen. 4:23a, p. 57 in Geller).

The comparison is done in order of major constituents of the first half-line: subject, verb, object. "PR" notes the form of synonymous parallelism which consists of noun paralleled by pronoun (here preposition plus pronoun). Note that noun // pronoun is assigned the semantic relationship "C" by Geller (p. 42). A term of semantic parallelism is not provided for the highly dissimilar verbs.

The formula is a simple one because of the strict three-element parallelism, with no deletions or compounds. Note that there is no way of indicating the chiasmus in the result formula—and that it does not stand out especially clearly in the preceding analysis.

2. *lhqšyb lḥkmh ʾznk*
tṭh lbk ltbwnh

Grammatical Structure: 3 (prep + inf constr a) 3 2-s
a 2-s 3
Transformation: none
Addition: none
Comparison: 3 (prep + inf constr a) : a :: A (List)
3 : 3 :: A (Syn)
2-s : 2-s :: A (List)
Restult: A A A
Deletion-compensation: none
Semantic parallelism: List, Syn, List
Transformation: none

In the notation of grammatical structure, 3 (pref + inf constr a) = adverbial phrase, consisting of a preposition plus the infinitive construct of a transitive verb (a), 2-s = direct object (2) with pronominal suffix (-s).

The simple formula is again owing to the strict three-element parallelism, with no deletions or compounds. The grammatical differentiation in the first comparison shows up well in Geller's system, with "a" at the end of the long first notation of structure and another "a" as the complete notation for the parallel verb.

3. *ky ʾm lbynh tqrʾ*
ltbwnh ttn qwlk

Grammatical Structure: ptcl ptcl 3 b
a 2-s 3
Transformation: none
Addition: ptcl ptcl
Reconstructed sentence: *ky ʾm lbynh tqrʾ*
(ky ʾm) ltbwnh ttn qwlk

Comparison: (ptcl ptcl : ptcl ptcl :: D)
3 : 3 :: D
b : a 2-s :: /A (Syn)
+ compensation

Result:
Formula: D /A (D)
Deletion-compensation: -ptcl ptcl + compensation
Semantic parallelism: D; Syn; (D)
Transformation: none

In the notation of grammatical structure, ptcl ptcl = two particles, 3 = adverbial phrase, b = intransitive verb, a = transitive verb, 2-s = direct object plus pronominal suffix.

This verse receives an "addition" in Geller's system (the repetition of *ky ʾm*) for "metrical" reasons, that is, *ky ʾm* here seems to function as a "grammatical unit" and hence as a "metrical unit" (Geller, pp. 6-10; cf. also my note above in "Semantic Parallelism: Geller's Categories").

For a discussion of the simple phrase *tqrʾ* parallel to the compound phrase *ttn qwlk*, see Geller, pp. 16-17. This compound is indicated by the symbol "/A" in the "Comparison" and "Result" entries (the slash before "A" indicates that the compound element is in the second half-line).

"+ compensation" in the "Comparison" rubric indicates that the compound (*ttn qwlk*) in the second half-line compensates quantitatively for the deletion of *ky ʾm* in the second half-line (see Geller, p. 51).

4. *ʾm-tbqšnh kksp*
wkmṭmwnym tḥpśnh

Grammatical Structure: ptcl a-s 3
& 3 a-s

Transformation: none
Addition: none
Reconstructed sentence: *ʾm tbqšnh kksp*
w(ʾm) tḥpśnh kmṭmwnym
Comparison: ptcl a-s : a-s :: A (List)
3 : & 3 :: A (List)

Result:
Formula: A A
Deletion-compensation: none
Semantic Parallelism: List; List
Transformation: none

In the notation of grammatical structure, ptcl = particle, a-s = transitive verb (a) with pronominal suffix (-s), 3 = adverbial phrase, & = coordinating conjunction.

ʾm is not noted as deleted/added because it is not a "metrical unit."

5. *ʾz tbyn yrʾt yhwh*
wdʿt ʾlhym tmṣʾ

Grammatical Structure: ptcl a 2-Cpn
2-Cpn a

Transformation: none

Addition: none

Reconstructed sentence: *ʾz tbyn yrʾt yhwh*
(*ʾz*) *tmṣʾ dʿt ʾlhym*

Comparison: ptcl a : a :: C
2-Cpn : 2-Cpn :: A/A (List; PN-Syn)

Result:

Formula: C A/A

Deletion-compensation: none

Semantic parallelism: List; PN-Syn

Transformation: none

In the notation of grammatical structure, ptcl = particle, a = transitive verb, 2-Cpn = direct object (2) in construct with a second noun (-C) which is a proper name (pn).

Comparison: the "C" ranking of semantic relationship is because of the semantic dissimilarity between *bn* 'understand' and *mṣʾ* 'find'. A/A = a compound phrase (*yrʾt yhwh*) in parallel with another compound phrase (*dʿt ʾlhym*), each element of both compounds being semantically similar to its corresponding element. The slash *between* the two "A's" indicates that the elements are both grammatically and semantically interchangeable (*yrʾt* ≃ *dʿt*, *yhwh* ≃ *ʾlhym*). The notation PN-Syn indicates that the proper name occurs in the first half-line (PN alone means that the proper noun occurs in the second half-line).

Note again (cf. above at "Semantic Parallelism: Geller's Categories") that Geller's system, because it is based on syntactic/grammatical relationships between half-lines, has no device for noting the half-line semantic parallelism of the two wisdom terms *tbyn* (*bn* 'understand') and *yrʾt* (*yrʾ* 'fear').

6. *ky-yhwh ytn ḥkmh*
mpyw dʿt wtbwnh

Grammatical Structure: ptcl 1pn a 2
3-s S & S

Transformation: none
Addition: none
Reconstructed sentence: *ky yhwh ytn ḥkmh*
(*ky*) *mpyw d'ʾt wtbwnh*
Comparison: ptcl lpn a : 3-s :: C/ (WP/PR)
2 : S & S :: /A (Syn)
\+ compensation
Result:
Formula C/ /A
Deletion-compensation: none
Semantic parallelism: WP; PR; Syn
Transformation: none

In the notation of grammatical structure, ptcl = particle, lpn = subject of verbal sentence, subject being a personal name, a = transitive verb, 2 = direct object, 3-s = adverbial phrase (3) with pronominal suffix (-s), S = subject of nominal sentence, & = coordinating conjunction.

In the analysis of compounds, *yhwh ytn* is treated as a compound in parallel with the simple phrase *mpyw* (the slash after "C" indicates that the compound is in the first half-line). *mpyw* is in "whole-part" relationship with *yhwh ytn* (*yhwh* // *yhwh*'s mouth) and contains a pronoun for *yhwh*. The "C" ranking of semantic relationship is because of the dissimilarity between the noun 'mouth' and the noun-plus-verb phrase *yhwh ytn*. In the second set of parallel phrases, the compound is in the second half-line (slash before "A") and the nouns are all first-rank semantic parallels.

7. *wṣpn lyšrym twšyh*
mgn lhlky tm

Grammatical Structure: & a 3 2
2 3-C
Transformation: none
Addition: + a
Reconstructed sentence: *wṣpn lyšrym twšyh*
(*wṣpn*) *mgn lhlky tm*
Comparison: (& a : a :: D)
3 : 3-c :: /A (Syn)
2 : 2 :: C (Met)
\+ compensation
Result:
Formula: /A C (D)
Deletion-compensation: -a + compensation
Semantic parallelism: Syn; Met; (D)
Transformation: none

In the notation of grammatical structure, & = coordinating conjunction, a = transitive verb, 3 = adverbial phrase, 2 = direct object, 3-C = adverbial phrase (3) in construct with a second substantive.

For the semantic relationships of the two parallel sets of phrases, see note above at "Semantic Parallelism: Geller's Categories."

8. *lnṣr ʾrḥwt mšpṭ*
wdrk ḥsydw yšmr

Grammatical Structure: 3 (prep + inf constr a) 2-C
& 2-C-s a

Transformation: none

Addition: none

Comparison: 3 (prep + inf constr a) : a :: A (Syn)
2-C :: & 2-C-s :: A/B (List; Concr-Abs)

Result:

Formula: A A/B

Deletion-compensation: none

Semantic parallelism: Syn; List; Syn, Concr-Abs

Transformation: none

In the notation of grammatical structure, 3 (prep + inf constr a) = adverbial phrase consisting of preposition plus infinitive construct of transitive verb (= a); 2-C = direct object containing a construct phrase; & = coordinating conjunction; 2-C-s = direct object containing a construct phrase with a pronoun (-s).

The slash between "A" and "B" indicates that the elements of the two compound phrases are interchangeable, grammatically and semantically (*ʾrḥwt ḥsydw // drk mšpṭ* would be possible). *mšpṭ* is here understood as having the abstract notion of justice, rather than the concrete one of 'ruling (handed down)', and is thus in "concrete-abstract" relationship with *ḥsydw* 'his pious one(s)'.

9. *ʾz tbyn ṣdq wmšpṭ*
wmyšrym kl-mʿgl-ṭwb

Grammatical Structure: ptcl a 2 & 2
& 2 ptcl 2-C

Transformation: none

Addition: + ptcl a

Reconstructed sentence: *ʾz tbyn ṣdq wmšpṭ*
(*ʾz tbyn*) *myšrym* (*w*)*kl-mʿgl-ṭwb*

Comparison: (ptcl a : ptcl a :: D)
2 : & 2 :: A (Syn)

& 2 : ptcl 2-C :: /B (Met)
+ compensation

Result:

Formula: A /B (D)
Deletion-compensation: -ptcl a + compensation
Semantic parallelism: Syn; Met
Transformation: none

In the notation of grammatical structure, ptcl = particle, a = transitive verb, 2 = direct object, & = coordinating conjunction, 2-C = direct object containing a construct phrase. For the analysis of *kl* as a particle, see Geller, p. 8.

In the comparison, I have treated the list of direct objects as two sets of parallels, one simple, the other containing a compound: *ṣdq // myšrym* (= 2 : & 2) and *wmšpṭ // kl-mʿgl-ṭwb* (= & 2 : ptcl 2-C). This is because *myšrym* does not form a grammatical double compound with *kl-mʿgl-ṭwb*. The phrases are in syntactic apposition and rhetorically dissimilar; moreover, the particle *kl* may indicate a caesura in the second half-line.

10. *ky-tbwʾ ḥkmh blbk*
wdʿt lnpšk ynʿm

Grammatical Structure: ptcl b 1 3-s
& 1 3-s b

Transformation: none
Addition: none
Reconstructed sentence: *ky tbwʾ ḥkmh blbk*
(ky) ynʿm dʿt lnpšk

Comparison: ptcl b : b :: C
1 : 1 :: A (Syn)
3-s : 3-s :: A (List)

Result:

Formula: C A A
Deletion-compensation: none
Semantic parallelism: Syn; List
Transformation: none

In the notation of grammatical structure, ptcl = particle, b = intransitive verb, 1 = subject, 3-s = adverbial phrase (3) plus pronominal suffix (-s), & = coordinating conjunction.

Geller's combination of grammatical analysis and semantic ranking shows its value here, where the tight parallels of the nouns and the partial grammatical parallelism of the verbs ("partial" because they are marked for different persons) might tend to hide the semantic dissimilarity. From the perspective of structural technique, this verse provides another example of one striking dissimilarity (the semantic dissimilarity of *bʾ* and *nʿm*) surrounded by good parallelisms.

11. *mzmh tšmr ʿlyk*
tbwnh tnṣrkh

Grammatical structure: 1 a 3(prep)-s
1 a-s

Transformation: none
Addition: none
Comparison: 1 : 1 :: A (Syn)
a 3(prep)-s : a-s :: A (Syn)
Result:
Formula: A A
Deletion-compensation: none
Semantic parallelism: Syn; Syn
Transformation: none

In the notation of grammatical structure, 1 = subject, a = transitive verb, 3(prep)-s = adverbial phrase consisting of a preposition plus a pronominal suffix (-s), a-s = transitive verb plus pronominal suffix.

Comparison: Geller refers to the verb plus preposition combination as a "compound verb" (p. 22—not to be confused with metrical "compounds," for this is precisely what the verb/preposition compound does not form!). In all of the examples of verb + direct object // verb + prepositional phrase in Geller's collection, however, the direct object is expressed by a noun and in all of these cases Geller takes the prepositional phrase as parallel to the direct object phrase (e.g., Deut. 32:11 *yʿr qnh // yrḥp ʿl gzlw* is analyzed as *yʿr // yrḥp* and *qnh // ʿl gzlw*). I have not found an example from his collection which would indicate how he would analyze the combination of verb = prepositional phrase // verb = pronominal suffix. I have assumes that he would consider the parallelism to be verb + preposition // verb. Since he specifically does not consider the prepositional phrase in a case such as this to constitute an element amenable to deletion-compensation analysis, he simply notes the difference in number of syllables between the parallel elements and does not use the notation proper for compound relationships. Thus the parallelism of *tšmr ʿlyk* and *tnṣrkh* would be noted *A. (The asterisk to the left of the indicator of rank of semantic parallelism indicates that the first half-line contains one more metrical unit than the second, while the grammatical units remain equal, i.e., *tšmr ʿlyk* constitutes two metrical units but one grammatical unit [p. 50].) The notation thus would not be A/ (grammatical and metrical compound phrase parallel to a simple phrase).

12. *lhṣylk mdrk rᶜ*
mʾyš mdbr thpkwt

Grammatical Structure: 3-s (prep + inf const a) 3-C
3 ,-R (a 2)
Transformation: none
Addition: + a
Reconstructed sentence: *lhṣylk mdrk rᶜ*
(*lhṣylk*) *mʾyš mdbr thpkwt*
Comparison: (3-s [prep + inf constr a] : a :: D)
3-C : 3 ,-R (a 2) :: Ø/A (Met, List)
+ compensation
Result:
Formula: Ø/A (D)
Deletion-compensation: -a + compensation
Semantic parallelism: Met; List; (D)
Transformation: none

In the notation of grammatical structure, 3-s (prep + inf constr a) = adverbial phrase (3) plus pronominal suffix (-s), the adverbial phrase being made up of preposition plus infinitive construct of a transitive verb (a), 3-C = adverbial phrase (3) made up of preposition plus noun in construct with another noun. (If *rᶜ* is analyzed as an adjective, the notation would be 3 ,-3 [cf. on 2 Sam. 22:17, p. 177 3 ,-R (a 2) = adverbial phrase (3) followed by attributive (,-) consisting of a relative clause (R) which is made up of a transitive verb (a) and a direct object (2).)

Comparison: The parallelism provided by the "added" verb in the second half-line is noted first (as "additions" always are), then that of the adverbial (prepositional) phrases. The latter consist of a compound phrase (*mdrk rᶜ*) in parallel with a double compound (*mʾyš mdbr thpkwt*). I have not found an example of a compound // double compound parallelism in Geller's sample of which the first word in the first half-line is parallel to two words in the second half-line (all examples that I have found are 1+1 // 1+2). My notation is meant to show that the semantically dissimilar phrases *mdrk* and *mʾyš mdbr* are parallel, as are the semantically similar single words *rᶜ* and *thpkwt*. The simple slash between the two letters denotes semantic and grammatical interchangeability (*mdrk thpkwt* // *mʾyš mdbr rᶜ* would be semantically acceptable).

13. *hᶜzbym ʾrḥwt yšr*
llkt bdrky-ḥšk

Grammatical Structure: ,-R (rel pr + part a) 2-C
3 (prep + inf constr b) 3-C

Transformation: none
Addition: none
Comparison: ,-R : 3 :: C
2-C : 3-C :: A/C (List; Ant)

Result:
Formula: C A/C
Deletion-compensation: none
Semantic parallelism: List; Ant
Transformation: none

In the notation of grammatical parallelism, ,-R (rel pr + part a) = relative clause consisting of a relative pronoun (*h*-) plus the participle of a transitive verb (a), 2-C = direct object consisting of nouns in construct (-C), 3 (prep + inf constr b) = adverbial clause consisting of a preposition plus the infinitive construct of an intransitive verb (b), 3-C = adverbial phrase with two nouns in construct (-C).

Comparison: I have considered the basic verbal elements to be parallel ("a" // "b" = transitive verb in parallel with intransitive verb). If I understand Geller correctly, these verb forms do not need transformation (for example, changing *llkt* to a participle to agree with *hʿzbym*). In the two compound phrases, the elements are grammatically but not semantically interchangeable (i.e., *yšr* ≠ *ḥšk*). The lack of semantic interchangeability is indicated by "/", the close semantic status of *ʾrḥwt* and *drky* by "A", and the antonymity (semantic dissimilarity) of *yšr* and *ḥšk* by "C".

14. *hśmḥym lʿśwt rʿ*
ygylw bthpkwt rʿ

Grammatical Structure: ,-R (rel pr + part b) 3-C (prep + inf constr a 2)
b 3-C

Transformation: none
Addition: none
Comparison: ,-R : b :: A (Syn)
3-C : 3-C :: C/D

Result:
Formula: A C/D
Deletion-compensation: none
Semantic parallelism: Syn; D
Transformation: none

In the notation of grammatical structure, ,-R (rel pr + part b) = relative clause consisting of a relative pronoun (*h*-) plus the participle of an intransitive verb (b), 3-C (prep + inf constr a 2) = an adverbial phrase consisting of a preposition plus the infinitive construct of a transitive verb plus a direct object of this verb, b = intransitive verb.

Comparison: Because of the grammatical parallel *bthpkwt*, I have viewed the infinitive construct *lʿśwt* primarily from its nominal side. Geller's system allows such an analysis, for in it these parallel elements, each with its following noun phrase, may be labelled "3-C". *hśmḥym*, on the other hand, is viewed primarily from its verbal aspect, again because of the parallel, which is a finite verb (*ygylw*). Again Geller's system allows this, by noting simply that *hśmḥym* is a relative clause.

15. *ʾšr ʾrḥtyhm ʿqšym*
wnlwzym bmʿglwtm

Grammatical Structure: rel pr S P
& P 3

Transformation: none

Addition: none

Reconstructed sentence: *ʾšr ʾrḥtyhm ʿqšym*
(*ʾšr*) *nlwzym bmʿglwtm*

Comparison: rel pr S : 3 :: A (List)
P : & P :: A (List)

Result:

Formula: A A

Deletion-compensation: none

Semantic parallelism: List; List

Transformation: none

In the notation of grammatical structure, rel pr = relative pronoun, S = subject of nominal sentence, P = predicate of nominal sentence, & = coordinating conjunction, 3 = adverbial phrase.

Transformation: No transformation of the Niphal form is required, for it is in parallel with an (intransitive) adjective. I do not believe that Geller's system requires that the subjects of the two predicates of a nominal bicolon, if different, be indicated as a transformation of an underlying sentence in which the referents would be identical (here *ʿqšym* = *ʾrḥtyhm*, *nlwzym* = *ʾšr*).

16. *lhṣylk mʾšh zrh*
mnkryh ʾmryh hḥlyqh

Grammatical Structure: 3 (prep + inf constr a) 3,-3
3-,R (2 a)

Transformation: none

Addition: + a

Reconstructed sentence: *lhṣylk mʾšh zrh*
(lhṣylk) mnkryh ʾmryh hḥlyqh
Comparison: (3 [prep + inf constr a] : a :: D)
3,-3 : 3-,R :: A + C (List + Syn; WP)
Result:
Formula: A/ C (D)
Deletion-compensation: -a
Semantic parallelism: List + Synonym; WP; (D)
Transformation: none

In the notation of grammatical structure, 3 (prep + inf constr a) = adverbial clause, consisting of preposition + infinitive construct of a transitive verb (a), 3,-3 = adverbial clause followed by attributive, 3-,R (2 a) = adverbial clause followed by relative clause which consists of a direct object and a transitive verb.

Addition: The verb must certainly be added. One might argue also that the reconstructed verse should be:

lhṣylk mʾšh zrh (ʾmryh hḥlyqh)
(lhṣylk) mnkryh ʾmryh hḥlyqh

which would, of course, require "adding" *ʾmryh hḥlyqh* to the first half-line. Note that when an "addition" is made to the first half-line, it is done at the level of "comparison," for true "addition" is permitted only in the second half-line (p. 47; example p. 63). However that may be, since the structure of vs. 16 is a reflection of vs. 12, where the reconstructed sentence

lhṣylk mdrk rʿ (mdbr thpkwt)
(lhṣylk) mʾyš mdbr thpkwt

would be impossible for semantic reasons (roads don't talk), I have considered vs. 16 to be structured like vs. 12.

Comparison: The ambiguity present in Geller's system of noting compounds becomes evident again here:

m	*ʾšh*	*zrh*	
m		*nkryh*	*ʾmryh hḥlyqh*

The obvious semantic parallelism (aside from the repetition of *m-*, which is not noted because it constitutes a minor element) is that of *zrh* and *nkryh*. There is no way in Geller's system, however, to make this obvious. One can only note the number of compound elements and their degree of divisibility (here grammatically divisible, but not semantically so). After the clearly parallel elements (*zrh* // *nkryh* = A, synonymous) are separated out, the elements *ʾšh* // *ʾmryh hḥlyqh* remain—tentatively identified as "whole-part" parallelism (the woman // her words; note that *hḥlyqh* is left stranded).

17. *hʿzbt ʾlwp nʿwryh*
wʾt-bryt ʾlhyh škḥh

Grammatical Structure: ,-R (rel pron + part a) 2-c
2-c a
Transformation: none
Addition: none
Comparison: ,-R (rel pron + part a) : a :: A (List)
2-c : 2-c :: C/C
Result:
Formula: A C/C
Deletion-compensation: none
Semantic parallelism: List
Transformation: none

In the notation of grammatical structure, ,-R (rel pron + part a) = relative clause consisting of relative pronoun (*h*-) plus participle of a transitive verb, a = transitive verb, 2-c = direct object consisting of two nouns in construct (-c).

Geller's system is highly useful in a verse such as this one, for the "comparison" shows explicitly that the two precisely similar structures 2-c exhibit no semantic parallelism, while the "list" parallelism (*ʿzb* // *škḥ*) exhibits only one like feature in the grammatical comparison ("a": both are transitive verbs).

18. *ky šḥh ʾl-mwt byth*
wʾl-rpʾym mʿgltyh

Grammatical Structure: ptcl b 3 1
3 1
Transformation: none
Addition: + ptcl b
Reconstructed sentence: *ky šḥh ʾl-mwt byth*
(ky šḥh) ʾl-rpʾym mʿgltyh
Comparison: (ptcl b : ptcl b :: D)
3 : 3 :: A (Abstr-Concr, WP, or PN)
1 : 1 :: B (List)
+ compensation

Result:
Formula: A B (D)
Deletion-compensation: -b + compensation
Semantic parallelism: Abstr-Concr (or WP, or PB); List
Transformation: none

In the notation of grammatical structure, ptcl = particle, b = intransitive verb, 3 = adverbial phrase, 1 = subject.

Addition: *ky* is shown as necessary for both elements of the reconstructed sentence and figures in the "addition" and in the "comparison" if it is associated with a major syntactic element (compare pp. 109-10, on Deut. 32:3, with p. 124, on Deut. 32:22).

Comparison: The major difficulty here is in assessing the nature of the parallelism *mwt* // *rpʿym*. If *mwt* is *abstract*, then the "shades" would be *concrete* denizens of the realm of death; if death is here the equivalent of Sheol, then the *rpʾym* are *part* of that realm; if *mwt* is the deity of that name, then the parallelism with *rpʾym* may be PN // PN.

19. *kl-bʾyh lʾ yšwbwn*
wlʾ-yśygw ʾrḥwt ḥyym

Grammatical Structure: ptcl 1-s neg b
& neg a 2-c
Transformation: none
Addition: + ptcl 1-s
Reconstructed sentence: *kl-bʾyh lʾ yšwbwn*
w(kl-bʾyh) lʾ yśygw ʾrḥwt ḥyym
Comparison: (ptcl 1-s : ptcl 1-s :: D)
neg b : & neg a :: B (Ant)
\+ 2-c
Result:
Formula: B (D)
Deletion-compensation: -1 + 2-c
Semantic parallelism: Ant; (D)
Transformation: none

In the notation of grammatical structure, ptcl = particle (taking the Hebrew noun *kl* as such), 1-s = subject with pronominal suffix, & = coordinating conjunction, neg = negative particle, b = intransitive verb, a = transitive verb, 2-c = direct object consisting of two nouns in construct (-c).

Addition: Note that only the word to be "added" into the second half-line is included here, while the compensating phrase of the actual second half-line is shown in the comparison (+ 2-c). On the problem of "adding" something to the first half-line, see here above on vs. 16. In the present instance, the "addition" to the first half-line would be more plausible than was the case in vs. 12 (taken above as model for vs. 16):

kl-bʾyh lʾ yšwbwn (ʾrḥwt ḥyym)
w(kl-bʾyh) lʾ yśygw ʾrḥwt ḥyym

None who enters unto her shall return (to the ways of life),
And none (who enters unto her) shall attain the ways of life.

Comparison: on the semantic structure of the verbs of movement in this verse, especially the antonymic nature of *yšwbwn* // *yśygw*, see notes above in "Semantic Parallelism: Notes" and "Semantic Parallelism: Grammatical Relationships."

20. *lmʿn tlk bdrk ṭwbym*
wʾrḥwt ṣdyqym tšmr

Grammatical Structure: ptcl b 3-c
2-c a
Transformation: none
Addition: none
Reconstructed sentence: *lmʿn tlk bdrk ṭwbym*
w(lmʿn) tšmr ʾrḥwt ṣdyqym
Comparison: ptcl b : a :: C
3-c : 2-c :: A/A (List)
Result:
Formula: C A/A
Deletion-compensation: none
Semantic parallelism: List
Transformation: none

In the notation of grammatical structure, ptcl = particle, b = intransitive verb, 3-c = adverbial phrase consisting of two nouns in construct (-c), 2-c = direct object phrase consisting of two nouns in construct, a = transitive verb.

Addition: If I understand Geller correctly, *lmʿn* would only be "added" into the second half-line if it were metrically independent, which does not seem to be the case here.

21. *ky-yšrym yšknw-ʾrṣ*
wtmymym ywtrw bh

Grammatical Structure: ptcl 1 a 2
& 1 b 3(prep)-s

Transformation: none
Addition: none
Reconstructed sentence: *ky-yšrym yšknw-ʾrṣ*
(ky) tmymym ywtrw bh

Comparison: ptcl 1 : & 1 :: A (Syn)
a : b :: B (List)
2 : 3(prep)-s :: C (PR)

Result:
Formula: A B C
Deletion-compensation: none
Semantic parallelism: Syn; List; PR
Transformation: none

In the notation of grammatical structure, ptcl = particle, 1 = subject, a = transitive verb, 2 = direct object, & = coordinating conjunction, b = intransitive verb, 3(prep)-s = adverbial phrase consisting of preposition plus pronominal suffix.

Transformation: I am assuming that no transformation of Niphal to transitive form is necessary, because the unit Niphal + preposition functions here exactly as would an intransitive Qal + preposition—which Geller specifically rejects as needing transformation (p. 22).

Comparison: For the "C" ranking for noun // preposition + suffix, see above "Semantic Parallelism: Geller's Categories," on vss. 1 and 21.

22. *wršʿym mʾrṣ yktrw*
wbwgdym ysḥw mmnh

Grammatical Structure: & 1 3 b
& 1 b 3(prep)-s

Transformation: none
Addition: none
Comparison: & 1 : & 1 :: B (WP)
3 : 3(prep)-s :: C (PR)
b : b :: B (List)

Result:
Formula: B C B
Deletion-compensation: none
Semantic parallelism: WP; PR; List
Transformation: none

In the notation of grammatical structure, & = coordinating conjunction, 1 = subject, 3 = adverbial phrase, b = intransitive verb, 3(prep)-s = adverbial phrase consisting of preposition plus pronominal suffix.

2.4.2.1 *Frequency of Formulae in Proverbs 2 as Compared with Geller's Sample*[25]

1. C C A	major	unattested
2. A A A	major	ten occurrences (p. 235)
3. D /A (D)	major	unattested
4. A A	minor	three occurrences (p. 291)
5. C A/A	major	unattested (but twice in Proverbs 2, see vs. 20)
6. C/ A/	major	unattested
7. /A C (D)	C /A (D) would be major	unattested with /x in first position
8. A A/B	major	unattested
9. A /B (D)	major	= Deut. 32:22 (pp. 246-47)
10. C A A	major	unattested
11. A A	minor	(see vs. 4)
12. C/A (D)	major	unattested
13. C A/C	major	unattested
14. A C/D	major	unattested
15. A A	minor	(cf. vs. 4)
16. A/C (D)	major	unattested
17. A C/C	major	= 2 Sam. 22:15 (p. 236)
18. A B (D)	major	three occurrences (pp. 252-54)
19. B (D)	minor	(cf. vs. 4)
20. C A/A	major	unattested
21. A B C	major	unattested
22. B C B	major	unattested

Comments:

1) There is in Proverbs 2 a greater number of "minor" formulae constituted by lines of two "grammatical units": vss. 4, 11, 15, 19 = 18% (I can find only three examples in Geller's listing: p. 291).

2) There is no verse in Proverbs 2 which exhibits no form of semantic parallelism (in vs. 19, which as analyzed as a b // c d e, the "b" and "c" elements are in antonymic parallelism). This contrasts with Geller's figure of 12% of non-parallel lines (p. 30).

3) There are many more "B"'s and "C"'s in my formulae (this is one reason why so many of Geller's "major" formulae are indicated as "unattested" above). On the other hand, with the exception of the formulae consisting of two grammatical units, there is a very high incidence of "major" formula types. If this is taken at face value (i.e., if my criteria for assigning "A" ranking have not been considerably more severe than Geller's[26]), it means that Proverbs 2 uses grammatical parallelism according to the standard mold for Hebrew poetry but inserts a far greater element of semantic dissimilarity into this time-honored mold. If such is the case, Geller's system has proven itself highly useful in pointing out the new usage to which grammatical parallelism has been put.

---

[25] See Ch. I, note 46, above.

[26] See Ch. I, note 23, above, for "B" used to indicate semantically close but otherwise unattested pairs.

4) A comparison with the distribution of formulae in the Ugaritic sample (see above, corresponding section) shows a much lower incidence of "minor" configurations and of non-parallel lines in Proverbs 2. The incidence of "B" and "C" rankings, though perhaps quite different from Geller's (who gives no statistics on this point), is in any case quite different in the two sample texts analyzed here; indeed, the proportions are reversed:

"B" in *ʿnt* I = 4/20[27] = 20% "C" in *ʿnt* I = 2/20 = 10%
"B" in Proverbs 2 = 8/61 = 13% "C" in Proverbs 2 = 16/61 = 26%

Thus Proverbs 2 is quite different from both Geller's sample and from *ʿnt* I in its greater use of weak semantic parallelism, while *ʿnt* I is quite different from both Geller's sample and Proverbs 2 in its use of different grammatical formulations ("minor" configurations) and of non-parallel lines. As to its use of semantic/grammatical parallelism, one could say that when *ʿnt* I is good it is very good (few "C"'s) but that when it is bad it is very bad (27% non-parallel lines). The poet of Proverbs 2, on the other hand, has produced a (new?) form of regularity by replacing the non-parallel lines of the other two corpora with a combination of grammatical and weak semantic parallelism. It would appear, therefore, that, typologically speaking, the poetry of Proverbs 2 represents an overall strengthening of the grammatical element in parallelism.

5) The fourth point mentioned above with regard to *ʿnt* I, viz., that Geller's system, by noting parallelisms first in terms of grammatical parallelism, can pass over parallelisms that are semantic but not grammatical, is also valid for Proverbs 2, for at least one clear instance of semantic parallelism is not noted there because of grammatical disparity (*tbyn* // *dʿt* in vs. 5).

2.4.3 *Grammatical Parallelism: Kaiser*

	Verb/Predicate	Subject	Object	Modifier
1.		*bny*		
	ʾm-tqḥ		*ʾmry*	
			wmṣwty	
	tṣpn			*ʾtk*
2.	*lhqšyb*			*lḥkmh*
			ʾznk	
	tṭh		*lbk*	*ltbwnh*
3.				*ky-ʾm lbynh*
	tqrʾ			*ltbwnh*
	ttn		*qwlk*	

[27] The proportions represent the number of "B" 's and "C" 's as compared with the total number of "A" 's, "B" 's, "C" 's, "D" 's, and "(D)" 's in the respective texts.

	Verb/Predicate	Subject	Object	Modifier
4.	*ʾm-tbqšnh*			*kksp*
				wkmṭmwnym
	tḥpśnh			
5.	*ʾz tbyn*		*yrʾt yhwh*	
			wdʿt ʾlhym	
	tmṣʾ			
6.		*ky-yhwh*		
	ytn		*ḥkmh*	*mpyw*
		dʿt wtbwnh		
7.	*wṣpn*			*lyšrym*
			twšyh	
			mgn	*lhlky tm*
8.	*lnṣr*		*ʾrḥwt mšpṭ*	
			wdrk ḥsydw	
	yšmr			
9.	*ʾz tbyn*		*ṣdq wmšpṭ*	
			wmyšrym	
			kl-mʿgl-ṭwb	
10.	*ky-tbwʾ*	*ḥkmh*		*blbk*
		wdʿt		*lnpšk*
	ynʿm			
11.		*mzmh*		
	tšmr			*ʿlyk*
		tbwnh		
	tnṣrk			
12.	*lhṣylk*			*mdrk rʿ*
				mʾyš mdbr
				thpkwt
13.	*hʿzbym*		*ʾrḥwt-yšr*	
	llkt			*bdrky-ḥšk*
14.	*hśmḥym*			*lʿśwt rʿ*
	ygylw			*bthpkwt rʿ*
15.		*ʾšr ʾrḥtyhm*		
	ʿqšym			
	wnlwzym			*bmʿglwtm*
16.	*lhṣylk*			*mʾšh zrh*
				mnkryh ʾmryh
				hḥlyqh
17.	*hʿzbt*		*ʾlwp nʿwryh*	
			wʾt-bryt ʾlhyh	
	škḥh			
18.	*ky šḥh*			*ʾl-mwt*
		byth		
				wʾl-rpʾym
		mʿgltyh		
19.		*kl-bʾyh*		
	lʾ-yšwbwn			
	wlʾ-yśygw		*ʾrḥwt ḥyym*	
20.	*lmʿn tlk*			*bdrk ṭwbym*
			wʾrḥwt ṣdyqym	
	tšmr			

	Verb/Predicate	Subject	Object	Modifier
21.		*ky-yšrym*		
	yšknw		*ʾrṣ*	
		wtmymym		
	ywtrw			*bh*
22.		*wršʿym*		*mʾrṣ*
	ykrtw	*wbwgdym*		
	ysḥw			*mmnh*

Comments: Most of the comments to the corresponding section on *ʿnt* I are applicable here. Again there are fewer entries in the subject column and again one must wonder about the propriety of assigning a normative word order. There are more instances of chiasmus in Proverbs 2 and these stand out rather clearly in the vertically adjacent entries.

2.4.4 *Grammatical Parallelism: O'Connor*[28]

1.	*bny ʾm-tqḥ ʾmry*	1 clause/3 constituents/3 units
	wmṣwty tṣpn ʾtk	1 clause/2 constituents/2 units
2.	*lhqšyb lḥkmh ʾznk*	1 clause/3 constituents/3 units
	tṭh lbk ltbwnh	1 clause/3 constituents/3 units
3.	*ky ʾm lbynh tqrʾ*	1 clause/2 constituents/2 units
	ltbwnh ttn qwlk	1 clause/3 constituents/3 units
4.	*ʾm tbqšnh kksp*	1 clause/2 constituents/2 units
	wkmṭmwnym tḥpśnh	1 clause/2 constituents/2 units
5.	*ʾz tbyn yrʾt yhwh*	1 clause/2 constituents/3 units
	wdʿt ʾlhym tmṣʾ	1 clause/2 constituents/3 units
6.	*ky yhwh ytn ḥkmh*	1 clause/3 constituents/3 units
	mpyw dʿt wtbwnh	1 clause/3 constituents/3 units
7.	*wṣpn lyšrym twšyh*	1 clause/3 constituents/3 units
	mgn lhlky tm	1 clause/2 constituents/3 units

[28] Reference above, Introduction, note 2. Verbal nouns and adjectives in the following analysis are classified according to the verbal side of their bivalent nature, in conformity with O'Connor's practice (e.g., p. 332, §§ 3.3.17, 18), rather than according to other aspects of their function in a verse; e.g., *lʿśwt* in vs. 14 was above analyzed as a modifier phrase (preposition + noun), here as a subordinate clause, *mdbr* in vs. 12 was above analyzed as part of an extended modifier phrase (second noun of a prepositional phrase), here as a subordinate clause. Even *hlky tm* in vs. 7 is analyzed here as verbal rather than nominal, though this case is more debatable: is the reference to "nominal" ("professional" as it were) "goers in integrity" or to those who are protected because they "go [verbally] in integrity"? For the semanto-syntactic gradation of "participles," see B. Kedar-Kopfstein, "Semantic Aspects of the Pattern *Qôṭēl*," *HAR* 1 (1977) 155-76.

8.	*lnṣr ʾrḥwt mšpṭ*	1 clause/2 constituents/3 units
	wdrk ḥsydw yšmr	1 clause/2 constituents/3 units
9.	*ʾz tbyn ṣdq wmšpṭ*	1 clause/3 constituents/3 units
	wmyšrym kl-mʿgl-ṭwb	0 clause/2 constituents/3 units
10.	*ky-tbwʾ ḥkmh blbk*	1 clause/3 constituents/3 units
	wdʿt lnpšk ynʿm	1 clause/3 constituents/3 units
11.	*mzmh tšmr ʿlyk*	1 clause/2 constituents/2 units
	tbwnh ynṣrk	1 clause/2 constituents/2 units
12.	*lhṣylk mdrk rʿ*	1 clause/2 constituents/3 units
	mʾyš mdbr thpkwt	1 clause/3 constituents/3 units
13.	*hʿzbym ʾrḥwt yšr*	1 clause/2 constituents/3 units
	llkt bdrky ḥšk	1 clause/2 constituents/3 units
14.	*hśmḥym lʿśwt rʿ*	2 clauses/3 constituents/3 units
	ygylw bthpkwt rʿ	1 clause/2 constituents/3 units
15.	*ʾšr ʾrḥtyhm ʿqšym*	1 clause/3 constituents/3 units
	wnlwzym bmʿglwtm	1 clause/2 constituents/2 units
16.	*lhṣylk mʾšh zrh*	1 clause/2 constituents/3 units
	mnkryh ʾmryh hḥlyqh	1 clause/3 constituents/3 units
17.	*hʿzbt ʾlwp nʿwryh*	1 clause/2 constituents/3 units
	wʾt-bryt ʾlhyh škḥh	1 clause/2 constituents/3 units
18.	*ky šḥh ʾl-mwt byth*	1 clause/3 constituents/3 units
	wʾl-rpʾym mʿgltyh	0 clause/2 constituents/2 units
19.	*kl-bʾyh lʾ yšwbwn*	1 clause/2 constituents/2 units
	wlʾ-yśyqw ʾrḥwt ḥyym	1 clause/2 constituents/3 units
20.	*lmʿn tlk bdrk ṭwbym*	1 clause/2 constituents/3 units
	wʾrḥwt ṣdyqym tšmr	1 clause/2 constituents/3 units
21.	*ky-yšrym yšknw-ʾrṣ*	1 clause/3 constituents/3 units
	wtmymym ywtrw bh	1 clause/2 constituents/2 units
22.	*wršʿym mʾrṣ ykrtw*	1 clause/3 constituents/3 units
	wbwgdym ysḥw mmnh	1 clause/2 constituents/2 units

The conclusion reached with regard to analysis by Geller's system, viz., that Proverbs 2 is characterized by significantly greater regularity of grammatical parallelism than was the case in *ʿnt* I, emerges just as clearly from analysis by O'Connor's system. As remarked above in the corresponding section on Proverbs 2, O'Connor does not compare *grammatical* patterns in a parallelistic fashion, preferring to deal with "half-lines." As was the case in *ʿnt* I, no significant macro-pattern of grammatical structures is visible in Proverbs 2, but there is significantly more parallelism between the half-lines than was the case in the Ugaritic text: where *ʿnt* I had not even one bicolon with identical patterns, Proverbs 2 has ten (vss. 2, 4, 5, 6, 8, 10, 11, 13, 17, 20) and several more verses show differences to the order of only one digit which are owing to various forms of deletion-compensation or pronominalization (vss. 1, 3, 7, 15, 16, 18, 19, 21, 22). This latter category is better represented in the Ugaritic text, though with more variation, e.g., in §§ II, III, IV there is a one-digit difference between all three of the levels. Another significant difference is that there are only two 0-clause half-lines in the twenty-two verses of Proverbs 2 but five in the eleven bicola of *ʿnt* I; the poet of Proverbs 2 makes, therefore, greater usage of relative clauses and of verbal nouns and adjectives in half-lines with a "deleted" verbal predicate (vss. 7, 12, 16) than did the poet of *ʿnt* I (only § VII).

As to the question of applicability of O'Connor's system, Proverbs 2 shows no deviations from O'Connor's constraints (as compared with the two debatable deviations in *ʿnt* I). The conclusions reached above regarding applicability are, therefore, strengthened by this text. The agreement with Geller's system as regards strictly grammatical parallelism, though not a feature of O'Connor's own argumentation, may also be seen as an indication of the suitability of his system of analysis. This granted, the strictures stated above regarding the magnitude of the contribution offered by this system of analysis still stand, viz., O'Connor's "constraints" constitute a sort of "meter" (syntactic, not phonological) and as such are as limited in their contribution to poetic analysis as are the contributions of any metrical analysis. On the problem of linking O'Connor's syntactic analysis with his analysis of tropes and on that of his organization of trope analysis, see the corresponding section above.

2.5 *Parallelism of Minor Elements* (see foldout at the end of the book)

2.5.0 *Parallelism of Minor Elements: Combinations*

1) *-y* (half-line, regular)
2) *ʾm* (near, distant)
3) *w-* (regular, near, distant)
4) *l-* (half-line, regular, near, distant)
5) *-k* (regular, near distant)
6) *-(n)h* (regular, near, distant)
7) *m(n)-* (half-line [non-repetitive], regular, distant)

8) *b-* (half-line [non-repetitive], near, distant)
9) *h-* (near, distant)

2.5.1 *Parallelism of Minor Elements: Comments*

As in *ʿnt* I, the highest incidence of parallelism of minor elements occurs in repetitive parallelism. The only good case of non-repetitive "regular" parallelism is *b- // l-* (vs. 10) and *l- // b-* (vs. 14). There are also three cases of half-line non-repetitive prepositional parallelism, all consisting of *l-* + infinitive followed by another preposition (vss. 12, 13, 16).

Also as in *ʿnt* I, there is very little repetitive parallelism of minor elements in half-line distribution (only vss. 1-2). Moreover, both instances are attenuated: in vs. 1 the 1 c.s. pronominal suffixes are on a singular then a plural noun, while the *l-*'s in vs. 2 have different syntactic functions (infinitive, local).

The repetitive parallelism of minor elements is clearly an important feature of the structure of Proverbs 2 in regular and near distributions. All the examples listed of regular parallelism clearly lend cohesiveness to the respective lines, with the possible exception of *w- // w-* in vss. 9 and 22. In the case of vs. 9, the parallelism is made especially weak by the lack of positional parallelism (unless *wmšpṭ* and *wmyšrym* be considered in chiastic position). In vs. 22, on the other hand, the weight lent to the verse by the repetition of *w-* before each half-line appears fitting for the conclusion of the poem.

There seems, to my mind, to be more disparity of structural importance in near distribution. The strongest examples are furnished by *-k* (vss. 2-3, 10-12), *h-* (vss. 13-14), and *-h* (3 f.s., vss. 16-19, 21-22). The last case is especially interesting, for the 3 f.s. suffix is clearly an important part of vss. 16-19, for it furnishes a rhyming element in that all cases but one consist of pronoun on plural noun. In vss. 21-22 the 3 f.s. suffix is singular and any link with vss. 16-19 is thus dubious; but the antecedent is the same in both cases and it is present in both verses (*ʾrṣ*). The result is a complex lexico-syntactic repetition of which *-h* is a minor but important element. The insistence on 2 m.s. suffixed forms in vss. 2-3 and 10-12 seems to contribute to the near linking of these verses in an important way. The relative function of the definite article is a clear linking element between vss. 13 and 14. Compared with these clear cases, others appear to be weaker structural elements (*ʾm*, *l-*, *b-*) while the *w-* has no near structural role that I can see.

The distant parallelism of minor elements appears, as was the case in *ʿnt* I, to have little importance unless linked with another element (e.g., *l-* + infinitive; *ʾz* linked with *tbyn*; *ky* because of its semantic import as marking a motivation) or in conjunction with another distribution (e.g., with near parallelism: *h-* in vss. 13, 14, 17; *-k* would not have the same strength if it were not clustered; *-h* [3 f.s.] is only important structurally when clustered in vss. 16-19 and again in vss. 21-22, not when considered uniquely as a distant structure [e.g., vs. 3 with vs. 16]).

2.6 *Positional Parallelism*

Positional parallelism is most evident in Proverbs 2 in the two major categories mentioned in the discussion of *ʿnt* I: 1) Close positional parallelism, when the forms to be compared are in grammatical parallelism, but are not semantically parallel; 2) Parallelism of major constituents (VSOM), when even grammatical parallelism is not close. There are several examples of the former: *tqḥ // tṣpn* (vs. 1), *tbyn // tmṣʾ* (vs. 5, chiastic position), *twšyh // mgn* (vs. 7, chiastic), *tbwʾ // ynʿm* (vs. 10, chiastic), etc. (see list at "Semantic Parallelism: Semantic Relationships," section C). Of the second category, perhaps the best example is vs. 14, where *lʿśwt rʿ* and *bthpkwt rʿ* are modifier clauses, but of very different function (preposition + infinitive, preposition + non-verbal noun). Other examples are furnished by the cases of parallelism of dissimilar verbal forms: *lhqšyb // tṭh* (vs. 2), *lnṣr // yšmr* (vs. 8), *hʿzbym // llkt* (vs. 13).

2.7.1. *Phonetic Parallelism: Repetition of Consonants*[29] (see foldout at the end of the book.)

2.7.1.1 *Phonetic Parallelism: Repetition of Consonants: Comments*

Comparing the chart of Proverbs 2 with that of *ʿnt* I reveals two major differences: 1) There is no immediately discernible link between consonantal frequency and a given word or motif in Proverbs 2 like the link between consonantal frequency and the "cup" motif in *ʿnt* I; 2) In the sequences of consonants, *m* appears in Proverbs 2 but not in *ʿnt* I, while the opposite is true of *d*. On the other hand, twelve of the thirteen consonants that appear in sequences in *ʿnt* I also appear in Proverbs 2, perhaps indicating that the sequences reflect little more than regular consonantal frequency (seventeen of the twenty-two Hebrew consonants appear in sequences in Proverbs 2!). The frequency of *d* in *ʿnt* I may be linked with the "cup" motif (*kd* being one of the words for wine container), and the frequency of *m* may be linked with the word *ḥkmh* 'wisdom' in Proverbs 2 (*k* forms a sequence in both texts, largely in both texts because it is a recurring pronominal morpheme; *ḥ* forms a minor sequence in Proverbs 2 but no part of the sequence depends on the word *ḥkmh* itself—indeed, if *ḥ* is linked with any one motif it is the "path" motif and the word *ʾrḥwt*). Three other consonants appear in sequences in Proverbs 2 but not in *ʿnt* I: *p*, *ṣ*, and *ś*. This is probably because the text of Proverbs 2 is longer than that of *ʿnt* I and these sequences could probably be found in other Ugaritic texts.

Examining the chart for Proverbs 2 in comparison with that for *ʿnt* I leads to conclusions very similar to those reached on the basis of the Ugaritic text alone: Parallelism of consonants is largely a feature of micro-parallelism. Most lines will show a good deal of repetition of consonants both within half-lines and between the two members of a bicolon. The principle seems to be that of proximity, however, for there is also a good deal of near parallelism of consonants. Indeed, in the absence of such semantically linked sequences as those found in the "cup" motif in the Ugaritic text, the sequences are probably made up of multiple near parallelisms rather than the result of a conscious attempt to produce extended sequences.

2.7.2 *Phonetic Parallelism: Repetition of Vowels*[30]

		Like Vowel in Accented Syllable	*Like Vowel in Final Syllable*	*Like Pattern of Vowels in Two Syllables with Like Consonant(s)*
1.	b^{e}nī^{y} ʾim-tiqqaḥ ʾămārāy ûmiṣwō^{w}tay tiṣpōn ʾittāk	-qa-, -rā- -ta-, -tā-	-aḥ, -āy -ay, -āk	
2.	l^{e}haqšī^{y}b laḥokmā^{h} ʾoznekā taṭṭe^{h} libb^{e}kā latt^{e}bū^{w}nā^{h}	-mā^{h}, -ne- -kā, -nā^{h}, -ṭe^{h}	-mā^{h}, -kā -kā, -nā^{h}	
3.	kī^{y} ʾim labbī^{y}nā^{h} tiqrāʾ latt^{e}bū^{w}nā^{h} tittēn qō^{w}lekā	-nā^{h}, rā- -nā^{h}	-nā^{h}, -āʾ -nā^{h}, -kā	
4.	ʾim-t^{e}baqšennā^{h} kakkāsep w^{e}kammaṭmō^{w}nī^{y}m taḥp^{e}śennā^{h}	-še- -śe-	-nā^{h} -nā^{h}	-šennā^{h} -śennā^{h}
5.	ʾāz tābī^{y}n yirʾat yahweh w^{e}daʿat ʾĕlōhī^{y}m timṣāʾ	-bī^{y}-, -ʾā- -hī^{y}-, -ṣā-	-ī^{y}n, -āz, -at -ī^{y}m, -āʾ, -at	
6.	kī^{y}-yahweh yittēn ḥokmā^{h} mippī^{y}w daʿat ût^{e}bū^{w}nā^{h}	kī^{y}, -mā^{h} -pī^{y}-, -nā^{h}	kī^{y}, -mā^{h} -ī^{y}w, -nā^{h}	
7.	w^{e}ṣāpan layšārī^{y}m tū^{w}šiyyā^{h} māgēn l^{e}hōl^{e}kē^{y} tōm	 -gē-, -kē^{y}	 -ēn, kē^{y}	
8.	linṣōr ʾorḥō^{w}t mišpāṭ w^{e}derek ḥăsī^{y}dō^{w} yišmōr	-ṣō-, -ḥō^{w}- -dō^{w}, -mō-	-ōr, -ō^{w}t -dō^{w}, -ōr	

[30] Each word, including separate particles, is here ascribed an accent. (One cannot, of course, judge by *maqqef* in deciding which words are accented, which not, for that indicator is inconsistently used, from a syntactic perspective. All such words must either be omitted or included in the accent count—I have decided to include them.)

		Like Vowel in Accented Syllable	*Like Vowel in Final Syllable*	*Like Pattern of Vowels in Two Syllables with Like Consonant(s)*
9.	*ʾāz tābīʸn ṣedeq ûmišpāṭ*	*-ʾā-, -pā-, -bīʸ-*	*-āz, -āṭ, -īʸn*	
	ûmēʸšārīʸm kol-maʿgal-ṭōʷb	*-rīʸ-*	*-īʸm*	
10.	*kīʸ-tābōʷʾ ḥokmāʰ bᵉlibbekā*	*-māʰ*	*-māʰ, -kā*	
	wᵉdaʿat lᵉnapšᵉkā yinʿām	*-kā, -ʿā-*	*-kā, -ām*	
11.	*mᵉzimmāʰ tišmōr ʿāleʸkā*	*-māʰ, -leʸ-*	*-māʰ, -kā*	*-eʸkā*
	tᵉbūʷnāʰ tinṣᵉrekkāʰ	*-nāʰ, -re-*	*-nāʰ, -kāʰ*	*-ekkā*
12.	*lᵉhaṣṣīʸlᵉkā midderek rāʿ*	*-ṣīʸ-*	*-kā, -rā-*	
	mēʿīʸš mᵉdabbēr tahpūkōʷt	*-ʾīʸ-*		
13.	*haʿōzᵉbīʸm ʾorḥōʷt yōšer*	*-ḥōʷ-, yō-*	*-er*	*-ōše-*
	lāleket bedarkēʸ ḥōšek	*ḥō-*	*-et, -ek*	*-ōše-*
14.	*haśśᵉmēḥīʸm laʿăśōʷt rāʿ*	*-śōʷ-, rā-*	*-ōʷt, rā*	*-ōʷt rāʿ*
	yāgīʸlūʷ bᵉtahpūkōʷt rāʿ	*-kōʷ-, rā-*	*-ōʷt, rā*	*-ōʷt rāʿ*
15.	*ʾăšer ʾorḥōtēʸhem ʿiqqᵉšīʸm*	*-še-, -he-, -šīʸ-*	*-er, -em, -īʸm*	*(-šīʸm)*
	ûnᵉlōʷzīʸm bᵉmaʿgᵉlōʷtām	*-zīʸ-*	*-īʸm*	*(-zīʸm)*
16.	*lᵉhaṣṣīʸlᵉkā mēʾiššāʰ zārāʰ*	*-šāʰ, -rāʰ*	*-kā, šāʰ, -rāʰ*	*-īʸlᵉkā*
	minnokriyyāʰ ʾămāreʸhā			
	heḥĕlīʸqāʰ	*-yāʰ, -qāʰ*	*-yāʰ, -hā, -qāʰ*	*-līʸqāʰ*
17.	*haʿōzebet ʾallūʷp nᵉʿūʷreʸhā*	*-ze-, -reʸ-*	*-et, -hā*	*-eʸhā*
	wᵉʾet-bᵉrīʸt ʾĕlōheʸhā šākēḥāʰ	*-et, -heʸ-*	*-et, -hā, -ḥāʰ*	*-eʸhā*
18.	*kīʸ šāḥāʰ ʾel-māwet bēʸtāh*	*kīʸ, -ḥāʰ, mā-, -tā-, ʾe-*	*kīʸ, -el, -et, -āh*	*(-ēʸtāh)*
	wᵉʾel-rᵉpāʾīʸm maʿgᵉlōteʸhā	*-ʾīʸ-, ʾe-, -teʸ-*	*-īʸm, -el, -hā*	*(-teʸhā)*
19.	*kol-bāʾeʸhā lōʾ yᵉšūʷbūʷn*	*lō-*	*-ōʾ, -ūʷn*	
	wᵉlōʾ-yaśśīʸgūʷ ʾorḥōʷt ḥayyīʸm	*lō-, ḥōʷ-, -śīʸ-, -yīʸ-*	*-ō, -ōʷt, -gūʷ*	
20.	*lᵉmaʿan tēlēk bᵉderek ṭōʷbīʸm*	*-bīʸ-*	*-īʸm*	
	wᵉʾorḥōʷt ṣaddīʸqīʸm tišmōr	*-qīʸ-, -ḥōʷ-, -mō-*	*-īʸm, -ōʷt, -ōr*	
21.	*kīʸ-yᵉšārīʸm yiškᵉnūʷ ʾāreṣ*	*kīʸ, -rīʸ-*	*kīʸ, -īʸm, -nūʷ*	
	ûtᵉīʸmīʸm yiwwātᵉrūʷ bāh	*-mīʸ*	*-īʸm, -rūʷ*	
22.	*ûrᵉšāʿīʸm mēʾereṣ yikkārētūʷ*	*-ʿīʸ-, -ʾe-*	*-īʸm, -tūʷ*	
	ûbōʷgᵉdīʸm yissᵉḥūʷ mimmennāʰ	*-dīʸ-, -me-*	*-īʸm, -ḥūʷ*	

2.7.2.1 *Phonetic Parallelism: Repeated vs. Non-Repeated Vowels*[31]

	Accented Syllables	*Final Syllables*
1.	4/7 = *a/ā*; 2/7 = *i/ī*; 1/7 = *ō*	Same
2.	3/6 = *ā*; 2/6 = *e*; 1/6 = *ī*	4/6 = *ā*; 1/6 = *ī*; 1/6 = *e*

[31] Though it does not well represent the Massoretic vocalic system, which is primarily qualitative rather than quantitative, the long and regular vowel grades are considered together here in order that this chart line up with the corresponding Ugaritic one.

3.	3/7 = *ā*; 2/7 = *i*/*ī*; 2/7 = *e*/*ē*	4/7 = *ā*; 2/7 = *i*/*ī*; 1/7 = *ē*
4.	2/5 = *i*/*ī*; 2/5 = *e*; 1/5 = *ā*	2/5 = *i*/*ī*; 2/5 = *ā*; 1/5 = *e*
5.	4/7 = *a*/*ā*; 2/7 = *ī*; 1/7 = *e*	Same
6.	3/7 = *a*/*ā*; 2/7 = *ī*; 2/7 = *e*/*ē*	Same
7.	2/6 = *a*/*ā*; 2/6 = *ē*; 1/6 = *ī*; 1/6 = *ō*	Same
8.	4/6 = *ō*; 1/6 = *ā*; 1/6 = *e*	Same
9.	3/8 = *a*/*ā*; 2/8 = *ī*; 2/8 = *o*/*ō*; 1/8 = *e*	Same
10.	4/7 = *a*/*ā*; 1/7 = *ī*; 1/7 = *ō*; 1/7 = *e*	5/7 = *ā*; 1/7 = *ī*; 1/7 = *ō*
11.	2/5 = *ā*; 2/5 = *e*; 1/5 = *ō*	4/5 = *ā*; 1/5 = *ō*
12.	2/6 = *ī*; 2/6 = *e*/*ē*; 1/6 = *ā*; 1/6 = *ō*	2/6 = *ā*; 2/6 = *e*/*ē*; 1/6 = *ī*; 1/6 = *ō*
13.	3/6 = *ō*; 2/6 = *e*/*ē*; 1/6 = *ī*	4/6 = *e*/*ē*; 1/6 = *ī*; 1/6 = *ō*
14.	2/6 = *ī*; 2/6 = *ō*; 2/6 = *ā*	2/6 = *ō*; 2/6 = *ā*; 1/6 = *ī*; 1/6 = *ū*
15.	2/5 = *e*; 2/5 = *ī*; 1/5 = *ā*	Same
16.	3/6 = *ā*; 2/6 = *ī*; 1/6 = *e*	6/6 = *ā*
17.	5/7 = *e*/*ē*; 1/7 = *ū*; 1/7 = *ī*	3/7 = *ā*; 2/7 = *e*; 1/7 = *ī*
18.	3/8 = *ā*; 3/8 = *e*; 2/8 = *ī*	Same (redistributed)
19.	4/8 = *o*/*ō*; 2/8 = *ī*; 1/8 = *e*; 1/8 = *ū*	4/8 = *o*/*ō*; 2/8 = *ū*; 1/8 = *ā*; 1/8 = *ī*
20.	2/7 = *e*/*ē*; 2/7 = *ī*; 2/7 = *ō*; 1/7 = *a*	Same
21.	3/7 = *ī*; 2/7 = *ū*; 2/7 = *ā*	3/7 = *ī*; 2/7 = *ū*; 1/7 = *e*; 1/7 = *ā*
22.	3/6 = *e*/*ē*; 2/6 = *ī*; 1/6 = *ū*	2/6 = *e*/*ē*; 2/6 = *ī*; 1/6 = *ū*; 1/6 = *ā*
	24 = Non-parallel (20%)	31 = Non-parallel (27%)
	119 = Parallel	112 = Parallel

2.7.2.2 *Phonetic Parallelism: Repetition of Vowels: Remarks*

Because of the very different morpho-phonological structure of biblical Hebrew as compared with Ugaritic (especially: loss of final short vowels, tonic and pretonic lengthening of historical short vowels), the distribution of vowels is very different in the two sample texts, in accented and final syllables (more long vowels in the Hebrew text and more variety of vowels) and in final syllables of half-lines (Ugaritic: *u* and *i*; Hebrew *ā* and *e*, the latter only once). Even counting the two vowel lengths as one (see ch. 2, note 31) there are more non-parallel vowels in the Hebrew text than in the Ugaritic one. This is also owing perhaps to the developed vowel system in Hebrew—would a text with a reconstructed archaic vowel system produce more regularity?

As was the case in the Ugaritic text (of which the vowels were in large part reconstructed) the highest incidence of vowel repetition is with the *a*-vowels (with a higher incidence of *ā* in Hebrew because of the *a* > *ā* shift). Indeed the vowel parallelism only becomes statistically striking when it consists of vowels other than *a*/*ā* (as in vss. 8, 13, and 15). Eleven of the twenty-two verses of Proverbs 2 show repetition of the final vowel of the line and in ten of these eleven cases the vowel is *ā*. The only exception is *e* in verse 13, where one of the two-syllable patterns exists (*yōšer* // *ḥōšek*). This is a slightly higher ratio than was found in the Ugaritic text (five of eleven). As for longer sequences at the end of the line, there are only four (vss. 11, 13, 14, and 18) and two of these are only partially parallel (vs. 11 *-eʾkā* // *-ekkāʰ*; vs. 18 *-ēʾtāh* // *-teʾhā*). This compares with two of eleven in the Ugaritic example, approximately the same ratio. There is no example in Proverbs 2 of repetition of identical pronominal elements at the end of half-lines like *-hu* // *-hu* in § V of *ʿnt* I (*-kā* // *kā* and *-hā* // *hā* do occur, but not with both in final position in the half-lines). As in the the Ugaritic text, Proverbs 2 has a good deal of repetition of vowels within the half-line, both in accented and in final position. The question of rhyme is quite a different one for Hebrew as compared with Ugaritic, because the accent usually falls on the final syllable in Hebrew but not so in Ugaritic. Thus the *OED* definition of rhyme as applied in English prosody cited above in the corresponding section on Ugaritic (likeness of last accented vowel and of all following sounds) is, in this rather strict definition, applicable to two of the eleven verses which have parallelism of final vowel of the half-lines (vss. 11, 14—the first example is not precisely parallel [*-k-* // *-kk-*], while the second includes the repetitive element *rāʿ*); there was no example of rhyme including the accented syllable in the Ugaritic text. There is likeness of the final accented vowel but not of accompanying consonant in three verses of Proverbs 2 (vss. 1, 6, 13 [*-ōšer* // *-ōšek*—one consonant identical the other not]). As to larger phonetic structures, there is in Proverbs 2 a fairly clear case of near patterning of final vowels: vss. 8-9 *mišpāṭ* // *-ō-*; *mišpāṭ* // *-ō-*.

Some general conclusions regarding phonetic parallelism in both Ugaritic and Hebrew: 1) The one indubitable feature seems to be a higher incidence of given consonants in one bicolon as compared with another (Margalit's "alliteration"); 2) This consonantalism clearly spills over into near distribution (i.e., material that is physically adjacent but structurally less closely related); 3) Though there are fewer vowels and their structural importance is thus more difficult to evaluate, the relatively low numbers of vowel sounds which occur only once in accented and final position in a given bicolon seems to indicate a desire to produce repetition at this level; 4) Beyond this general repetition, *patterns* of vowel repetition appear to be desirable but not mandatory (that they occur relatively frequently indicates their desirability; that they do not occur more frequently indicates that the feature was "stylistic" rather than "prosodic"); 5) These patterns are not limited to any one slot within the poetic unit (e.g., in a given aceentual pattern or at the ends of the half-lines: *-šennā*^{h} // *-śennā*^{h} [vs. 4] are accented alike but do not occur in the same position in the sentence while *-ōšer* // *-ōšek* [vs. 13] do occur at the ends of their half-lines and are accented alike [but do not have a common final consonant!]); 6) They may occur in conjunction with consonantal parallelism, either complete or partial (as in the third column of the preceding chart [and the corresponding Ugaritic chart]) or in a given slot without accompanying consonantal parallelism (as in most of the examples in the first and second columns of these charts). 7) Because of the small number of vowels, any structure is unlikely to extend beyond the bicolon unless it be linked to consonantal parallelism or even to repetitive lexical or morpheme parallelism. An example of near parallelism which includes lexical repetition and an associated vowel parallelism was cited above (vss. 8-9). An example of morpheme parallelism is provided by the several (3) f.s. morphemes which include *-ā-* in vss. 16-19, the "female evil" section.

2.8 *Length Compensation*

	Equivalent Elements			*Deleted Elements*	*Compensatory Elements*	*Total*
1.	*b*^{e}*nī*^{y}	+ *tiqqaḥ*	+ *ʾămārāy*	+ *ʾim*[32]		
	ʾittāk	+ *tiṣpōn*	+ *ûmiṣwō*^{w}*tāy*			
	1/2/5	+ 1/2/6	+ 1/3/9	+ 1/1/3		= 4/8/
	1/2/7	+ 1/2/7	+ 1/4/11			3/8/
2.	*l*^{e}*haqšī*^{y}*b*	+ *laḥokmā*^{h}	+ *ʾoznekā*			
	taṭṭe^{h}	+ *latt*^{e}*bū*^{w}*nā*^{h}	+ *libb*^{e}*kā*			
	1/3/9	+ 1/3/8	+ 1/3/8			= 3/9/
	1/2/6	+ 1/4/11	+ 1/3/8			3/9/
3.	*labbī*^{y}*nā*^{h}			+ *kī*^{y} *ʿim*	+ *tiqrāʾ*	
	latt^{e}*bū*^{w}*nā*^{h}				+ *tittēn qō*^{w}*lekā*	
	1/3/9			+ 2/2/6	+ 1 /2 /7	= 4/7/
	1/4/11				+ 1 + 1/2 + 3/7 + 8	3/9/
4.	*t*^{e}*baqšennā*^{h}	+ *kakkāsep*		+ *ʾim*		
	taḥp^{e}*śennā*^{h}	+ *w*^{e}*kammaṭmō*^{w}*nī*^{y}*m*				
	1/4/12	+ 1/3/9		+ 1/1/3		= 3/8/
	1/4/11	+ 1/5/15				2/9/
5.	*tābī*^{y}*n*	+ *yirʾat*	+ *yahweh*	+ *ʾāz*		
	timṣāʾ	+ *w*^{e}*daʿat*	+ *ʾĕlōhī*^{y}*m*			
	1/2/7	+ 1/2/6	+ 1/2/6	+ 1/1/4		= 4/7/
	1/2/6	+ 1/3/7	+ 1/3/9			3/8/

[32] Minor deleted elements are included in this column as well as the "metrically" important ones that Geller would consider to be truly deletable. This was not a feature of the corresponding Ugaritic chart because particles did not play a conspicuous role in that poem.

			kī^{y}	+ *yahweh yittēn* + *ḥokmā^{h}*	
				+ *mippī^{y}w* + *da^{c}at ût^{e}bū^{w}nā^{h}*	
			1/1/3	+ 1 + 1/2 + 2/6 + 7 + 1/2/6	= 4/7/22
				+ 1/2/7 + 1 + 1/2 + 4/5 + 10	3/8/22
tū^{w}šiyyā^{h}			+ *w^{e}ṣāpan*	+ *layšārī^{y}m*	
māgēn				+ *l^{e}hōl^{e}kē^{y} tōm*	
1/3/9			+ 1/3/8	+ 1 /3 /10	= 3/9/27
1/2/7				+ 1 + 1/4 + 1/10 + 4	3/7/21
linṣōr	+ *ʾorḥō^{w}t*	+ *mišpāṭ*			
yišmōr	+ *w^{e}derek*	+ *ḥăsī^{y}dō^{w}*			
1/2/7	+ 1/2/7	+ 1/2/7			= 3/6/21
1/2/7	+ 1/3/7	+ 1/3/8			3/8/22
			ʾāz tābī^{y}n	+ *ṣedeq ûmišpāṭ*	
				ûmē^{y}šārīm kol-ma^{c}gal-ṭō^{w}b	
			1+1/1+2/4+7	+ 1+1 /2+3 /5+9	= 4/8/25
				1+1+1+1/4+1+2+1/12+3+6+4	4/8/25
tābō^{w}ʾ	+ *ḥokmā^{h}*	+ *b^{e}libbekā*	+ *kī^{y}*		
yin^{c}ām	+ *w^{e}da^{c}at*	+ *l^{e}napš^{e}kā*			
1/2/7	+ 1/2/6	+ 1/4/10	+ 1/1/3		= 4/9/26
1/2/7	+ 1/3/7	+ 1/4/10			3/9/24
m^{e}zimmā^{h}				+ *tišmōr ^{c}ālē^{y}kā*	
t^{e}bū^{w}nā^{h}				+ *tinṣ^{e}rekkā^{h}*	
1/3/8				+ 1 + 1/2 + 3/7 + 9	= 3/8/24
1/3/8				+ 1 /4 /11	2/7/19
			l^{e}haṣṣī^{y}l^{e}kā	+ *midderek rā^{c}*	
				mēʾī^{y}š m^{e}dabbēr tahpūkō^{w}t	
			1/5/13	+ 1 + 1 /3 + 1 /8 + 4	= 3/9/25
				1 + 1 + 1/2 + 3 + 3/7 + 9 + 10	3/8/26
ha^{c}ōz^{e}bī^{y}m	+ *orḥō^{w}t*	+ *yōšer*			
lāleket	+ *b^{e}darkē^{y}*	+ *ḥōšek*			
1/4/11	+ 1/2/7	+ 1/2/6			= 3/8/24
1/3/8	+ 1/3/8	+ 1/2/6			3/8/22
haśś^{e}mēḥī^{y}m	+ *la^{c}ăśō^{w}t*	+ *rā^{c}*			
yāgī^{y}lū^{w}	+ *b^{e}tahpūkō^{w}t*	+ *rā^{c}*			
1/4/12	+ 1/3/8	+ 1/1/4			= 3/8/24
1/3/9	+ 1/4/12	+ 1/1/4			3/8/25
ʾorḥōtē^{y}hem		+ *^{c}iqq^{e}šī^{y}m*	+ *ʾăšer*		
b^{e}ma^{c}g^{e}lō^{w}tām		+ *ûn^{e}lō^{w}zī^{y}m*			
1/4/12		+ 1/3/9	+ 1/2/5		= 3/9/26
1/5/14		+ 1/4/11			2/9/25
			l^{e}haṣṣī^{y}l^{e}kā	+ *mēʾiššā^{h} zārā^{h}*	
				minnokriyyā^{h} ʾămārē^{y}hā heḥĕlī^{y}qā^{h}	
			1/5/13	+ 1 + 1 /3 + 2 /9 + 6	= 3/10/28
				1 + 1 + 1/4 + 4 + 4/12 + 11 + 10	3/12/33

17.	haʿōzebet	+ allū^{w}p	+ n^{e}ʿū^{w}re^{y}hā			
	šākēḥā^{h}	+ b^{e}rī^{y}t	+ ʾĕlōhe^{y}hā	+ weʾet		
	1/4/10	+ 1/2/7	+ 1/4/11			= 3/1
	1/3/9	+ 1/2/6	+ 1/4/11	+ 1/2/5		4/1
18.	ʾel-māwet		+ bē^{y}tāh	+ kī^{y}šāḥā^{h}		
	w^{e}ʾel-r^{e}pāʾī^{y}m		+ maʿg^{e}lōte^{y}hā			
	1 + 1/1 + 2/3 + 6		+ 1/2/7	+ 1 + 1/1 + 3/3 + 6		= 4/9
	1 + 1/2 + 3/5 + 9		+ 1/5/14			3/1
19.	lōʾ y^{e}šū^{w}bū^{w}n			+ kol-bāʾe^{y}hā		
	w^{e}lōʾ-yaśśī^{y}gū^{w}				+ ʾorḥō^{w}t ḥayyī^{y}m	
	1 + 1/1 + 3/3 + 9			+ 1+1/1+3/3+9		= 4/8
	1 + 1/2 + 3/5 + 9				+ 1 + 1/2 + 2/7 + 7	4/9
20.	tēlēk	+ b^{e}derek	+ ṭō^{w}bī^{y}m	+ l^{e}maʿan		
	tišmōr	+ w^{e}ʾorḥō^{w}t	+ ṣaddī^{y}qī^{y}m			
	1/2/7	+ 1/3/7	+ 1/2/7	+ 1/3/7		= 4/1
	1/2/7	+ 1/3/9	+ 1/3/10			3/8
21.	y^{e}šārī^{y}m	+ yišk^{e}nū^{w}	+ ʾāreṣ	+ kī^{y}		
	ût^{e}mī^{y}mī^{y}m	+ yiwwat^{e}rū^{w}	+ bāh			
	1/3/9	+ 1/3/8	+ 1/2/6	+ 1/1/3		= 4/9
	1/4/11	+ 1/4/11	+ 1/1/4			3/
22.	ûr^{e}šāʿī^{y}m	+ mēʾereṣ	+ yikkārētū^{w}			
	ûbō^{w}g^{e}dī^{y}m	+ mimmennā^{h}	+ yiss^{e}ḥū^{w}			
	1/4/11	+ 1/3/8	+ 1/4/12			= 3/
	1/4/11	+ 1/3/9	+ 1/3/8			3/

2.8.1 *Length Compensation: Remarks*[33]

1. The imbalance in "words" is caused by the additional particle *ʾim* in the first half-line, which is here listed in the "deleted elements" column (though it would certainly not be so listed in a system such as Margalit's or Geller's, which are based on stress patterns). For the purpose of this analysis, of such particles, only separable particles are listed in the "deleted elements" column. The syllable count is balanced by the object phrase of the second half-line having one more syllable than that of the first half-line, while the "vocable" count is not perfectly balanced. Since the "compensation" is not effected lexically, there is nothing in the "compensatory elements" column.

2. The syllable count is balanced by short // long in the verb + modifier clauses of the second half-line (3 + 3 // 2 + 4). In this case, the vocable count is also balanced in these phrases.

[33] For general introductory remarks, see the corresponding section above on the Ugaritic text. For relationship between quantitative and rhetorical concerns, see especially Ch. I, note 89.

3. The deletion-compensation phenomenon is very clear in vs. 3, with the particle(s) *ky ʾm* replaced by a longer verb phrase which consists of verb + object (on the semantic equivalence of the two forms of the verb phrase, see above at "Semantic Parallelism"). It is also clear that the poet "overcompensated" in terms of both syllable count and vocable count. With *ky ʾm* given one "unit valence" in a system such as Margalit's, however, the lines would be considered balanced (see above at "Quantitative Analysis": "Verse-units").

4. For the listing of *ʾim* as a deleted element, see on vs. 1. Once again the line has suffered "overcompensation," caused here by the longer modifier phrase in the second half-line. Note that the two major changes required in this verse to bring it closer to the Hebrew of the earlier periods would result in the same syllable count, for though one syllable would be added in the Piel form (*tabaqqišanna*) one would disappear from the segholate noun (*kakkasp*).

5. The deletion of *ʾāz* in the second half-line is compensated for by the addidion of *w*- in the second half-line and by a longer divine element. Note that if anaptyxis were removed from *daʿat* the line would have a balanced syllable count of 7 // 7.

6. For the relationship of *yhwh ytn* and *mpyw*, see above at "Semantic Parallelism" and at "Grammatical Parallelism: Geller." This verse contains not only an example of double compensation (compound phrase // simple phrase + simple phrase // compound phrase) but also an increase of quantity in the second half-line to compensate for the deletion there of *kīʸ*. This is accomplished perfectly in vocable count but not in syllable count. Removing the anaptyctic vowel from *daʿat* would give an equal syllable count but produce an imbalance in the vocable count.

7. This verse provides an excellent example of undercompensation: Not only does the first half-line include a verb that is deleted in the second half-line, but the object phrase is also longer in the first half-line than is its complement in the second (*tūʷšiyyāʰ* // *māgēn*). The compound modifier phrase *lᵉhōlᵉkēʸ tōm* is not sufficient to achieve perfect balance. Vs. 7 contains the only example in Proverbs 2 of chiasmus coupled with deletion of a major element (cf. also vs. 15 which has chiasmus plus deletion of the minor element *ʾšr*).

8. There is no compensation at all in this line, each pair of parallel terms being roughly equivalent in quantity. Some syllabic balance could be restored by considering *derek* as a single syllable (> *dark*).

9. Faced with a line containing only "list" parallelism, one wonders if the quantitative balance which exists according to all three methods of counting was not purposeful, intended to impose some order on what might have been chaos. In this case, the monophthongization of *ṣedeq* would produce syllabic imbalance (though Stuart's method would allow the *û*- at the beginning of the second half-line to be removed to restore the balance[34]).

10. This verse contains only one deleted element, the minor element *kīʸ* and compensation is found in the subject phrase of the second half-line. Counting *daᶜat* as a single syllable would in this case result in syllabic imbalance and in an even greater imbalance in the syllable count.

11. Here is a prime candidate for a 3 // 2 "meter," in that *ᶜāleʸkā* is, in spite of being a particle, a "metrical" entity because of its three syllables and is not, by any method of counting, counterbalanced by the energic verbal form of the second half-line. In spite of the 3 // 2 parallelism of words (and of "verse-units"), however, the syllable count does not show extreme imbalance—indeed the 3 // 2 structure is shown equally well here by the vocable count (24 // 19).

12. A form of "list" parallelism, in which a modifier (*rᶜ*) is paralleled by a (suppressed) relative clause, results in a very good quantitative balance. If *derek* is counted as a single syllable, the syllable balance is improved (8 // 8) but not that of the vocable count (24 // 26). The futility of such revocalizations is illustrated in this verse and in several others (see concluding remarks, below) but equally well illustrated is the necessity of looking at more than one form of quantitative balance. The structural sister-verse to this one, vs. 16, can legitimately be said to contain overcompensation in the second half-line (10/28 // 12/33) but can vs. 12 be said to contain undercompensation on the basis of syllable count (9 // 8) when the vocable count shows *over*compensation (25 // 26)?

13. The compensation in this line takes place in the first two words of the first half-line (long + short // medium + medium). Note that restoring ancient forms in this line would involve a great number of changes but would not produce balance of syllable count:

haᶜ(ᶜ)ōzibīm ʾuraḥōt yušr = 8
lalikt bidarakê ḥušk = 7

14. In this case the compensation is strictly symmetrical in the first two words of each half-line: 4+3 // 3+4 (syllable count).

---

[34] *Studies* (reference above, Ch. I, note 61), p. 31.

15. Balance is achieved by compensating for *ʾăšer*, deleted in the second half-line, by the use of two words in the second half-line which are longer than the two corresponding words in the first half-line: 4+3 // 5+4 (syllable count). The balance of syllables and vocable units is nearly perfect in this case (9/26 // 9/25). restoring more archaic forms results in the same number of syllables (lose one in *ʾašr*, gain one in *ʾuraḥōtêhim*).

16. The balancing of the second half-line was not so successful as that of vs. 12, though removing the secondary *ḥatef-seghol* in the final verb would give a better balanced syllable count (10 // 11).

17. There is an imbalance in the second half-line, and there would be an even greater imbalance if the first word of the first half-line were considered as consisting of three syllables (*haᶜ*[ᶜ]*ōzibt*) rather than four. Removing *ʾt*, one of the "prosaic" particles,[35] would provide a better balance and taking the conjunction *w-* with it would give a perfect balance of syllables (9 // 9). The balance is impaired, therefore, by archaizing the participle but improved if *wʾt* is removed.

18. There is slight overcompensation in the increased length of each of the two words in the second half-line. Removing the *w-* at the beginning of the second half-line does not help, for if we are to resort to such procedures the bisyllabic *māwet* of the first half-line would also have to be reduced to one syllable (result: syllable count of 7 // 9), while *kīʸ* is another particle subject to deletion (result: syllable count of 6 // 9).

19. The subject is deleted from the second half-line, while there is no object in the first half-line. The object clause is here given as a "compensatory element" (i.e. for the deleted subject) in accordance with Geller's system. Restoration of a more archaic form of the text would not help the syllabic imbalance for if the particle *w-* were removed *ʾorḥōʷt* should be restored as *ʾuraḥōt* (or the like, in any case the plural stem was historically bisyllabic).

20. The compensation here is provided entirely by word-length, especially that of *ṣaddīʸqīʸm*. This use of long syllables almost brings the vocable count up to parity (28 // 26), while the disparity of the syllable count is relatively greater (10 // 8). This disparity may be removed, however, by restoring a more archaic form of the text:

lamaᶜn talik bidark ṭōbīm = 8
ʾuraḥōt ṣaddīqīm tašmur = 8

---

[35] See above and Ch. II, note 34.

21. The first two words of the second half-line carry the compensatory load in this verse and they succeed not only in making up for the deleted *kīʸ* but for the shorter modifier phrase of the second half-line (*bāʰ*) as well.

22. The modifier clauses are better balanced here than in the preceding verse (1/3/8 // 1/3/9) and so are each of the other parallel pairs (the modifier clause of the second half-line does provide one vocable count towards counterbalancing the long verb in the first half-line but this is a minimal compensation). Here again a more archaic text would have had a more balanced syllable count (with monosyllabic *ʾarṣ* the syllable count would be 10/10).

Finally, an explicit rendering is in order of the results of computing deletion-compensation on the basis of a text rewritten in a more archaic form of Hebrew than that found in the Massoretic text.[36] Because of the difficulties of determining vowel length in a reconstructed archaic text, only syllable count will be considered here.

A. No significant changes to consider: vss. 1, 2, 3, 11, 14 (considering the infinitive construct to be originally bisyllabic; see § D on vs. 8)

B. No difference in syllable count results from changes: vss. 4, 15

C. Equal balance: vss. 5 (7 // 8 > 7 // 7), 6 (7 // 8 > 7 // 7), 12 (9 // 8 > 8 // 8), 22 (11 // 10 > 10 // 10)

D. Better, but unequal, balance: vss. 8 (6 // 8 > 8 // 7; if the infinitive construct is reconstructed as monosyllabic, the balance is 7 // 7; the same change in vs. 14 would result, however, in imbalance), 16 (10 // 12 > 10 // 11), 20 (10 // 8 > 8 // 9)

E. Worse: vss. 7 (9 // 7 > 10 // 7), 9 (8 // 8 > 9 // 8), 10 (9 // 9 > 9 // 8), 13 (8 // 8 > 8 // 7), 17 (10 // 11 > 9 // 11), 18 (9 // 10 > 8 // 10), 19 (8 // 9 > 8 // 10), 21 (9 // 9 > 8 // 9)

Only four verses show a perfectly balanced syllable count as a result of reverting to a more archaic form of Hebrew, and only three more show improvement. On the other hand, eight verses suffer imbalance as a result of archaizing, and half of these were perfectly balanced before the text was retroverted. Thus Proverbs 2 provides little comfort for the view that more exact deletion-compensation and hence better quantitative parallelism are to be found in a more archaic linguistic form of a poem. Perhaps the system will work better with earlier poetry but the empirical results to date are not encouraging.[37]

---

[36] See Ch. II, note 34 and bibliography in Stuart.

[37] *Studies* (reference above, Ch. note 61), p. 31.

2.9 *Distribution of Parallelisms (Repetitive, Semantic, Minor Elements, Grammatical, Positional)*[38]

A. Half-line Parallelism

1) *-y* + *y* (vs. 1) (repetitive: minor element)
2) *l-* + *l-* (vs. 2) (repetitive: minor element)
3) *tbyn* + *yrʾat* (vs. 5) (semantic: list)
4) *dʿt* + *tbwnh* (vs. 6) (semantic: synonymous)
5) *ṣdq* + *mšpṭ* (vs. 9) (semantic: list)
6) *myšrym* + *kl-mʿgl-ṭwb* (vs. 9) (semantic: list)
7) *l-* + *m(n)-* (vs. 12) (grammatical: minor element)
8) *l-* + *b-* (vs. 13) (grammatical: minor element)
9) *thpkwt* + *rʿ* (vs. 14) (semantic: part // whole)
10) *l-* + *m(n)-* (vs. 16) (grammatical: minor element)
11) *bʾyh* + *lʾ-yšwbwn* (vs. 19) (semantic: antonymic; note weakness of grammatical parallelism)
12) *l-* + *b-* (vs. 20) grammatical: minor element)

B. "Regular" Parallelism

1) *bny* // *ʾtk* (vs. 1) (semantic: noun // pronoun)
2) *ʾmry* // *mṣwty* (vs. 1) (semantic: list)
3) *-y* + *-y* // *-y* (vs. 1) (repetitive: minor element)
4) *tqḥ* // *tṣpn* (vs. 1) (grammatical)
5) *l-* + *l-* // *l-* (vs. 2); (*l-* // *l-* (vss. 3, 7) (repetitive: minor element)
6) *lhqšyb* // *tṭh* (vs. 2) (semantic: list; note weakness of grammatical parallelism)
7) *ḥkmh* // *tbwnh* (vss. 2, 6; cf. #21) (semantic: synonymous)
8) *ʾznk* // *lbk* (vs. 2) (semantic: list)
9) *-k* // *-k* (vss. 2, 10, 11) (repetitive: minor element)
10) *bynh* // *tbwnh* (vs. 3) (repetitive)
11) *tqrʾ* // *ttn qwlk* (vs. 3) (semantic: synonymous)
12) *tbqšnh* // *tḥpśnh* (vs. 4) (semantic: list)
13) *k-* // *k-* (vs. 4) (repetitive: minor element)
14) *-nh* // *-nh* (vs. 4); *-h* // *-h* (vss. 17, 18) (repetitive: minor elements)
15) *ksp* // *mṭmwnym* (vs. 4) (semantic: list)
16) *tbyn* // *tmṣʾ* (vs. 5) (grammatical)
17) *tbyn* // *dʿt* (vs. 5) (semantic: synonymous; note weakness of grammatical parallelism)

---

[38] As in the corresponding section above, grammatical and positional parallelism are only listed when semantic parallelism is missing.

18) *yrʾat* // *dʿt* (vs. 5) (semantic: list)
19) *yhwh* // *ʾlhym* (vs. 5) (semantic, proper name // common noun)
20) *yhwh* // *mpyw* (vs. 6) (semantic: whole // part, proper noun // pronoun)
21) *ḥkmh* // *dʿt* + *tbwnh* (vs. 6; cf. # #7, 30) (semantic: synonymous)
22) *yšrym* // *hlky tm* (vs. 7; note weakness of grammatical parallelism); *yšrym* // *tmymym* (vs. 21) (semantic: synonymous)
23) *twšyh* // *mgn* (vs. 7) (grammatical; metaphorical)
24) *lnṣr* // *yšmr* (vs. 8; note weakness of grammatical parallelism); *tšmr* // *tnṣrk* (vs. 11) (semantic: synonymous)
25) *ʾrḥwt* // *drk(y)* (vss. 8, 13); *drk* // *ʾrḥwt* (vs. 20) (semantic: list)
26) *mšpṭ* // *ḥsydw* (vs. 8) (semantic: abstract // concrete)
27) *ṣdq* + *mšpṭ* // *myšrym* + *kl-mʿgl-ṭwb* (vs. 8) (semantic: list)
28) *w-* // *w-* (vss. 9, 22) (repetitive: minor element)
29) *tbwʾ* // *ynʿm* (vs. 10) (grammatical)
30) *ḥkmh* // *dʿt* (vs. 10; cf. #21) (semantic synonymous)
31) *b-* // *l-* (vs. 10) (grammatical: minor elements)
32) *lbk* // *npšk* (vs. 10) (semantic: list)
33) *mzmh* // *tbwnh* (vs. 11) (semantic: synonymous)
34) *m(n)-* // *m(n)-* (vss. 12, 16, 22) (repetitive: minor element)
35) *mdrk rʿ* // *mʾyš mdbr* (vs. 12) (grammatical: *mdrk* // *mʾyš*, *rʿ* // *mdbr*)
36) *rʿ* // *thpkwt* (vs. 12), *rʿ* // *thpkwt rʿ* (vs. 14) (repetitive + semantic: whole // part; cf. #42)
37) *hʿzbym* // *llkt* (vs. 13) (positional; weak grammatical [both are verbs])
38) *yšr* // *ḥšk* (vs. 13) (semantic: antonymic)
39) *hśmḥym* // *ygylw* (vs. 14) (semantic: synonymous; note weakness of grammatical parallelism)
40) *l-* // *b-* (vs. 14) (grammatical: minor elements)
41) *lʿśwt* // *bthpkwt* (grammatical [modifier phrases]; positional)
42) *rʿ* // *rʿ* (vs. 14; cf. #36) (repetitive)
43) *ʾrḥtyhm* // *mʿglwtm* (vs. 15) (semantic: list)
44) *-hm* // *-(h)m* (vs. 15) (repetitive: minor elements)
45) *ʿqšym* // *nlwzym* (vs. 15) (semantic: list; note weakness of grammatical parallelism)
46) *ʾšh zrh* // *nkryh* (vs. 16) (semantic: list + synonymous)
47) *hʿzbt* // *škḥh* (vs. 17) (semantic: list) (note weakness of grammatical parallelism)
48) *ʾlwp* // *bryt* (vs. 17) (grammatical)

49) *nʿwryh* // *ʾlhyh* (vs. 17) (grammatical)
50) *ʾl* // *ʾl* (vs. 18) (repetitive: minor element)
51) *mwt* // *rpʾym* (vs. 18) (semantic: abstract // concrete *or* whole // part *or* proper name // proper name)
52) *byth* // *mʿgltyh* (vs. 18) (grammatical; semantic [whole // part] if *mʿgltyh* has a concrete meaning "path [to her house]" as well as an abstract meaning "her conduct," "conduct which relates to her")
53) *lʾ* // *lʾ* (vs. 19) (repetitive: minor element)
54) *yšwbwn* // *yśygw* (vs. 19) (grammatical; cf. # A 11)
55) *tlk* // *tšmr* (vs. 20) (grammatical)
56) *ṭwbym* // *ṣdyqym* (vs. 20) (semantic: whole // part)
57) *yšknw* // *ywtrw* (vs. 21) (semantic: list)
58) *ʾrṣ* // *bh* (vs. 21); *mʾrṣ* // *mmnh* (vs. 22) (semantic: noun // pronoun)
59) *ršʿym* // *bwgdym* (vs. 22) (semantic: whole // part)
60) *ykrtw* // *ysḥw* (vs. 22) (semantic: list)

C. Near Parallelism

1) *l-* (vss. 2, 3; 7, 8; 12, 13, 14) (repetitive: minor element)
2) *ḥkm*, *byn*, *yrʾ*, *ydʿ*, *twšyh*, *mzmh* (vss. 2, 3, 4, 5, 6, 7; 9, 10, 11) (repetitive + semantic: list + synonymous)
3) *ʾzn* // *lb . . . qwl* (vss. 2, 3) (semantic: list)
4) *-k* (vss. 2, 3; 10, 11, 12) (repetitive: minor element)
5) *ʾm* (vss. 3, 4) (repetitive: minor element)
6) *w-* (vss. 4, 5, 6, 7, 8, 9, 10; 17, 18, 19, 20, 21, 22) (repetitive: minor element)
7) *yhwh* // *ʾlhym . . . yhwh* // *mpyw* (vss. 5, 6) (repetitive + semantic: proper noun // common noun, whole // part, proper name // pronoun)
8) *yšr*, *tm*, *mšpṭ*, *ḥsd*, *ṣdq*, *ṭwb*, *nʿm* (vss. 7, 8, 9, 10; 20, 21) (repetitive [only *mšpṭ*, vss. 8, 9] + semantic: list, synonymous)
9) *ʾrḥwt*, *drk*, *mʿgl* (vss. 8, 9; 12, 13; 19, 20) (repetitive + semantic: list)
10) *tšmr* // *tnṣrk . . . lhṣylk* (vss. 11, 12) (semantic: list)
11) *rʿ*, *thpkwt*, *ʿqšym*, *nlwzym*, *ḥšk* (vss. 12, 13, 14, 15) (semantic [the repetitive parallelism is not in near distribution]: list, whole // part; note near antonymic parallelism of negative terms with *mzmh* // *tbwnh* in vs. 11 and with *yšr* in vs. 13)
12) *h-* // *h-* (vss. 13, 14) (repetitive: minor element)
13) *b-* (vss. 13, 14, 15; 20, 21) (repetitive: minor element)
14) *-h* (vss. 16, 17, 18, 19; 21, 22) (repetitive: minor element)

15) *mwt . . . ḥyym* (vss. 18, 19) (semantic: antonymic)
16) *bʾyh . . . tlk* (vss. 19, 20) (semantic: list)
17) *yšrym // tmymym . . . ršʿym // bwgdym* (vss. 21, 22) (semantic: antonymic)
18) *yšknw // ywtrw . . . ykrtw // ysḥw* (vss. 21, 22) (semantic: antonymic)
19) *ʾrṣ // bh . . . ʾrṣ // mmnh* (vss. 21, 22) (repetitive + semantic: noun // pronoun + minor elements)

D. Distant Parallelism
1) *ʾm* (vss. 1, 3, 4) (repetitive: minor element)
2) *ʾmr, dbr, ʾmr* (vss. 1, 12, 16) (repetitive + semantic: synonymous)
3) *ṣpn, ksp, mṭmwnym* (vss. 1, 4, 7) (repetitive + semantic: list)
4) *l-* (vss. 2, 3, 7, 8, 12, 13, 14, 16, 20; cf. # #22, 23) (repetitive: minor element)
5) *ḥkm, byn, yrʾ, ydʿ, twšyh, mzmh* (vss. 2, 3, 5, 6, 7, 9, 10, 11) (repetitive + semantic: list, synonymous)
6) *ʾzn, lb, qwl, ph, npš* (vss. 2, 3, 6, 10) (repetitive + semantic: list)
7) *-k* (vss. 2, 3, 10, 11, 12, 16) (repetitive: minor element)
8) *ky* (vss. 3, 6, 10, 18, 21) (repetitive: minor element)
9) *ttn . . . ytn* (vss. 3, 6) (repetitive)
10) *-(n)h* (vss. 4, 16, 17, 18, 19, 21, 22) (repetitive: minor elements)
11) *w-* (vss. 4, 5, 6, 7, 8, 9, 10, 15, 17, 18, 19, 20, 21, 22) (repetitive: minor element)
12) *ʾz* (vss. 5, 9) (repetitive: minor element)
13) *yhwh, ʾlhym* (vss. 5, 6, 17) (repetitive, semantic: proper name // common noun)
14) *-w* (vss. 6, 8) (repetitive: minor element)
15) *m(n)-* (vss. 6, 12, 16, 22; cf. #23) (repetitive: minor element)
16) *yšr, tm, mšpṭ, ḥsd, ṭwb, ṣdq* (vss. 7, 8, 9, 20, 21) (repetitive + semantic: list, synonymous)
17) *hlk, bwʾ, šwb* (vss. 7, 10, 13, 19, 20) (repetitive + semantic: list, antonymic)
18) *nṣr, šmr, hṣyl* (vss. 8, 11, 12, 16, 20) (repetitive + semantic: list, synonymous)
19) *ʾrḥwt, drk, mʿgl* (vss. 8, 9, 12, 13, 15, 18, 19, 20) (repetitive + semantic: list)
20) *kl* (vss. 9, 19) (repetitive: minor element)
21) *b-* (vss. 10, 13, 14, 15, 20, 21; cf. #22) (repetitive: minor element)

22) *b-* // *l-* . . . *l-* // *b-* (vss. 10, 14), *l-* + *b-* (vss. 13, 20) (repetitive + grammatical: minor elements)
23) *l-* + *m(n)-* (vss. 12, 16) (repetitive + grammatical: minor elements)
24) *r*ᶜ, *thpkwt*, *ḥšk*, ᶜ*qšym*, *nlwzym*, *ršᶜym*, *bwgdym* (vss. 12, 14, 15, 22) (repetitive + semantic: list, whole // part)[39]
25) ʾ*yš* . . . ʾ*šh* (vss. 12, 16) (semantic: list)
26) *h-* (vss. 13, 14, 17) (repetitive: minor element)
27) ᶜ*zb* . . . *škḥ* (vss. 13, 17) (repetitive + semantic: list)

E. Combinations

Combinations of the various distributions are not listed, for the list would be a simple combining of the combinations of repetitive parallelism ("Repetitive Parallelism: Distribution," § E) with those of semantic parallelism ("Semantic Parallelism: Distribution," § E). This is true because other items considered are either included in one of the two preceding categories ("minor elements" are in the list of repetitive parallelisms) or else they have only been invoked in particular instances (those forms of parallelism which are characterized by few variables: non-semantic grammatical parallelism, positional parallelism, and phonetic parallelism). Moreover, in putting together a list of combinations one would have to deal with the problem of preparing a side-by-side listing of single unities (repetitive parallelism) and double or multiple unities (semantic parallelism)—compare the two lists just cited.

2.9.1 *Distributions of Parallelisms: Remarks*[40]

Half-line parallelism plays less clearly in Proverbs 2 than in ᶜ*nt* I the role of strengthening lines which show weakness in other forms of parallelism. One clear case of such a function, however, is vs. 14, where *r*ᶜ // *r*ᶜ strengthens the weak parallelism of *l*ᶜ*śwt* and *bthpkwt*. The main environment of half-line parallelism in Proverbs 2 is that of lines which feature some form of deletion: vss. 6 (verb deleted), 9 (ditto, half-line parallelism in second half-line), and 19 (subject phrase deleted in second half-line, no object phrase in first half-line). Otherwise, the only purpose seems to be to accumulate similar terms: vss. 5 (the "semantic cognate" accusative phrase *tbyn yr*ʾ*t*) and 9 (a list of similar direct objects, again after *tbyn*). Half-line parallelism of minor elements does not play a major role in the structure of this chapter, though there are three clear cases:

[39] Elements of # 24 are in various distributions of antonymic parallelism with ## 5 and 16. The macrodistribution is ABAB, i.e., ## 5 + 16 (vss. 2-11), # 24 (vss. 12-15), # 16 (vss. 20-21), # 24 (vs. 22).

[40] For a general discussion, see corresponding section on ᶜ*nt* I.

(1) the grammatical parallelism in the repeated 1 c.s. endings in vs. 1 (*bny* + *ʾmry*), (2) the combination of repetitive and grammatical parallelism in the distant structure *lhṣylk m(n)-* (vss. 12 and 16), and (3) the same combination of types of parallelism, also in a distant structure, in *llkt bdrky . . . lmʿn tlk bdrk* (vss. 13, 20).

"Regular" distribution of parallelisms is undoubtedly the major structural characteristic of Proverbs 2. All verses but one show some form of semantic parallelism in "regular" distribution (the exception is vs. 19, which compensates for a lack of clear semantic parallelism by an accumulation of verbs of movement, half-line antonymic parallelism, and a "regularly" distributed grammatical parallelism). Semantic parallelism is clearly the strongest element in these "regular" structures, though there is an appreciable number of parallelisms that do not show good semantic balance (those labelled "(weak) grammatical" in the preceding list: # #4, 16, 23, 29, 35, 37, 41, 48, 49, 52 [?], 55, viz. 11 out of 60). Repetitive parallelism in "regular" distribution is not a major structural feature of this chapter (only two cases of non-minor elements, vss. 3, 14, # #10 and 42 in preceding list). The twenty-one occurrences (eleven entries: # #3, 5, 9, 13, 14, 28, 31, 40, 44, 50, 53) of parallelism of minor elements in "regular" distribution seems to indicate, on the other hand, that such repetition was considered stylistically correct. Grammatical parallelism was not indicated in the preceding chart unless semantic parallelism was lacking and phonetic parallelism was not indicated at all; it was the conclusion of the respective sections above that both of these forms of parallelism function primarily within the bicolon (and secondarily across the colon boundary, i.e., in "near" distribution).

The clearest result of isolating the "near" distribution of parallelisms is the emergence of clusters of concepts: the "wisdom" terms (#2), the "moral"terms (#8), and the "evil" terms (#11), with the conclusion to the chapter made up of near parallelisms of the last two of these concepts ("moral" in vs. 21, "evil" in vs. 22). Other clusters are made up of fewer terms: parts of the body (#3), divine names (#7), and terms for "ways" (#9). Antonymic parallelism plays a minor but important role: in the conclusion to the "evil woman" section (vss. 18-19 *mwt . . . ḥyym*) and in the positive and negative terms in vss. 11-13, 21-22. The clearest case of a minor element in near distribution making an important structural contribution is that of the definite article functioning as a relative pronoun in vss. 13-14 (also in distant distribution in vs. 17). Several of the minor elements do make their contribution, however, to the rhetorical structure of the chapter, e.g., *-k* (#4) and *-h* (#12). Repetitive parallelism of major elements is much more frequent in near distribution than in "regular" distribution (seven cases as opposed to two, respectively, and of these two one shows grammatical dissimilarity and the other has been questioned textually). This situation is reversed for the minor elements for they appear less frequently in near distribution than in "regular" distribution (seven entries as opposed to eleven, respectively). The distinctive aspect of these ratios seems not to be the lower ratio of parallelisms of minor elements in near distribution as compared with those in "regular" distribution, for this situation pertained also in *ᶜnt* I (though the numbers were so small there as to make a judgement based on them uncertain), but the much higher incidence of major-element repetitive parallelism in near distribution as compared with "regular" distribution. It is safe to conclude that the poet who created Proverbs 2 did not consider the repetition of a same word within a colon to be an acceptable structural device, whereas such repetition was acceptable across colon boundaries.

The most important parallelisms in distant distributions include and expand the clusters of near parallelisms (##5, 16, 24 of § D). There are other more subtle uses of the device, however: *ʾmr*, *dbr*, *ʾmr* (#2), used to contrast the father's speech with that of the "evil man" and of the "evil woman"; *ṣpn*, *ksp*, *mṭmwnym* (#3), used first as a metaphor for the value of wisdom, then for YHWH's reciprocal action toward the wise son; the verbs of movement (#17), used to point up the difference between the wise (*hlky tm*, vs. 7; *tlk bdrk ṭwbym*, vs. 20) and the unwise (*llkt bdrky ḥšk*, vs. 13; *bʾhy*, vs. 19) and as a strengthening device in a line lacking tight semantic parallelism (vs. 19). When semantically strong enough, distant synonymous parallelism is structurally important (*ʾyš* . . . *ʾšh*, #25) but, as in *ᶜnt* I, distant semantic parallelism is usually linked with other distributions and with repetitive parallelism. One clear example of structurally important distant parallelism of minor elements is *h-* . . . *h-* . . . *h-* (#26), in a combination of near and distant parallelism strengthened by repetitive and grammatical parallelism (*hᶜzbym* . . . *hᶜzbt*). Two other combinatory structures that contain minor elements are *lhṣylk m*(*n*)- (vss. 12 and 16) and *llkt bdrky* . . . *lmᶜn tlk bdrk* (vss. 13 and 20). It is the collocation of the minor elements in near parallelism, however, that, when repeated in the distant structures and in combination with the repetitive parallelism of major elements, allows these minor elements to appear clearly as structural devices. Without this collocation of two minor elements and without the other elements of the distant structure, the minor elements would not have stood out so clearly—as one may surmise from the many other repeated minor elements which do not stand out as parts of clearly discernable distant structures.

These conclusions may be restated now in terms of types of parallelism. Repetitive parallelism of major elements is not an important feature in half-line and "regular" distribution. This is in striking contrast with ʿ*nt* I and, within the narrow limits of the two poems examined, is a striking confirmation of W. F. Albright's view of repetitive parallelism as an early feature of Northwest Semitic poetry that tends to be abandoned in later poetry.[41] On the other hand, repetitive parallelism figures very significantly in near and distant distributions in Proverbs 2. Especially when considered in conjunction with the accompanying semantic parallelisms, repetitive parallelism provides some of the major recall features of Proverbs 2. This use of repetitive parallelism in conjunction with semantic parallelism constitutes a textbook case of the use of redundancy to avoid loss of information through "channel noise": semantic parallelism is considered sufficient within a bicolon but it must be strengthened by repetition of roots and words when used at greater distances. Such an explanation by "information theory" is not, of course, a complete explanation of the poetic device: repetitive parallelism was an age-old device when Proverbs 2 was composed and its author made use of the technique. The *distribution* of this repetition, however, being so different in Proverbs 2 as compared with our sample text from an earlier era, may perhaps be explained at least in part along the lines just attempted.

Semantic parallelism is undoubtedly the main structural feature of Proverbs 2, with the structure of virtually every bicolon somehow dependent on it. It is most important in "regular" distribution, though it occurs in all distributions. In near and distant structures it is frequently linked with repetitive parallelism (see preceding paragraph for one element of an explanation of this linking).

Because of the many features of grammar and the many gradations of semantics, grammatical parallelism is tied in with semantic parallelism in a multitude of ways. Above in "Semantic Parallelism: Semantic Relationships" and "Semantic Parallelism: Grammatical Relationships" I have attempted to chart the major relationships between grammar and semantics. These may now be discussed in terms of the relative contribution of semantic and grammatical parallelism to poetic structure. Of fifty-five regular parallelisms (counting occurrences, not number of parallel pairs; see "Semantic Parallelism: Grammatical Relationships"), twenty-two have precisely or virtually the same grammatical form, another fourteen have minor differences, and nineteen have more serious differences, though of these nineteen, ten are built on a same major grammatical

[41] *Yahweh and the Gods of Canaan* (Garden City, NY: Doubleday, 1968).

form (e.g., noun or verb) while three others, though not built on a same form, have phonetic parallelism either because they end in a same morpheme (*ʿqšym* // *nlwzym*, vs. 15, and *ršʿym* // *bwgdym*, vs. 17) or because two different morphemes happen to sound alike (*lʿśwt* // *bthpkwt*, vs. 14). Thus of the fifty-five occurrences, forty-eight either have a same (22) or a similar (14) form or show partial grammatical parallelism (12). Put otherwise, 87% of the regular parallelisms in Proverbs 2 have some form of grammatical parallelism while one example (2%) has two phonetically identical morphemes.

Viewing now the relationship between grammar and semantics from the perspective of semantic strength (again counting occurrences, rather than semantic pairs; see "Semantic Parallelism: Semantic Relationships"), of fifty-five regular parallelisms,[42] forty-one (74%) show various degrees of synonymity, two (4%) are antonymic, while ten (18%) rely primarily on grammar and only two (4%) are seriously deficient in both semantic and grammatical balance (they are in what I have above called positional parallelism, though both are not only in similar positional slots in the half-lines but in similar syntactic slots as well, viz., in prepositional phrases). There is, therefore, a high degree of correlation between semantics and grammar, though either can stand more or less alone and this occurs in Proverbs 2 approximately the same number of times for the two types of parallelism: there are ten occurrences of grammatical parallelism without semantic balance and eight occurrences of semantic parallelism without grammatical equivalence (20% of the total of forty-one occurrences of synonymous parallelism).[43] One may conclude, therefore, that semantic and grammatical similarity usually go hand in hand

---

[42] In order to reach the number of fifty-five occurrences in 'Semantic Parallelism: Semantic Relationships," the compound phrases in § A9 and 25 and in § C5 must each be counted as two occurrences. These were broken down according to their different grammatical relationships in the chart of "Semantic Parallelism: Grammatical Relationships."

[43] See above, Ch. I, note 39, for Berlin's and Watson's use of the phrase "grammatical parallelism" primarily to note grammatical disparity rather than grammatical likeness. I believe that the two texts sampled here and the work of Collins and Geller show that the study of grammatical parallelism must present grammatical dissimilarity in terms of the surrounding similarities rather than taking grammatical similarity as the norm, with discussion accorded only to the dissimilarities. The method of presentation adopted here has also shown varying grades of grammatical dissimilarity. (And my rather simple system of three grades could certainly be diversified in order to show many more nuances of gradation.) Moreover, the charts just alluded to have shown that the opposite form of disparity, viz., grammatical similarity coupled with semantic dissimilarity, is even more frequent (three to two in *ʿnt* I, ten to eight in Proverbs 2) than the grammatical dissimilarity discussed by Berlin and Watson. This is *prima facie* evidence for studying these two types of parallelism (along with the others, of course) in tandem and for seeing them as mutually compensating forms of parallelism.

but that in a significant number of cases the poet will insert or allow disparity to intrude. Both types of parallelism are equally important for the structure of a bicolon but the relatively limited number of grammatical features, as compared with concepts and lexical items, precludes grammatical parallelism, in isolation from other types of parallelism, from being a strong linking device in distant structures.

The parallelism of minor elements is indeed a minor, though not unimportant, element in the structure of Proverbs 2. The contribution of these elements becomes apparent only in repetitive structures and only in conjunction with other elements (examples cited above, this section). The inclusion of these minor elements in larger poetic structures appears, therefore, to be intended to strengthen structures built primarily of stronger materials rather than to form independent poetic structures—at least if these latter exist I have not been able to pick them out. This was also the case in *ʿnt* I and is, indeed, to be expected because of the relatively unimportant phonetic and semantic contribution that these particles are capable of making. It is worth noting that in the few cases in Proverbs 2 where minor elements assume important phonetic proportions (*ky ʾm* in vs. 3, *ʾšr* in vs. 15, and *lmʿn* in vs. 20), they are not accompanied by a parallel term. It would appear, therefore, that when minor elements are long enough to assume an important phonetic position or when they are clustered in order to form such an entity, their principal role is to advance the argument of the poem and that their place in the second half-line is properly filled by deletion-compensation rather than by parallelism.

Phonetic parallelism (of both vowels and consonants) is clearly visible in half-lines and in "regular" distribution. There is also a significant degree of phonetic recall across verse boundaries, producing near parallelism. There are only sporadic instances of vowel + consonant combination structures (i.e., "rhyme" in one sense or another). Extended phonetic structures in Proverbs 2 appear to be dependent upon morpheme repetition (e.g., *-ā-* in vss. 16-19). Phonetic parallelism is not necessarily nor even especially frequently linked with specific semantic pairs as grammatical parallelism usually is (see above, this section) but appears as a higher-than-expected ratio of certain vowels and consonants within a half-line, a line, or across adjacent line boundaries. This relative lack of strength in building larger structures is again related to the nature of phonetic parallelism: because of the relatively few variables and the brevity of each of them, sound parallelism cannot extend beyond a few syllables unless joined with lexical or grammatical parallelism.

CHAPTER THREE

A COMPARISON OF UGARITIC AND HEBREW PARALLELISM

On the basis of this "trial cut" into Ugaritic and Hebrew poetry, narrow but deep, with all the dangers inherent in any attempt to generalize on the basis of so narrow a sounding, some tentative comparisons may be made. We may begin with a summary of results attained for each of the texts studied and then attempt some comparisons.

3.1. *A Brief Commentary on the Parallelism of ʿnt I and Proverbs 2*

3.1.1 *ʿnt* I

§ I. Grammatical parallelism functions without deletion: VO // VO. The second half-line contains an expanded form of the object phrase which compensates, indeed overcompensates, for the fact that *ʾaliyāna* is longer than *zabūla*.

§ II. The parallelism of this section and of § IV is irregular by all of the major forms of analysis proposed in recent years in that it consists of three verbs. The unusual shortness of the first half-line may indicate that this entire line should be analyzed as the first segment of a tricolon. The analysis proposed above is intended to line up more clearly the three three-verb structures in this text and to negate the large quantitative differences between the first and second lines of the putative tricola (§§ II and IV): 3/12/27 // 3/9/21 and 3/12/27 // 3/8/17. As analyzed here, the bicolon consists of three verbs, the second and third of which form a closer semantic pair than does the first with either of the other two. In both of the bicola the single verb of the second half-line overcompensates quantitatively, by every "metric" system except simple word count and Margalit's verse-unit count, for the two verbs of the first half-line.

§ III. The verb is deleted from the second half-line and the object and modifier phrases of the second half-line are expanded (indeed, over-expanded) by compounding in order to compensate for this deletion. These phrases are also reversed in order to compensate for this deletion. These phrases are also reversed in order, producing a partially chiastic ordering of major consituents (VOM // MO).

§ IV. See on § II.

§ V. As in § III the verb is deleted in the second half-line and the object and modifier phrases are expanded, this time both by word length (the object phrase) and by compounding (the modifier phrase), and again overcompensation is the result by all systems of counting except those of words and of verse-units. The parallelism of the modifier phrases includes a special form of number parallelism: singular noun // word for "pair" + dual noun.

§ VI. This is the first bicolon of this text to have only very weak semantic parallelism (*bk // nmt*) and virtually no grammatical parallelism in "regular" distribution (only *dā* carries over the accusative phrases of the first half-line). Moreover, it is in grammatical enjambment with the preceding and following bicola. Its weakness of parallelisms in regular distribution is compensated for by half-line parallelism in the first half-line (*rb // ʿẓm*). It is linked phonetically to the preceding bicolon by the repetition of both *k* (present in the two words for 'cup' in § V) and *r* (present in the second word for 'cup' *krpn*). The grammatical enjambment entails grammatical parallelism: the two singular object phrases in § V are echoed in § VI by four phrases in the accusative case (*bīka rabba ʿaẓuma . . . dā*). This enjambment continues into the next section, which is in turn internally more regular and which includes the same pair of object phrases as in § V (*ks // krpn*). Thus § VI is a central unit in a three-unit structure and it is bound into the structure by grammatical parallelism (a high incidence of substantives and a particle in the accusative case) and by the more regular parallelism of the enclosing units.

§ VII. As just noted, the enjambment continues into § VII but in this case the bicolon is very precisely balanced by means of virtually exact repetition of forms in each of the half-lines: semantic, grammatical (morphological and syntactic), phonetic, and positional parallelism are all very strong. The one compound, *ks qdš*, is apparently present more for semantic reasons than for compensatory ones, for *qdš* is the key word in the line (it explains why the cup cannot be seen by the two subjects of the two clauses); in any case, it results in a somewhat longer first half-line.

§ VIII. Passing from the "cup" section to the "drinking" section, we see that the parallelistic structure is very similar to that of the previous bicolon, with one important difference. In this case, the exactness of the grammatical and positional parallelism, coupled with the half-line repetitive parallelism *ymsk bmskh*, has created an environment in which the very weak semantic parallelism *lqḥ* // *msk* ('take' // 'mix') passes almost unnoticed. The semantic parallelism of the modifier phrases is not quite so weak but is definitely of the same "functional" or "sequential" type (*ḫmr* // *msk* 'type of wine' // 'mixture'). Finally, the poet has in this case produced nearly perfect quantitative balance by spreading ten syllables over three words in the second half-line to counterbalance the compound *ʾalp kd* in the first half-line.

§ IX. This is the second bicolon without good semantic and grammatical parallelism in "regular" distribution. Its coherence is assured, however, by distant repetitive and grammatical parallelism with §§ II and IV, though the relationship of the three-verb structure to the surrounding context is different: In §§ II and IV the three verbs formed either a bicolon (as analyzed here) or the first segment of a tricolon, whereas the comparative brevity of the three verbs and the following line segment which depends syntactically on the three-verb sequence indicate that the three-verb sequence in § IX is the first segment of a bicolon. The semantic parallelism of the bicolon itself is "functional" or "sequential" in that the instrument mentioned in the second half-line accompanies the singing mentioned in the first half-line. The phonetic parallelism is quite good: *-āma* // *-âma*, *b-d* // *b-d*, *-a-ī-* // *-a-ī-*, and so is the quantitative balance (3/9/20 // 3/9/22)—something that cannot be said for the following bicolon. By means of the repetitive parallelism of *yšr*, § IX is more closely linked to the following unit than was the case with §§ II and IV. In spite of the lack of the types of parallelism by which Northwest Semitic poetry has generally been characterized, therefore, one can say that this bicolon is locked into the structure of the poem as a whole by a combination of distant repetitive and semantic parallelism, by near repetitive parallelism, by "regular" phonetic parallelism, and by half-line grammatical and semantic parallelism.

§ X. This is the third bicolon of this short sample which does not contain a "regular" distribution of good semantic or grammatical parallelism. It is a simple, prosaic sentence: VS // M + M. As was the case with the preceding unit, however, the structure of the unit as a bicolon can be determined by syntactic and (rough) quantitative criteria and the place of the unit within the structure of the larger poem is assured by various other types of parallelism: the repetitive parallelism of *yšr* with the same form of the word in the preceding bicolon, the repetitive parallelism of *bʿl* with both the following bicolon and with the first (preserved) unit of the poem, the near semantic parallelism *nʿm . . . ṭb*, and the good but not especially remarkable phonetic parallelism in both half-line and "regular" distributions (see charts of phonetic parallelism of both consonants and vowels above). As to quantitative balance, the length of the formulaic compound *bṣrrt ṣpn* leads to overbalancing of the second half-line by all systems except word count and verse-unit count.

§ XI. The new narrative section which begins with this unit is launched by a nicely balanced unit which contains good semantic and grammatical parallelism and a complex but almost impeccable quantitative balance (single word // double compound; the double compound does not result in overcompensation because each of its terms is shorter than any of the words in the first half-line). This unit is also characterized by near and distant repetitive parallelism (*bʿl*, *bt*/*bnt*, *ʿn*) and by distant semantic parallelism (*ytmr* with the verbs of seeing in §§ VI and VII). The parallelism of the object phrases has the particular forms of common noun // proper name, whole // part (*pdry* is one of a group), repetitive (*bnt* // *bt*), and because of its genealogical form, a second proper name (common noun // proper name + proper name).

3.1.2 *Proverbs 2*

1. One of the principal differences between the two sample texts stands out immediately in vs. 1, viz., the higher incidence of chiastic structures in Proverbs 2. The perfect ABC // CBA chiastic structure has no parallel in *ʿnt* I. The perfect regularity is weakened (or: diversified) by the fact that the B elements do not show good semantic parallelism (a b c // c′ d a′) and that the A elements are formed on different grammatical bases (noun // preposition). As to quantitative balance, the poet of Proverbs 2 produced a more consistent balance than was observed in *ʿnt* I and vs. 1 is no exception to that generality.

2. Chiasmus characterizes the second verse also, this time of the second and third elements only. Once again the verb forms show a degree of dissimilarity, though here the difference is grammatical (infinitive // finite form) rather than semantic. Otherwise the parallelism of all types is tight to the point of triteness.

3. The first case of deletion-compensation occurs here: the minor elements *ky ʾm* form a metrically important entity which, when deleted in the second half-line, is compensated for by the verb + noun compound *ttn qwlk*.

4. Except for the deletion of *ʾm* in the second half-line, this verse is precisely balanced from the grammatical and semantic perspectives, including the minor elements *-nh* // *-nh* and *k-* // *k-*, though the longer modifier phrase in the second half-line has slightly overcompensated for the deleted *ʾm*. Chiasmus again accompanies the lack of deletion-compensation of major elements.

5. Only the minor element *ᵓz* is deleted and this is well compensated for in the second half-line. Once again chiasmus (ABC // BCA) characterizes a line which does not contain deletion-compensation of major elements.

6. This is the first bicolon in Proverbs 2 made up of two different types of sentences (verbal // nominal). The semantic parallelism is nonetheless very good because *mpyw* contains two forms of semantic parallelism with *yhwh* (whole // part, proper name // pronoun). There is also a form of functional parallelism between *ytn* in the first half-line and the preposition *m*(*n*)- in the second half-line ("functional" rather than "grammatical" because *ntn m*(*n*)- is not a regular idiom for either speech or gift-giving, and thus *m*(*n*)- is functioning somewhat as an equivalent of *ntn* rather than as part of a syntagm *ntn m*(*n*)-). Neither the grammatical/syntactic differences nor the deletion of the minor element *ky* have been allowed to produce quantitative imbalance.

7. This is the only verse in the chapter to contain both chiasmus (of the object phrases: ABC // CB) and deletion-compensation of a major element (verb deleted, modifier phrase expanded). The parallelism of the object phrases constitutes a metaphor, a rhetorical form that can contain the most disparate elements (here 'intelligence' serves as a 'shield').

8. Once again chiasmus characterizes a verse which lacks deletion-compensation. The semantic parallelism is very tight, though one twist is thrown in by making *mišpāṭ* parallel to *ḥăsīʸdōʷ* rather than to *ḥesed* producing a parallelism of abstract // concrete. Another of the grammatical dissimilarities so characteristic of this chapter (vss. 2, 13, 14, 17) is found in this verse as well (*lnṣr* // *yšmr*). Again a verse characterized by very tight semantic parallelism has had some variety interjected by devices that do not essentially affect the semantic balance.

9. The parallelism here consists of a list of object phrases following the single verb. The elements of the list are homogeneous except for the one metaphorical element *mᶜgl*. As was the case with § IX of *ᶜnt* I, the unorthodox parallelistic balance is accompanied by good quantitative balance. (This was not the rule in *ᶜnt* I, however, for § VI were seen to be indifferently balanced and § X poorly so.)

10. Again a line with no deletion-compensation of major elements (only the minor element *ky* is deleted) is chiastically arranged (ABC // BCA). The nearly perfect grammatical parallelism permits the poor semantic parallelism of *tbwᵓ* and *ynᶜm*. A quite astonishing, albeit coincidental, detail of agreement with *ᶜnt* I (§§ IX and X) is the near parallelism of *ynᶜm* with *ṭwb* in vs. 9, though the order of occurrence of the two roots is reversed here.

11. The special form of compounding which consists of verb + prepositional phrase // verb + suffixed pronominal suffix occurs here. The verse is very well balanced grammatically and semantically but in this case the deletion of the prepositional phrase from the second half-line is not compensated for lexically and the longer verb from in the second half-line does not fully compensate for the lexical deletion. Even so, the disparity is not significant, especially in syllable count (only a one-syllable difference).

12. Vss. 12-13 begin a unit containing structures that are closely imitated in vss. 16-17. Those parallel structures introduce rhetorically separate but parallel units of the discourse. The parallelism of vs. 12 is characterized by deletion of the verb in the second half-line accompanied by compensation in the modifier clause. The poor semantic parallelism of the inner elements (*drk* // *ʾyš mdbr*) is balanced by repetitive and semantic parallelism of the outer units (*m*(*n*)- // *m*(*n*)- . . . *rʿ* // *thpkwt*), by the likeness of the syntactic structures (with the exception of the deleted verb), and by good quantitative balance.

13. The repetitive parallelism of the minor element *h*- at the beginning of vss. 13 and 14 ties these verses together and ties them in with the parallel structure in vss. 16-19 (*h*- in vs. 17). This function of the minor element (definite article) is proven by its rarity in this chapter, for it only occurs these three times—there would be many occurrences in a piece of standard prose of the same length. This rarity is heightened by the equivalence of syntactic function: in each of the three appearances the definite article functions as a relativizing particle. As in vss. 2, 8, 14, and 17, the regularity of structure is broken by grammatical dissimilarity of the verbs; in the present instance the semantic parallelism of the verbs is sequential rather than synonymous, as well. Finally, the aberrant nature of the evil man's conduct is underlined by one of only two instances of antonymic parallelism in "regular" distribution in this chapter (*yšr* // *ḥšk*); the other is in the "evil woman" section (vs. 19).

14. One of the nicest mixtures of similarity and dissimilarity of all sorts is found in vs. 14. The A elements are semantically close but grammatically dissimilar (participle // finite). The B elements are semantically unrelated and grammatically dissimilar (verbal noun // common noun), but syntactically (prepositional phrases) and phonetically similar ($-\bar{o}^{w}t$ // $-\bar{o}^{w}t$, not identical morphemes!). The C elements are repetitive as well as being in regular and half-line semantic parallel with the B element of the second half-line (*rʿ* // *thpkwt rʿ*). All this fitted into a quantitative balance that is virtually perfect.

15. The rare use of *h-* in vss. 13-14 is reflected in the even rarer use of the relative pronoun *ʾšr* in vs. 15. As the relative *h-* was replaced by verb forms not requiring its use in the second half-lines of vss. 13-14, *ʾšr*, here used to introduce nominal sentences, is deleted from the second half-line of vs. 15. Once again what appears to be a very tightly balanced bicolon contains a twist, this time in the syntax: *ʾrḥtyhm* has as subject the 'ways', whereas the subject of *nlwzym* is (the antecedent of) *ʾšr*. This is accomplished by the minor element *b-* before *mʿglwtm*. All three of the particles of this verse only occur once. When *ʾšr* is viewed as a minor element (i.e., defined lexically rather than metrically), this verse is in agreement with the general practice of the poet of using chiasmus only when deletion-compensation of major forms is not present.

16. The semantic and grammatical structure of this verse is similar to that of vs. 12, though the semantic distribution is different: (natural) compound // single word, with good semantic balance (*ʾšh zrh* // *nkryh*; the corresponding phrases in vs. 12 were semantically unrelated: *drk rʿ* // *ʾyš*). The expanding clauses are each unrelated to anything in their own verses but contain distant semantic parallelism: *mdbr thpkwt* // *ʾmryh hḥlyqh* (the semantic parallelism is in the first words of each phrase, the words in second position are both semantically and grammatically unrelated). *ʾmryh* in vs. 16 closes the progression of words for speech which began with the father's words to his son in vs. 1. The sequence of forms characterized by the (3) f.s. morpheme with *-ā-* begins here and continues through vs. 19. Though the syntactic structure of vs. 16 is very similar to that of vs. 12, the compensatory process did not lead to the same quantitative balance in the two verses, for vs. 16 contains a two-syllable over-compensation in the second half-line.

17. The most blatant case of semantic dissimilarity hidden in regular grammatical, phonetic, and positional structures is to be found in this verse: both *ʾlwp* // *bryt* and *nʿwryh* // *ʾlhyh* get "C" in ranking of semantic proximity. This semantic dissimilarity is balanced by grammatical likeness (both direct object phrases, construct chains, with 3 f.s. pronominal suffixes on the plural second noun), phonetic parallelism (*-eʸhā* // *-eʸhā*), and position between two semantically similar, though grammatically dissimilar, verbs (*hʿzbt* // *škḥh*). Could the piling up of parallelistic "irregularities" of this verse have been intended to reflect the irregularity of the evil woman's life? This verse contains the only occurrence of the definite direct object marker *ʾt* in this chapter. Is it a later "prosaic" addition or a further irregular feature (emending it out would give a 10 // 10 syllable count)? Again the partial chiasmus (ABC // BCA) occurs in a verse which does not contain deletion-compensation.

18. Both the particle and the verb of the first half-line are deleted in the second and again overcompensation has occurred. Again there is no chiasmus when a major element is deleted.[1]

19. The deletion-compensation structure is of a particular sort: a major element (subject) of the first half-line is deleted in the second half-line and compensated for by the insertion of another major element (object). There is a form of double deletion here, for the minor element *kl* is also deleted in the second half-line. There is a form of antonymic parallelism of the main verbs if one considers the direction of motion: *šwb* = return, *hśyg* = attain (opposite movements). However that may be, the "functional" parallelism is synonymous, with the 'return' being the safe return from the evil woman's house and life being what is 'attained'. It is the piling up of verbs of movement (including *bʾyh* of the first half-line) that provides the only semantic parallelism present in this verse. Each of the three verbs of movement has contributed its part to the scene and whatever semantic dissimilarity exists among them has played, under the overarching category of verbs of movement, a part in creating the scene: *bwʾ* = resorting to the woman, *šwb* = (not) returning from the encounter, *hśyg* = (not) attaining life. The near parallelism of *mwt* // *rpʾym* . . . *ḥyym* (vss. 18-19) constitutes a near antonymic structure, in which *mʿgltyh* and *ʾrḥwt* (also vss. 18-19) contribute, for the 'paths' of verse 18 are negatively polarized by context whereas the 'ways' of vs. 19 are positively polarized by *ḥyym*. Given the syntactic enjambment with

[1] Given the great variety of semantic parallelism, as well as of other types in Proverbs 2, the proposal to emend *byth* to *ntybth* in this verse strikes me as unlikely (see Loretz' recent discussion in "Ugaritische und hebräische Lexikographie (III)," *UF* 14 [1982] 141-48—with previous bibliography). I see no basis in parallelism alone for such an emendation. *ntyb(h)* does not appear elsewhere in this poem whereas *ʾrḥwt* and *mʿgl* are repeated. If any emendation is suggested, therefore, it should be *ʾrḥ(w)th*: with near and distant repetitive parallelism so striking a feature of the structure of this chapter, the intrusion of *ntybh* would be surprising indeed. The many gradations of semantic and grammatical parallelism which occur throughout this chapter indicate to me, however, that the claim that *kl bʾyh* in vs. 19, because it is not *kl bʾym ʾlyh*, must refer to a feminine antecedent other than the evil woman (cf. Loretz, p. 144) emanates from a lack of comprehension of the varieties of grammatical structure that can go into a Hebrew poem. The structure itself is certainly not impossible for, though *bʾyh* only occurs once, other like verbs occur frequently in such constructions. *qmy*, for example, occurs more frequently than does *qmym ʿly*! As argued above in the note on "Semantic Parallelism," the parallelism of *byth* and *mʿgltyh* is "functional" (i.e., the "house" and the "path" form a sort of "list" parallelism, referring to the external elements of a domicile), for at least one nuance of the parallelism is that of the material "path" which leads to the material "house": anyone who takes the path to that house may as well be taking the path that leads straight to the domicile of the shades. (The other main nuance, of course, is that of the conduct associated with the woman and with those who resort to her—the nuance of conduct would be strengthened by the emendation, but at the expense of the nuance of the domicile.)

vs. 20 which *lmʿn* provides and the continuation of the 'path' motif in that verse, it becomes clear that vs. 19 is the middle unit of a three-verse structure. Looking ahead at vs. 20, we see that it is very regular in structure, incorporating only one major dissimilarity (the semantic dissimilarity of *tlk* // *tšmr*). Vss. 18-20 provide, therefore, the clearest case in this poem of a near structure sustaining the weakness of a poetic line (the weakness of semantic parallelism of vs. 19). It is difficult to label the chiasmus of this verse for, though the verbs certainly occupy chiastic grammatical slots, the other elements are neither semantically nor grammatically related, resulting in a structure AB // BCD (and if the verbs are considered semantically antonymic the semantic parallelism becomes a b // c d e). To coin a term, the structure of this verse is "zedastic" (in form of Z) rather than chiastic (in form of X).

20. We return in vs. 20 to a regular form of chiasmus, the presence of which conforms to the general rule for this chapter in that only a minor element is deleted (*lmʿn*) in the verse. The precise grammatical balance and tight semantic parallelism of four of the main elements (*drk ṭwbym* // *ʾrḥwt ṣdyqym*) permit lack of semantic parallelism in the remaining pair (*tlk* // *tšmr*). Moreover, the combination of the phrases produces a good "functional" parallelism: 'going' in a way is the equivalent of 'keeping' to the way, especially in a moral context, for *šmr* is a standard part of idioms denoting observance of norms.

21-22. These verses contain a combination of very tight parallelisms of all sorts within each verse and antonymic near parallelism between the two verses. The antonyms extend to all words except the common denominator between the two, the word *ʾrṣ*, and the conjunction *w*-. This extends even to the prepositions: *b*- in vs. 21, *m*(*n*)- in vs. 22. This near structure does not, therefore, play the role of strengthening an otherwise weak unit but is a marrying of two internally synonymous units for the purpose of creating a larger antonymic one. Only the second verse contains an element of chiasmus (ABC // ACB), again not in the presence of deletion-compensation of major elements. The quantitative balance is very close in both verses. The structure of these two verses seems to be set up, then, in what might be called a cadential form of "major chords," the first stressing the beatitude of the righteous, the second beating out the destruction of the wicked.

3.2 *Comparing the Two Texts*

What strikes one immediately on comparing the parallelistic structures of these two texts is how much more "regular" are the structures in

Proverbs 2 than in ᶜ*nt* I. Comparing these texts with the "early Hebrew poetry" sampled by Geller and the poetry of the prophetic books sampled by Collins, which texts also appear less regular than Proverbs 2, leads to the conclusion that late wisdom poetry reflects a conscious seeking for regularity of grammatical and semantic symmetry to an extent not witnessed in the earlier traditions. Does this reflect simply the scholarly tendencies (i.e., attention to "rules") of wisdom circles or does it reflect a general evolution of Northwest Semitic poetry from primitive, relatively untrammeled forms to more "civilized" forms? Perhaps we will not have the definitive answer to that question until the Ugaritic "Book of Proverbs" is found.

This regularity means that systems of analysis intended to assess the balance of grammatical and semantic elements, such as Collins' and Geller's, "work better" for Proverbs 2 than for ᶜ*nt* I or even, for that matter, than for the poetry that those two authors analyzed. On the other hand, their systems are useful for analyzing a continuous text of less regular poetry, for those systems point out clearly where imbalances occur.

Granting this increased regularity, however, it must also be stressed that the poet's craft did not consist in creating a series of perfectly aligned structures. For in every verse of Proverbs 2 some "twist" was found: if the semantic structure was regular, a grammatical dissimilarity could be introduced (the most characteristic of these grammatical discordances is the five-fold occurrence of parallelism of a non-finite form, infinitive or participle, with a finite verbal form: vss. 2, 8, 13, 14, 17); if the grammatical structure was regular, semantic dissimilarity could be introduced (e.g., *tqḥ* // *tṣpn* in vs. 1); surrounding elements that were semantically similar permitted semantic dissimilarity of grammatically similar elements (e.g., *tbyn* // *tmṣ*ʾ, in vs. 5); lines from which no major element was deleted could be arranged chiastically (only vs. 7 contained both deletion-compensation of a major element and chiasmus); two regular lines could surround a line lacking major forms of parallelism (vss. 18-20—even here, though, there are more parallel elements in vs. 19 than in those bicola of ᶜ*nt* I which require outside support). The game seems to have been, therefore, to produce a mixture of regularity and dissimilarity within an approximately balanced quantitative structure.

Another important difference between the two texts sampled here is the decrease in usage of repetitive parallelism in "regular" distribution between the time of ᶜ*nt* I and that of Proverbs 2. Both texts make use of near and distant repetitive parallelism, but there is virtually no repetition of same words within a bicolon in the later text (there is one case of root parallelism in vs. 3, and one precise repetition in vs. 14).

A final principal difference in structure is in the ordering of major elements: there is a much greater use of chiastic arrangements in Proverbs 2 than in ʿ*nt* I. This may have been, as hinted above, a varying feature introduced to counteract the increased regularity of semantic and grammatical parallelism.

The two texts are alike in that the parallelistic center of both is undoubtedly the bicolon (this is true in general even if some of the lines of ʿ*nt* are to be reanalyzed as tricola), though repetitive and semantic parallelism are used to link individual bicola and groups of bicola together into larger rhetorical units.

There is no clear metrical structure in either text, in the narrow sense of the term "meter." The closest one can come to meter is in the analysis by a stress-counting system but even that system does not provide evidence for a true meter, but simply for a preponderance of 3 // 3 lines in Proverbs 2[2] (but not in ʿ*nt* I!). This relatively greater quantitative regularity in the biblical text probably does, however, reflect the grammatical/semantic regularity of the poem and it incites one to ask if a tendency towards the development of stricter metrical systems may not have originated within wisdom poetry. Was this a tendency natural to wisdom thinking which only became overt under the influence of classical metrical systems? Finally, though narrative and rhetorical units stand out clearly in both texts there is no evidence in either for strophes as metrically conceived units.[3]

3.3. *Comparing the Systems of Analysis*

Three major new systems of analysis have been compared in this study, those of Collins, Geller, and O'Connor. The strengths and weaknesses of each of these systems may now be briefly discussed.

Collins' system notes configurations of major syntactic elements (verb, subject, object, and modifier phrases) and establishes that certain configurations ("line types") are more frequent than others. The weaknesses of the system are that it has not been so conceived as to deal with the entire corpus of ancient Hebrew poetry (only about 40% is analyzable by Collins' method), that it deals neither with other elements of grammatical parallelism (morphological and morpho-syntactic) nor with other types of parallelism (semantic, phonetic), and that it deals primarily with the line (bicolon, tricolon) and not with larger structures.

---

[2] One might argue that the short half-lines mark ends of strophes (vss. 4, 11, 15), but vs. 20, at one of the major rhetorical breaks of the poem is 3 // 3, while the following verse is 3 // 2 and is part of one of the strongest near structures of the poem.

[3] See especially my article in *JANES* 10 cited above in Ch. I, note 7.

Geller has attempted a notation which takes into consideration meter, semantic parallelism, and grammatical parallelism. The weakness of the notational system is that its very all-inclusiveness makes it nearly impenetrable to all but the total devotee of the method. As to the elements of the system: ''meter'' is useful only as a rough approximation, Geller's new divisions of grammatical parallelism are a step beyond what had previously been done (and are more useful than O' Connor's categories, in my estimation),[4] and his notation of grammatical parallelism is half-way between Collins' attention to major syntactic elements and a system which would note every detail of morphology (person, gender, number, verbal stem, etc.—cf. my attempts at a gradation of morphological parallelism at ''Semantic Parallelism: Grammatical Relationships''). Another feature of Geller's analysis is the specific notation of ''deletion-compensation.'' The study of the poet's method of balancing his line segments requires such an analysis, though it need not be stated in strictly metrical terms. The major weaknesses are: the opacity of the notational system already mentioned, the failure to consider all aspects of grammatical parallelism (how could Collins' system and Geller's be integrated?), the failure to observe phonetic parallelism, and lack of consideration of poetic units larger than the line.

O'Connor's system is also presented as a total system of analysis in that it covers both metrical and rhetorical structures: it replaces meter by a system of syntactic constraints, includes attention to semantic parallelism, (O'Connor's ''tropes''), then goes on to analyze what I classify as ''regular,'' near, and distant semantic structures. The rejection of meter *per se* can only be applauded, the system of constraints has proven itself to be generally applicable to the texts studied here, while the attempt to work microparallelism into microparallelistic structures deserves the highest praise. On the negative side, one can cite an overemphasis of the half-line and a resultant down-playing of the importance of the line as the major building block of Hebrew poetry, the failure to observe phonetic parallelism, and the lack of a systematic study of the main types of parallelism (repetitive, semantic, and grammatical [as well as the phonetic parallelism which is generally ignored]) in all four major

[4] What is really needed is a thorough-going study of the sense-relations of words in parallel using the categories developed by philosophical and linguistic semanticists. See J. Lyons, *Semantics* (Cambridge: Cambridge University Press, 1977) vol. 1, pp. 270-335. I do not mean to imply by this statement any basic disagreement with Kugel's (reference above, Introduction, note 2) view of parallelism as a concept (''seconding'') rather than as a list of techniques; simply that (as I stated in ''Types and Distributions of Parallelism in Ugaritic and Hebrew Poetry'' at the 1982 Society of Biblical Literature Annual Meeting) calling a forest a forest does not preclude a detailed analysis and description of the trees that make up the forest.

distributions.[5] One result of the present study has been to show that the analysis of each type of parallelism according to each of the possible distributions will offer insight into the structure of the poem.

3.4 *Whither Hence?*

My own conclusion to this overview of analytical systems is that no one system of notation can encompass the manifold nuances of linkage that occur at every level of analysis. The present study has gone to the opposite extreme of separating out each type of analysis into a list or chart with varying amounts of explanatory support. Moreover, judging from my own perceptions of these poems, the detailed nature of the analysis has not been vain, for each stage of analysis has shown what each type of parallelism, in its various distributions, contributes to the total structure. I am convinced, therefore, that the modern critic who wishes to come to some realization of why the ancient poet placed a given word in a given slot in a given poem or, to phrase this in another way, of what the detailed structure of a given poem is, must go through the steps of analysis followed here—though the precise number and nature of the steps will surely not be identical to the ones followed here. Having said this, though, I am not convinced that every literary study of an ancient poem must include in its final published form the detailed apparatus behind the final prose analysis, nor, if such an apparatus should ever be deemed necessary by some eventual Governing Board of Literary Analysis, am I prepared to say just what that apparatus must include and what its form must be. Charts cannot replace lucid prose criticism. But a chart can provide a measure of proof for the prose assertions. Only time and the practice of the skill can sharpen the method of presentation. In any case, it is time to pass from the study of isolated verses in search of a form and a notational system that characterized the works of Collins and Geller, and to a lesser extent that of O'Connor, to a literary analysis of given works of poetry more along the lines of traditional literary criticism.[6] The present work is not intended to be a model for such a study but rather for the apparatus behind such a study.

---

[5] For a more detailed weighing of the strengths and weaknesses of O'Connor's system, see my review cited above in Ch. I, note 7 as well, of course, as the assessments of other reviewers (see especially Watson's review in *Biblica* 64 [1983] 131-34 and Wansbrough's articles in *BSOAS* cited above in Ch. I, note 62).

[6] For some preliminary bibliography, see the article cited in Introduction, note 1, above, and the comments and bibliography in Landy, *JSOT* 28 (1984) 61-98.

APPENDIX I

UGARITIC AND HEBREW POETRY: PARALLELISM

Communication prepared for the First International Symposium on the Antiquities of Palestine, Aleppo, September, 1981

In this communication I wish to continue my overview of Northwest Semitic poetry[1] with a brief look at parallelism. To some extent this communication constitutes a response to my own call for increased study of parallelism as the principal structural device in Ugaritic and Hebrew poetry.[2] In my previous study I claimed that meter, in the strictest sense of the term at least, was not the constitutive feature of Ugaritic and Hebrew poetry. Rather, it was claimed, parallelism is the constitutive feature of Ugaritic and Hebrew poetry, with the parallelism expected to fit into certain quantitative bounds too loosely defined to merit the appellation 'meter'. Thus I considered Bishop Lowth to be correct when, well over two centuries ago now, he claimed that *parallelismus membrorum* was the principal feature of Hebrew poetry[3] and, in my opinion, attempts since that time to discover a metrical system within Hebrew have all been in vain.

Until relatively recently, Lowth's main categories of parallelism (synonymous, antithetic, synthetic[4]) were accepted as a sufficient catalogue of forms. The third category, synthetic, was often felt to be too all-embracing,[5] but the overall approach was considered satisfactory, especially when the varieties of formal distribution of the parallel elements were explored.[6] In the last fifty years, however, two other types of parallelism have received increased recognition and more refined distinctions have been proposed for analyzing the previously recognized forms of parallelism.

---

[1] Cf. D. Pardee, "Ugaritic and Hebrew Metrics," in *Ugarit in Retrospect: Fifty Years of Ugarit and Ugaritic* (Winona Lake, Indiana: Eisenbraun: 1981) 113-130.

[2] See the conclusion to the article just cited (n. 1).

[3] G. B. Gray, *The Forms of Hebrew Poetry* (New York: Ktav, 1972 [reprint of 1915 edition]) 48-49.

[4] Cf. Gray, ibid.; Robert G. Boling, " 'Synonymous' Parallelism in the Psalms," *JSS* 5 (1960) 221-255, esp. p. 221.

[5] Gray, ibid., pp. 49-52.

[6] Gray, ibid., pp. 64-83; Louis I. Newman, "Parallelism in Amos," in *Studies in Biblical Parallelism* by Louis I. Newman and William Popper (University of California Publications: Semitic Philology, vol. 1, nos. 2 and 3, pp. 57-444; August 6, 1918) 137-185.

The first of these other facets of parallelism to receive recognition as a major consitutive feature of (at least early) Northwest Semitic poetry was repetitive parallelism. In the broad sense of the term, all parallelism is a form of repetition, at least in the cases of synonymous and antithetic parallelism[7] (for parallelistic devices used to strengthen "synthetic" parallelism, see below at "Distribution of Parallelisms"). In its narrow sense, however, the phrase "repetitive parallelism" is used to refer to the verbatim repetition of the same word, though even here problems of definition arise as to the relationship between repetitive parallelism and paronomasia. W. F. Albright claimed to have first emphasized the importance of repetitive parallelism in Ugaritic poetry[8] and in his major work on Canaanite-Hebrew relationships he uses repetitive parallelism as a typological device for dating Hebrew poetry.[9] M. Dahood included repetitive parallelisms in his catalogue of parallel pairs found in both Ugaritic and Hebrew,[10] though in his introductory remarks on method he attempts no defense of this inclusion beyond empirics and polemics.[11]

Two remarks are necessary to place the use of repetitive parallelism in the broader context of parallelism as a structural device. First, repetitive parallelism is not a monolithic device including only absolutely verbatim repetition. It, like any other poetic device, may be varied so as to appear in different lights. The least controversial form of variation occurs when the basic grammatical form of the word to be repeated is maintained, with change provided, for example, by the distribution of a prefixed preposition, an added pronominal suffix, or a different mood in the verb

---

[7] See, for example, Roman Jakobson, "Grammatical Parallelism and its Russian Facet," *Language* 42 (1966) 399-429, esp. pp. 399-400. For some idea of parallelistic devices in other traditions, see Ruth Finnegan, *Oral Poetry* (Cambridge: Cambridge University Press, 1977) 98-109; Heda Jason, *Ethnopoetry* (Bonn: Linguistica Biblica Bonn, 1977) 65-66; Vladimir N. Toporov, "William Butler Yeats: 'Down by the salley gardens.' An Analysis of the Structure of Repetition," *PTL: A Journal for Descriptive Poetics and Theory of Literature* 3 (1978): 95-115; John S. Miletich, "Oral-Traditional Style and Learned Literature: A New Perspective," *PTL* 3 (1978) 345-356.

[8] *Yahweh and the Gods of Canaan* (Garden City, N.Y.: Doubleday, 1969 [Anchor Edition]) 5, n. 10. Here he refers to a pre-Ugaritic article of his ("The Earliest Forms of Hebrew Verse," *JPOS* 2 [1922] 69-86) but gives no reference supporting his antecedence over Ginsberg in recognizing repetitive parallelism in Ugaritic.

[9] For Albright as a typologist, see Frank Moore Cross, Jr., "William Foxwell Albright: Orientalist," *BASOR* 200 (1970) 7-10, esp. pp. 9-10. The existence of the phenomenon of repetitive parallelism must, of course, be kept rigorously separate from use of the phenomenon as a typological dating device. The existence of the phenomenon is proven without doubt by the Ugaritic poetic corpus, but, to my knowledge, only Albright has attempted to turn the device into a dating technique (though his conclusions are accepted to various degrees by his students). It should be noted that his sampling of Hebrew poetry was small and, in part at least, predetermined by other considerations.

[10] "Ugaritic-Hebrew Parallel Pairs," pp. 71-382 in *Ras Shamra Parallels*, vol. 1 (L. R. Fisher, ed.; Rome: Pontifical Biblical Institute, 1972), and pp. 1-39 in vol. 2 (1975).

[11] *RSP I* (1972) 79-80.

(e.g., ʿnt I 10-11 *bdh* // *bklʾat ydh* [*b*- vs. *b*- . . .]). A more extensive change involves a like grammatical form but with the change effected in the form of the word itself (e.g., ʿnt I 10-11 *bdh* // *ydh* [*badihu* // *yadêhu*?]; ʿnt I 15, 23 [distant parallelism] *tʿn* . . . *yʿn*; ʿnt I 23-24 *bnth* // *bt*). Finally, there are cases of repetition of forms from the same root but of different grammatical categories (e.g., ʿnt I 17 *ymsk bmskh*). All these forms of repetitive parallelism involve various forms of *figurae etymologicae* but, with the last especially, we are also approaching paronomasia and the validity of the term "repetitive parallelism" is at least partially tied up in the problem of root perception in the ancient world.[12]

This second remark with respect to repetitive parallelism is that, with the exception of the third category of variation just mentioned, it brings together all other forms of parallelism: repetitive parallelism, in the narrow sense of the term being used here, brings together into one pair of words semantic, grammatical (both morphological and syntactic), and phonetic parallelism. (Even with the grammatical parallelism excluded, repetitive parallelism constitutes a great concentration of like elements.) Thus repetitive parallelism functions as the strongest recall device in distant parallelism: if the same word is repeated at ten lines' distance it is more likely to be noted than another word meaning the same thing, than a like grammatical form with different meaning, or than the repetition of a single sound or grouping of sounds. In the sample Ugaritic text analyzed as the basis for this paper (ʿ*nt* I), repetitive parallelism was found to be the strongest linking device, used for the purpose of binding units together as small as the half-line (*ymsk bmskh*, l. 17) and as large as eight bicola (*qm* . . . *qm*, ll. 4, 18).

Semantic parallelism has, of course, been recognized for the longest time and has received the greatest amount of attention in traditional biblical studies. For the purposes of the present discussion I wish to focus on three recent aspects of the study of semantic parallelism.[13] The first

---

[12] Cf. James Barr, *The Semantics of Biblical Language* (Oxford: University Press, 1961); idem, "Hypostatization of Linguistic Phenomena in Modern Theological Interpretation," *JSS* 7 (1962) 85-94; John F. A. Sawyer, "Root Meanings in Hebrew," *JSS* 12 (1967) 37-50; idem, *Semantics in Biblical Research* (Studies in Biblical Theology, Second Series 24; Naperville, IL: Allenson, 1972).

[13] Many basic historical and literary questions remain with respect to the whole phenomenon of parallelism, having to do both with questions of origin and with questions of extent. For example: J. C. de Moor and P. van der Lugt have claimed that "the principle of *parallelismus membrorum* was invented by the Sumerians and was taken over by the Akkadians and other Semitic peoples of the ancient world" ("The Spectre of Pan-Ugaritism," *BiOr* 31 [1974] 3-26, quotation from p. 7). If this statement is to be understood as implying an original invention followed by a set of linear borrowings, all occurring relatively late in human history, one must ask how the principle of parallelism came to be a feature of the poetry of so many disparate cultures arount the world (cf. references cited in n. 7, above).

feature to be discussed is the increased study of varieties of semantic parallelism. The need for further categorization arose from the recognition that Lowth's three categories were so all-comprehensive as to contain little probitive value. Many attempts have been made over the years to improve on Lowth's categories. I will only cite here one recent example which appears to be as useful as any proposed to date. S. A. Geller, in his published dissertation *Parallelism in Early Biblical Poetry*,[14] to which repeated reference will be made below in discussing grammatical parallelism, has set forth six main categories (synonym, list, antonym, merism, identity, and metaphor) with "synonym" and "list" each having several sub-categories (under "synonym" appear epithet, proper noun, and pronoun; and under "list" appear whole-part, concrete-abstract, and number). This new break-down of forms of semantic parallelism is a modernization of Lowth's system, in which "list" partially overlaps with Lowth's "synonymous" and "synthetic,"[15] including repetitive parallelism ("identity"), and refining some of the categories which formerly would have been forced into the "synonym" or "antonym" categories (e.g., "merism": is the parallelism of 'heaven' and 'earth' synonymous or antithetic? However that may be, it is certainly merismous.) Attempts at refinement of the semantic categories of parallelism such as Geller has proposed are certainly to be applauded as forcing us to reject the fuzzy thinking which results from an attempt to press too many features into too few categories of classification.

The second aspect of modern research into the nature of semantic parallelism is the relationship of parallelism and tradition. This has come to the fore since the discovery of the Ugaritic poetic texts, with their many resemblances to Hebrew poetry. In simplest terms the controversy is this: Did the Northwest Semitic poets have at their disposal a "thesaurus" of parallel pairs into which they could delve according to need or did they work with a "principle of parallelism" which allowed them to create parallel pairs as needed?

The history of the discussion has been admirably presented as the introductory chapter in William R. Watters' book *Formula Criticism and the Poetry of the Old Testament*.[16] There Watters describes how the separate strains of study into Yugoslavian and Homeric formulaic poetry (M.

---

[14] Harvard Semitic Monographs 20; Missoula, Montana: Scholars Press, 1979.

[15] Geller's system will not include many examples of Lowth's "synthetic" parallelism because of the former's increased interest in grammatical considerations (i.e., a list of semantically related roots is not enough for Geller; there must be grammatical parallelism as well). My own greatest difficulty in working with Geller's categories has been in attempting to distinguish between "synonym" and "list".

[16] BZAW 138 (1976).

Parry, A. B. Lord[17]) and of Hebrew/Ugaritic parallelism (H. L. Ginsberg, U. Cassuto, M. Held, S. Gevirtz[18]) were brought together in the study of Hebrew parallelism as formulaically derived (R. C. Culley, W. Whallon[19]). The most important steps in this development were: 1) Culley's attempt to discover a Homeric-style formulaic system in the Psalter[20]; 2) The early discoveries in the likeness of Ugaritic and Hebrew parallelistic devices[21]; 3) Gevirtz' application of the concept of traditional pairs to the text criticism of the Hebrew Bible[22] and, to a lesser extent, to that of the Ugaritic texts.[23] The conception of the Northwest Semitic poets as working with a collection of formulae and "fixed pairs" has reached its logical high-point in the work of W. Whallon, who sees the product of any given poet as almost entirely based on tradition, with very little creative input,[24] and of M. Dahood, who speaks of a "dictionary of paired words" and "the Canaanite thesaurus from whose resources Ugaritic and Hebrew poets alike drew,"[25] and who proceeds to reproduce such a dictionary.[26] In summing up this trend, Watters uses the phrases "stockpile" and "rigidly fixed container of acceptable word pairs."[27]

The theory of a "thesaurus" of "fixed pairs" or of fixed phrases has been countered with the theory that the poet was not working with a collection of individual pairs and phrases, but with the *principle* of parallelism: "We believe that once the principle of parallelism has been adopted, the creation of many of these pairs took place in a spontaneous, quite natural way."[28] "Given that parallelism is employed in both

---

[17] M. Parry, *The Making of Homeric Verse: The Collected Papers of Milman Parry* (A. Parry, ed.; Oxford: Clarendon Press, 1971); A. B. Lord, *The Singer of Tales* (Cambridge, MA: Harvard University Press, 1960).

[18] H. L. Ginsberg, "The Rebellion and Death of Baᶜlu," *Orientalia* n.s. 5 (1936) 161-198, esp. pp. 171-173; U. Cassuto, *The Goddess Anath* (Jerusalem: Magnes, 1971 [original Hebrew edition 1951]) 25-32; M. Held, "Studies in Ugaritic Lexicography and Poetic Style," Ph.D. dissertation Johns Hopkins University, 1957; S. Gevirtz, *Patterns in the Early Poetry of Israel* (Studies in Ancient Oriental Civilization 32; Chicago: The University of Chicago Press, 1963).

[19] R. C. Culley, *Oral Formulaic Language in the Biblical Psalms* (Toronto: University of Toronto Press, 1967); W. Whallon, *Formula, Character, and Context: Studies in Homeric, Old English, and Old Testament Poetry* (Cambridge, MA: Harvard University Press, 1969).

[20] *Oral Formulaic Language* (reference in n. 19).

[21] Perhaps best summed up in Held's still unpublished dissertation (reference in n. 18); see also Boling, " 'Synonymous' Parallelism" (reference in n. 4).

[22] *Patterns* (reference in n. 18).

[23] "The Ugaritic Parallel to Jeremiah 8:23," *JNES* 20 (1961) 41-46.

[24] *Formula* (reference in n. 19).

[25] *RSP I* (1972) 74.

[26] Ibid., pp. 89-382; *RSP II* (1975) 5-39.

[27] *Formula Criticism*, pp. 68, 77.

[28] De Moor and van der Lugt, *BiOr* 31 (1974) 7.

Ugaritic and Hebrew poetry, it is to be expected *a priori* that common synonyms, antonyms and complementary terms would be employed in pairs in both literatures . . . .''[29] ''We shall end our discussion with the conclusion that word pairs which *repeat* are common associations fostered by limited vocabulary. Those pairs which *do not repeat* were probably created by the author with which they are found.''[30]

Let me conclude this portion of my overview by remarking that the reaction of scholars such as de Moor and van der Lugt, Craigie, and Watters is salutary and necessary. The modern images of ''dictionary,'' ''thesaurus,'' and ''stockpiles'' have a scholastic aura about them and they fail to account for the high quality of the works of art which, under close examination, the Northwest Semitic poems reveal themselves to be.[31] On the other hand, these criticisms appear to me to vacillate to the other extreme of the pendulum: Though Craigie expresses himself very circumspectly, Watters allows for virtually no influence of tradition in the choice of a given parallel pair. At most he speaks of ''borrowing'' (i.e., one poet borrowing from another)[32] and ''idiom.''[33] I would prefer to have seen a much more extensive discussion of how borrowing would have taken place and of just what Watters means by ''idiom'' in the context of parallel pairs and repeated phrases. For it appears to me impossible to rule tradition out of poetic production in an ancient society—just as impossible as to rule creativity completely out of an artistic production. Though the extent of each element is certainly variable, and though the study of traditionalism is more the work of anthropologists and sociologists rather than of philologists, it is nonetheless inconceivable to me to devise a theory of artistic production which absolutely excludes either element. This said, however, I believe that we must accept that it was the principle of parallelism which was the guiding principle of poetic production, rather than a hide-bound tradition, but that, at least in the forms of poetry which have come down to us, the production of poetry

---

[29] P. C. Craigie, ''The Problem of Parallel Word Pairs in Ugaritic and Hebrew Poetry,'' *Semitics* 3 (1973) 48-58, quotation from p. 49.

[30] Watters, *Formula Criticism*, p. 78.

[31] P. B. Yoder has stated explicitly the only possible form in which the ''stockpiling'' hypothesis could have any validity: '' . . . Held thought of a 'dictionary of parallel words', only it was an oral dictionary, which the poet had in his head, not a written dictionary on his bookshelf'' (''A-B Pairs and Oral Composition in Hebrew Poetry,'' *VT* 21 [1971] 470-489, quotation from p. 483). Such a form of stockpiling is, of course, possible, indeed well known from research into oral composition, and the resolution of the question of whether it existed or not boils down to questions of evidence, empirics, statistics, etc. (cf. Watters' statistical argument cited below in n. 34).

[32] *Formula Criticism*, pp. 71-73.

[33] Ibid., p. 73.

had reached a highly sophisticated level and traditional forms and usages had taken their place as a part of the poet's craft.[34]

The third feature of semantic parallelism which has come to the fore in recent years but which still merits a great deal more study is its international character. This aspect was mentioned in earlier studies[35] but new progress has been made in recent years with the conscious seeking out in other Semitic languages of parallel pairs which are cognate or equivalent to the Ugaritic-Hebrew pairs.[36] According to Watters,[37] S. E. Loewenstamm and Y. Avishur are preparing a catalogue of all the parallel pairs which occur in Hebrew, Ugaritic, Akkadian, and Aramaic. This work should eventually be broadened to include the other Semitic languages and to include the study of parallelistic devices in Semitic languages which rely on poetic devices other than parallelism as main structural features (meter, rhyme, etc.). And, finally, once the Semitic picture becomes clear, the various aspects of parallelism within the Semitic languages should be compared with the uses of parallelism in other linguistic groups. Such broad studies may do something to cure the

---

[34] My position is, therefore, the mirror-image of, but otherwise not so far removed from Yoder's: "The stock of formulas which a poet has at his disposal is the result of a poetic tradition which hands these formulas on generation after generation because they are useful and pleasing. Individual poets may add to the inherited stock of formulas[3] [Note 3: That is, the poet, in the course of his 'career' creates a few idiosyncratic formulas . . .] but these additions will be few, since the tradition is the work of many hands" (*VT* 21 [1971] 478). On the basis of an extensive sampling (all of Isaiah, Lamentations, and Job), Watters has come up with a quite consistent ratio of 2:1 for parallel pairs which are "original" vs. those which are attested in more than one source (*Formula Criticism*, p. 79). This ratio could, of course, decrease if our corpus were to grow, but there is no way of knowing this without actually having the larger corpus and it therefore appears safer for the present to give the principle of parallelism (i.e., a large margin of creativity in the choice of parallel pairs) precedence over stockpiling (i.e., extensive traditional constraints on creativity). Whichever way the balance tips, it is absolutely necessary, in my opinion, to exclude theories which rely entirely on one of these options. For the combination of tradition with one principle or method of composition (oral composition), see the quotations I gathered in footnote 50 of my article in *Retrospect* (reference above in n. 1). Here is another: " . . . the oral poet is one who, at the moment of performance, makes spontaneous and therefore original realizations of inherited, traditional impulses" (M. N. Nagler, *Spontaneity and Tradition: A Study in the Oral Art of Homer* [Berkeley and Los Angeles: University of California Press, 1974] xxi).

[35] Gray, *Forms of Hebrew Poetry* (1915) 38-46; Newman, "Parallelism in Amos" (reference above, n. 6; 1918) 57-119.

[36] De Moor and van der Lugt, *BiOr* 31 (1974) 3-26; Craigie, *Semitics* 3 (1973) 48-58; cf. also Craigie, "Parallel Word Pairs in the Song of Deborah (Judges 5)," *Journal of the Evangelical Theological Society* 20 (1977) 15-22; idem, "Deuteronomy and Ugaritic Studies," *Tyndale Bulletin* 28 (1979) 155-169.

[37] *Formula Criticism*, pp. 26-27. Cf. Avishur's published work: "Pairs of Synonymous Words in the Construct State (and in Appositional Hendiadys) in Biblical Hebrew," *Semitics* 2 (1971): 17-81; "Word Pairs Common to Phoenician and Biblical Hebrew," *UF* 7 (1975) 13-47; "Studies of Stylistic Features Common to the Phoenician Inscriptions and the Bible," *UF* 8 (1976) 1-22.

study of Northwest Semitic poetry of the narrow provincialism from which it now suffers.[38]

Let us pass now to the third and newest area of study of parallelism: grammatical parallelism. First, it is important to see what we mean by "grammatical parallelism." Roman Jakobson, in his article most often cited by students of Semitic poetics,[39] "Grammatical Parallelism and its Russian Facet,"[40] may confuse the first-time reader by launching immediately into a discussion of classical *parallelismus membrorum*—which most of us identify with semantic parallelism. Jakobson makes clear later in his article that, whatever he may mean by the specific phrase "grammatical parallelism," he sees parallel structures at all levels of language:

> Pervasive parallelism inevitably activates all the levels of language—the distinctive features, inherent and prosodic, the morphologic and syntactic categories and forms, the lexical units and their semantic classes in both their convergences and divergences acquire an autonomous poetic value. This focusing upon phonological, grammatical, and semantic structures in their multiform interplay does not remain confined to the limits of parallel lines but expands throughout their distribution within the entire context; therefore the grammar of parallelistic pieces becomes particularly significant. The symmetries of the paired lines in turn vivify the question of congruences in the narrower margins of paired hemistichs and in the broader frame of successive distichs. The dichotomous principle underlying the distich may develop into a symmetrical dichotomy of much longer strings . . .[41]

Jakobson includes various forms of phonetic parallelism with the more generally recognized forms of parallelism, explicitly separating off only rhyme:

> Rhyme has been repeatedly characterized as a condensed parallelism, but rigorous comparison of rhyme and pervasive parallelism shows that there is a fundamental difference. The *phonemic* equivalence of rhyming words is compulsory, whereas the linguistic level of any correspondence between two parallelled terms is subject to a free choice. The fluctuating distribution of different linguistic levels between variables and invariants

---

[38] Cf. Watters, *Formula Criticism*, p. 2.

[39] E.g., by Edward L. Greenstein, "Two Variations of Grammatical Parallelism in Canaanite Poetry and Their Psycholinguistic Background," *JANES* 6 (1974) 87-105.

[40] *Language* 42 (1966) 399-429.

[41] Ibid., pp. 423-424. Analyzing the first two sentences of this statement seems to indicate that Jakobson sees three principal levels of parallelistic analysis: phonological, grammatical, and semantic, with the second level sub-divided into two areas, morphological and syntactic. However that may be, such a scheme represents reasonably well the state of parallelistic analysis in Northwest Semitic poetry today: 1) Semantic parallelism, the object of traditional analysis; 2) Grammatical parallelism, represented by Geller (morphological) and Collins (syntactic) [see below, this section]; 3) Phonetic parallelism, in its infancy [see below].

> imparts a highly diversified character to parallelistic poetry and provides it with ample opportunities to individualize the parts and to group them with respect to the wholes.[42]

Indeed, from a perusal of some of Jakobson's treatments of poetry, one realizes that for him any one level of analysis is insufficient.[43]

The two scholars who have proposed forms of analysis of Northwest Semitic poetry (Hebrew poetry in both cases) on the basis of grammatical parallelism have made a clear distinction between semantic and grammatical parallelism. T. Collins[44] specifically downplays the results of semantic analysis in the introduction to his method, while S. A. Geller[45] analyzes both semantic and grammatical parallelism, but as separate steps in the overall process. There are further differences between the two systems of analysis: Collins' analysis is almost uniquely syntactic (rather than morphological and/or phonetic) and within the larger category of syntax, centered on the phenomenon of word order. Thus he analyzes every poetic unit according to only four categories: subject, verb, object, and modifier phrases. All lesser categories are subsumed under these four major categories. Then the order of these constituents is observed and the various attested structures are analyzed and grouped together into "line-types." Geller's system, on the other hand, incorporates a very minute description of the poetic unit according to standard morphologico-syntactic analysis (subject, object, adverb; transitive verb, intransitive verb, passive/reflexive verb; participle, subject of nominal sentence, predicate of nominal sentence, etc., with eighteen additional features noted). This precise analysis enables him to note very explicitly the grammatical relationship of the two halves of a poetic line and, more explicitly, to note exactly which elements are present in one line and missing from another ("deletion"). On the other hand, his final "formula" for the poetic structure of a line is based primarily on semantic considerations rather than on grammatical ones (i.e., it does not note verb // verb but semantic content of verb // semantic content of verb). Moreover, in his analysis and in his final "formula," Geller includes "metrical" information. One point in common between Collins' and

---

[42] *Language* 42 (1966) 426-427.

[43] "Those oral traditions that use grammatical parallelism to connect consecutive lines, for example, Finno-Ugric patterns of verse . . . and to a high degree also Russian folk poetry, can be fruitfully analyzed on all linguistic levels—phonological, morphological, syntactic, and lexical: we learn what elements are conceived as equivalent and how likeness on certain levels is tempered with conspicuous difference on other ones" ("Closing Statement: Linguistics and Poetics," pp. 350-377 in *Style in Language* [ed. T. A. Sebeok; Cambridge, MA: M.I.T. Press, 1960] quotation from p. 369).

[44] *Line-Forms in Hebrew Poetry* (Studia Pohl: Series Maior 7; Rome: Pontifical Biblical Institute, 1978).

[45] *Parallelism* (reference above, n. 14).

Geller's systems is that neither is capable of noting parallelistic structures that extend beyond the individual poetic unit (bicolon or tricolon).

Since these systems are new and since I have spent some time applying them to my sample Ugaritic text,[46] it may be of use for me to give a brief initial impression. Collins' system has the advantage of focusing quite sharply on one aspect of parallelism and of doing it well. Moreover, though Geller's system may do more things it does not do the one thing that Collins' system does; thus they are complementary rather than overlapping. Collins' system suffers, however, from the limitations imposed by the tight focus: 1) His devaluating of traditional semantic parallelism is completely unmerited—his system should be complementary to semantic analysis, it cannot in any way replace it. 2) His own system can only include about 40% of Hebrew poetry in its notation—it should be expanded to include a higher percentage of the corpus. 3) By its limitation to the higher orders of syntax and to word order, it cannot take into its purview all the other levels of poetic analysis which Geller's system and modern work in poetics have shown to be so important.

In its inclusiveness, Geller's system is superior to Collins'. As it includes three of the main areas of poetic analysis, meter, semantics, and grammar, it has made a giant step towards a more comprehensive method of describing Northwest Semitic poetry. It is far from being perfect, however. 1) The first criticism I have regards only the format of Geller's system: it is too compact, including too much information in too few symbols. Not only does it take a great deal of effort and concentration to decipher the sigla and formulae by which the analysis is noted, but some of the notations themselves verge on the ambiguous (especially the notation of compound phrases). The elegance of a compact system has a great deal to say for it, but the general usefulness and communicative value for students of the poetry being analyzed must also be considered and, in my opinion, relatively few students are going to take the time to master Geller's notational system. 2) Alongside the first criticism must be placed another: For all that it does note, Geller's system still does not note enough. It is too linked to the individual poetic unit to touch on any type of feature which may link two poetic units (enjambment, relativization, cross-unit parallelism, etc.).[47] Moreover, it includes no notation of

[46] *ʿnt* I (the detailed analysis, along with a similar analysis of a biblical Hebrew text, is published here above).

[47] I might add that Collins' system cannot handle long units, either, but it breaks down over such features, while Geller's system, because it is microanalytically descriptive, simply ignores such features. Take, for example, the following three bicola from *ʿnt* I (ll. 10-15):

ytn ks bdh	He puts a cup in his hand,
krpn bklʾat ydh	A goblet in his two hands;

phonetic parallelism. Thus Geller's system notes what it notes too compactly but it does not note enough.

I submit that there is not a compact solution to the problem of a notation for Northwest Semitic poetry. Only an analysis of the intricacies of structure will reveal the depths of meaning,[48] and, at least at the present state of Hebrew-Ugaritic poetic analysis, these intricacies must be made clear to an audience previously more interested in content than in form (and thus primed to miss the indissolubility of the two). Such a detailed analysis must include an analysis of the individual poetic unit and of the structure of a given work as a whole (and eventually, of course, of the place of the work within the literary and cultural world from which it sprang). It must include considerations of quantitative/rhythmic measure (''meter'' to the extent that it exists); of semantic relationships at all levels of the work; of grammatical relationships, including morphological and syntactic relationships, at all levels of the work; and of phonetic relationships (to the extent that a sound pattern may be perceived as a structural device).[49] It is, however, simply too much to ask of any one notational system to include all of the information garnered from these different analyses. I see no other solution than to include in one's analysis a different notation for each level of interpretation: repetitive, semantic, grammatical, and phonetic parallelism, in some cases with more than one notation for each category. For example, the major rubrics of my analysis of *ʿnt* I are the following:

Text
Vocalization
Translation
Quantitative analysis
  Word count

---

bk rb ʿẓm rʾi	A large vessel, mighty to look upon,
dnmt šmm	Belonging to the furnishings of the heavens;
ks qdš ltphnh ʾaṯt	A holy cup (which) women may not see,
krpn ltʿn ʾaṯrt	A goblet (which) ʾAṯirat may not eye.

Collins' system breaks down because the second and third bicola are dependent on the first and thus do not have a complete independent sentence structure (the second bicolon consists of one long object clause containing juxtaposition in *bk rb* + *ʿẓm rʾi* and genitive relativization in *dnmt šmm*, while the third bicolon consists of two object clauses with elliptical relativization: ''A holy cup [which] . . .''). Geller's system goes blithely on analyzing everything in its path: the second bicolon is analyzed descriptively but may not be put into a formula because semantic and grammatical parallelism are missing (such ''synthetic'' parallelism occurs, of course, elsewhere and is only an accidental feature of the continued syntax); the third bicolon is easily analyzable because of the clear semantic and grammatical parallelism. But Geller's system leaves completely unnoted that the second and third bicola are syntactically dependent on the first. Moreover, both systems are so centered on the individual poetic unit that considerations of syntactic linkage between poetic units virtually fall within the pale of the extraneous.

Syllable count
Vocable count
"Verse-units"[50]
Repetitive parallelism
Distribution
Grammatical forms
Semantic parallelism
Distribution
Grammatical forms
Grammatical parallelism
Collins
Geller
Kaiser[51]
Parallelism of minor elements[52]
Positional parallelism
Phonetic parallelism
Consonants
Vowels
Length compensation
Distributions of parallelism

What I find important about these multiple notations is that new insights into the structure of the text in question emerged from each of the analyses behind the notations. There is no doubt that I have reached the point of diminishing returns in parallelistic analysis and that further notations would add relatively little to the perception of the text in question, but the fact remains that I have gained new insights from each level of analysis and my notational system is sufficiently redundant to convey this information to anyone who knows Ugaritic. The difficulty, of course, is that the analysis ends up being far longer than the work being ana-

---

[48] "My hypothesis is that the grammatical and other patterns are giving meaning in a more complex and tightly packed way than we expect from our familiarity with traditional methods of describing language" (J. McH. Sinclair, "Taking a Poem to Pieces," pp. 129-142 in *Linguistics and Literary Style* [ed. Donald C. Freeman; New York: Holt, Rinehart and Winston, 1970] quotation from p. 129 [here reprinted from *Essays on Style and Language*, ed. Roger Fowler; New York: Humanities Press, 1966]). This need for detailed analysis appears to me to be even greater for texts in dead languages than for texts in a given reader's mother tongue, for in the case of dead languages virtually no information may be perceived by intuition—thus vertually the entire burden of interpretation lies on the shoulders of analysis.

[49] This list presupposes a solid philological underpinning, but it says little about those features of the poetic work which fall under the heading of general literary analysis; imagery comes immediately to mind (I hope to treat imagery in a future article).

[50] B. Margalit, "Introduction to Ugaritic Prosody," *UF* 7 (1975) 289-313.

[51] Yet a third system of notation has been devised by Mrs. Barbara Kaiser, a doctoral student at the Divinity School of the University of Chicago. It has the advantage of noting all distributions of parallel grammatical elements.

[52] The ordering of the last five categories in this list was a function of the present overview; these categories would be reordered in the systematic analysis of a given text.

lyzed. At the present time I see no solution to this problem. A Hebrew or Ugaritic poem is a work of art and works of art have elicited floods of comment since the dawn of criticism.[53] Should the situation be different for Northwest Semitic poetry?

Allow me to proceed now to my plea for increased attention to certain neglected aspects of parallelism. It should be made clear immediately that these aspects have been included in one or another of previous discussions of parallelism in one form or another; my plea is, therefore, not based on total neglect, but is in favor of a consistently detailed treatment.

1) *Parallelism of minor elements*. Here I refer to those elements which are usually not included in a stress-count or word-count metrical system and which tend, therefore, to be passed over in the study of parallelism. They are included in Geller's descriptive notation of poetic lines, but are not included in his final formula. Dahood, in *Ras Shamra Parallels*,[54] regularly notes the particles, especially when these are in repetitive parallelism. I have noted several such parallelisms in *ʿnt* I, a text which makes very light use of particles. These include repetitive and semantic parallelisms (they are all grammatically parallel) in all distributions (see below at § 5). Two, especially, serve as markers of one of the principal structural elements of this poem and are thus worthy of citation and comment here:

Ll. 4-5)	*qm yṯʿr*	He arises, prepares,
	wyšlḥmnh	And causes him to eat.
8-9)	*ndd yʿšr*	He arises, serves,
	wyšqynh	And causes him to drink.
18-19)	*qm ybd wyšr*	He arises, chants, and sings;
	mṣltm bd nʿm	Cymbals (are) in the hands of the goodly one.

The structure of these lines is clearly and unequivocally marked out by the three-verb sequence in each, but the repetition and positioning of the *w*-, before the third verb and the third verb only, in each case, as well as the pronominal suffix on the third verb in the first two bicola (transitive verbs), lends a nice touch, rounding out the structure, making it precisely parallel in a number of respects.

[53] Cf., for example, Roland Posner's description of two centuries of work on a single poem by Goethe: "Linguistic Tools of Literary Interpretation: Two Centuries of Goethe Criticism," *PTL: A Journal for Descriptive Poetics and Theory of Literature* 3 (1978) 71-93. As J. Lotman has remarked, the description of a literary work in all its possible aspects "would be so vast that in practice to do it in one research paper is a barely realizable task" (cited from Ann Shukman, "The Canonization of the Real: Jurij Lotman's Theory of Literature and Analysis of Poetry," *PTL* 1 [1976] 317-338, quotation from p. 333).

[54] See the list of terms discussed, *RSP I* (1972) 89-95, and *RSP II* (1975) 5.

A second fairly clear structural use of a minor element is the repetition of the 3 m.s. pronominal suffix -(*n*)*h* in ll. 5-11, where *bʿl* is in each case the antecedent. The use of the pronoun tends to bind together the 'serving' unit (ll. 2-11) and the repetition of the suffix in l. 17 binds together the 'drink' unit (ll. 10-17) with the 'serving unit'. The perfection of the structure appears broken by the suffix on *ltphnh* in l. 14, which has *ks* as its antecedent, rather than *bʿl*. Here "positional parallelism" (see next section) comes into play, however, for in all cases where the antecedent of the suffixed pronoun is *bʿl* the word carrying the pronoun is in final position in its half-line, while *ltphnh*, with *ks* as its antecedent, is not in final position.

2) *Positional parallelism.* I do not expect this term to become a primary one in the description of Northwest Semitic parallelism, for it is not frequently useful as a descriptive tool. It only refers to the positioning in a poetic line of the respective elements. Thus a "typical" line a b c // a′ b′ c′ exhibits semantic and grammatical parallelism as well as "positional" parallelism (i.e., the parallel terms are in the same respective positions). If the semantic and grammatical parallelism of such a "typical" line is strong, the concept of position is not exceptionally useful. If, on the other hand, one of the major parallelistic features is missing, the relative position of the words appears to carry the parallelistic load. Take, for example,

ʾalp kd yqḥ bḫmr One thousand *kd*-measures he takes from the *ḫmr*-wine,
rbt ymsk bmskh Ten thousand he mixes into his mixture.
(*ʿnt* I 15-17)

It is not until one breaks the parallelism down into its various components (or until one seeks out other instances of the parallelisms) that one realizes that *yqḥ* (*lqḥ*) and (*y*)*msk* make a very poor semantic pair. It is a combination of various other types of parallelism which permit this pair, so semantically dissimilar, to function as a parallel pair: internal repetitive parallelism (*ymsk bmskh*), grammatical parallelism (*yqḥ* // *ymsk*), and, finally, positional parallelism. The two words are so locked into their respective positions that *yqḥ* and *ymsk* are almost automatically labelled as b and b′ until one considers their semantic dissimilarity.

Another part of *ʿnt* I which responds to the concept of positional parallelism is the bicolon in ll. 18-19:

qm ybd wyšr He arises, chants, and sings;
mṣltm bd nʿm Cymbals (are) in the hands of the goodly one.

The positional parallelism is here operative on several levels. First, in the three-verb sequence which is like that, already discussed, in ll. 4-5 and 8-9: the repetitive (*qm*, l. 4) and semantic parallelism (*ndd*, l. 8) of the first verb of l. 18 with the first verb of the previous similar bicola, linked with the unusual poetic structure of three verbs in sequence, provides a combination of repetitive, semantic, grammatical, and positional parallelism that leaves little doubt about the structural significance of l. 18. There remains, however, the problem of l. 19, which shows no semantic or grammatical parallelism with l. 18. Here one may expand positional parallelism to include position of a larger unit within the larger structure: rather than one word being locked into the structure by its position within a colon, we have here an entire half-line which is locked into place by the surrounding structure. This is visible in at least two features of the surrounding text: a) Ll. 18-19 are surrounded by otherwise clear bicola, making it likely that ll. 18-19 also form a bicolon; b) The three-verb structure already discussed is, in each of its two previous occurrences, followed by a fourth verb beginning the next bicolon (*ybrd*, l. 6; *ytn*, l. 10). Here that slot is filled by *yšr* in l. 20, coming after the unit formed by ll. 18-19. Notice further that this structure is strengthened by the fourth verb being repetitive of the third verb of the sequence (*yšr*, ll. 18, 20). Thus l. 19 is so locked into the structure of the entire poem that it can exhibit a rather radical form of "synthetic" parallelism without becoming lost and turning into a true "orphan line."

Finally, I recall your attention to the example of the 3 m.s. pronominal suffixes in ll. 5, 6, 9, 10-11, 14, 17, 23, already mentioned in § 1: in all cases where the antecedent is *bʿl* the word bearing the pronominal suffix is in final position in its half-line; where the antecedent is *ks* (*ltphnh*, l. 14) the word is not in final position. Since the parallelism is one of minor elements, and since it would be almost too much to expect so neat a pattern to be repeated frequently, one might discount the validity of the argument from position. There is no denying its presence in *ʿnt* I, however, and increased attention to such "minor" phenomena may open our eyes to intricacies of structure which would otherwise pass unnoticed.

3) *Phonetic parallelism.* I do not feel at home in the phonetic aspects of modern linguistic discussion and hope that I may be permitted to found my plea for increased attention to phonetic phenomena on reference to the work of such scholars as Roman Jakobson (see, most recently, *The Sound Shape of Language*, by Jakobson and Linda R. Waugh,[55] which is, of course just the latest in a long series of discussions by Jakobson of the phonetic aspects of linguistic and poetic structures[56]). I may refer further

---

[55] Bloomington, IN: Indiana University Press, 1979.

[56] The most famous is, perhaps, " 'Les Chats' de Charles Baudelaire," in collaboration with C. Lévi-Strauss, *L'Homme* 2 (1962) 5-21. See now the analysis of E. E. Cummings' poem "love is more thicker than forget" in *Sound Shape*, pp. 222-230. For other approaches to the technique, see, for example, A. L. Johnson, "Anagrammatism

to Margalit's claim, with respect to alliteration, that "To be significant, a letter should occur: (a) at least three times per seven verse-unit verse; and/or (b) twice in a single word or once in each of two adjacent words (especially at the beginning); and/or (c) as a repeated sequence of two or more adjacent letters, not necessarily in the same order, and not necessarily in the scope of a single word."[57] Margalit's rules may indeed by valid, but we need more study by persons well attuned to modern linguistic study of phonetics before we can be sure of the ground on which we tread.

One special problem of the ancient Northwest Semitic languages is that of vowels, or rather the lack thereof. I have yet to see a discussion of the phonetic aspect of modern poetry that ignores the vocalic structure, yet that is precisely what we are forced to do, at least with Ugaritic, where the vowels must be almost entirely reconstructed—what one does with biblical Hebrew depends on one's perception of the reliability of the Masoretic vowel system. I would suggest that for Ugaritic poetry it is necessary to attempt a phonetic analysis based on the reconstructed vocalic system but that the practitioners of such an artificial analysis should be sure to state clearly the precarious nature of the evidence and hence of the results.

Finally, I must state that the necessity of noting the phonetic features of Ugaritic poetry was sharply impressed upon my mind by my very rudimentary phonetic analysis of the Ugaritic sample text examined for

---

in Poetry: Theoretical Preliminaries," *PTL* 2 (1977) 89-118; the chapter entitled "Sounds" in P. M. Wetherill's *The Literary Text: An Examination of Critical Methods* (pp. 3-35; Oxford: Blackwell, 1974); the four articles on "Sound Texture" by David I. Masson, Ants Oras, Dell Hymes, and Masson again (all reprinted from elsewhere) in *Essays on the Language of Literature* (eds. S. Chatman, S. R. Levin; Boston: Houghton Mifflin, 1967).

[57] *UF* 7 (1975) 311. According to the Oxford English Dictionary, "alliteration" is used in two primary senses: for "the commencing of two or more words in close connexion, with the same letter, or rather the same sound," and for "the commencement of certain accented syllables in a verse with the same consonant or consonantal group." It is clear from Margalit's definitions and examples that he is making no attempt to fit his alliteration into his metrical scheme according to the OED definition (i.e., he does not limit alliteration to first syllables, nor to accented syllables, nor to any combination thereof). Given our lack of knowledge about Ugaritic metrics and accentuation, I tend to agree with Margalit that the phenomenon to be noted in Ugaritic poetry is repetition of same and similar consonants (it may be noted in passing that the Jakobsonian approach may trace phonetic patterns irrespective of position and meter). It must be made clear, however, that it is this phenomenon that we are studying and not traditional "alliteration" (for the latter has, of course, been applied in the past to biblical Hebrew; cf. O. S. Rankin, "Alliteration in Hebrew Poetry," *JTS* 31 [1929-1930] 285-291). Margalit has eliminated the second of the definitions in the OED in his preliminary statement that alliteration "belongs to the category of the aesthetic rather than the strictly prosodic" (*UF* 7, p. 310). The first definition is, however, only eliminated by implication, that is, by including non-initial consonants as examples of aliteration.

this study. Though I have reconstructed the vowels, no phonetic pattern emerged to my untutored eye except some sporadic cases of assonance. In the case of consonantal patterning, however, at least one clear pattern emerged, that of *k* and *q* in the 'drink' section of ʿ*nt* I (ll. 10-17):

ytn k*s* *bdh*	He puts a cup in his hand,
k*rpn* *b*k*l*ʾ*at ydh*	A goblet in his two hands;
*b*k *rb* ʿ*ẓm r*ʾ*i*	A large vessel, mighty to look upon,
dnmt šmm	Belonging to the furnishings of the heavens;
k*s* q*dš ltphnh* ʾ*aṯt*	A holy cup (which) women may not see,
k*rpn lt*ʿ*n* ʾ*aṯrt*	A goblet (which) ʾAṯirat may not eye.
ʾ*alp* k*d y*q*ḥ bḫmr*	One thousand *kd*-measures he takes from the *ḫmr*-wine,
*rbt yms*k *bms*k*h*	Ten thousand he mixes into his mixture.

Since all the words for vessels here contain *k* it is fairly obvious that the phonetic play is meant to link sound and meaning. It is perhaps also worth noting that the second word for the drinking vessel contains a *r*, which also reappears rather frequently in the line following the first appearance of *krpn*:

bk r*b* ʿ*ẓm* rʾ*i*
dnmt šmm

ks qdš ltphnh ʾ*aṯt*
*k*r*pn lt*ʿ*n* ʾ*aṯ*r*t*

ʾ*alp kd yqḥ bḫm*r
r*bt ymsk bmskh*

On a more restricted level, there appear to be several phonetic bonds within bicola:

*yt*n *ks* bdh *krp*n b*kl*ʾ*at y*dh	n // n; b // b; dh // dh
bk rb ʿ*ẓ*m *r*ʾ*i* *dn*m*t š*mm	m // m, mm
ks qdš lt*phnh* ʾaṯt *krp*n ltʿn ʾaṯ*r*t	lt // lt; n // n, n; ʾaṯt // ʾaṯ-t
ʾ*alp kd* y*qḥ* b*ḫ*m*r* *rbt y*m*sk* bm*skh*	y // y; b // b; m // m, m

Though several of these phonetic parallelisms are founded on repetitive parallelism, there is no discounting their existence, When the clear macro-binders (*k* & *q*, *r*) are linked up with the inner-colonic binders, a surprising number of the consonants is seen to form patterns. I rest my case for phonetic parallelism here in the hope that someone more qualified to pursue such a study will do so.

4) *Length compensation*. C. H. Gordon long ago noted the phenomenon of "ballast variants,"[58] which he defined as follows: "If a major word in the first stichos is not paralleled in the second, then one or more of the words in the second stichos tend to be longer than their counterparts in the first stichos."[59] The most comprehensive recent study of length compensation of which I am aware is Geller's in *Parallelism in Early Biblical Poetry*. He carries out the study of compensation at two levels of his analysis, which he (correctly) terms "deletion-compensation."[60] The deletion is noted first by adding the deleted element into the sentence which is reconstructed as underlying the poetic line, then the deletion is noted again in the final formula as a 'missing' repetitive parallelism. For example, in

ytn ks bdh	He puts a cup in his hand,
krpn bklʾat ydh	A goblet in his twohands. (*ʿnt* I 10-11)

the verb missing in the second line is noted as 'added' in the reconstructed sentence:

ytn ks bdh
(*ytn*) *krpn bklʾat ydh*[61]

Then the reconstructed repetitive parallel *ytn* // (*ytn*) is noted in the final formula, in parentheses to make its reconstructed nature clear.

The second notational level of analysis for deletion-compensation is in the specific notation of the compounds wherein the compensation is to be

---

[58] *Ugaritic Grammar* (Rome: Pontifical Biblical Institute, 1940) § 12.11; *Ugaritic Handbook* (Rome: Pontifical Biblical Institute, 1947) § 13.107; *Ugaritic Manual* (Rome: Pontifical Biblical Institute, 1955) § 13.107; *Ugaritic Textbook* (Rome: Pontifical Biblical Institute, 1965) § 13.116.

[59] This definition is repeated verbatim in each of the four editions of Gordon's Ugaritic grammar just cited. The phenomenon of compensation was, of course, noted long before Gordon with application to Hebrew poetry (cf. Gray, *Forms* [1915] 74-83; Newman, "Parallelism" [reference in n. 6; 1918] 141-147).

[60] For modern linguistically oriented studies of deletion, see, for example, Greenstein, *JANES* 6 (1974) 87-105; G. L. Dillon, "Literary Transformations and Poetic Word Order," *Poetics* 5 (1976) 1-22, esp. pp. 2-5.

[61] Geller's notational format is: *ytn* *ks bdh* / *krpn bklʾat ydh*

found (in the above example *bdh* // *bklʾat ydh*). For this Geller has a complicated system of notation which includes marking of both semantic and metrical features (see above, the discussion of grammatical parallelism).

While warmly welcoming Geller's progress in noting compensation features, I would nonetheless make three brief criticisms: 1) The notation of the compounds is too compact for the information contained therein to be readily assimilable (cf. above on this point); 2) The separating out of deletion (noted in the grammatical analysis) and compensation (noted in the compounding formulae) tends to obscure the inseparable relationship between the two. In a notational system such as I am promoting here, where the various aspects of parallelism are analyzed and noted separately, there should be a place for analysis of deletion-compensation as two aspects of a single phenomenon. 3) Because the notational system used by Geller is already too charged, it cannot note, along with compounding and deletion-compensation, features of compensation or lack thereof which do not fall into those two categories. For example, in the text just cited, Geller's system would note that *bklʾat ydh* is an expansion of *bdh*, but it must pass to yet another section of the analysis (metrical information *per se*)[62] to note that *krpn* is also an expansion of *ks* (not noted with compensation because it corresponds to no deletion), one which happens to result in a quantitative over-expansion (syllable-count = 8 // 10). I see no obvious reason why this form of compensation should be separated from deletion-compensation and compounding (the reason cannot be metrical, for no form of compensation results in consistently equivalent quantitative parallelism—see next paragraph). Nor can Geller's system note such cases as ll. 8-9 *ndd yʿšr* // *wyšqynh* (syllable count 6 // 6), where the lack of deletion in the bicolon precludes a notation of compensation in the second half-line (unless *ndd yʿšr* is considered a compound or unless the line is to be reconstructed as verb + verb // (verb) + verb, i.e., with deletion of a fourth verb). A separate descriptive analysis of all forms of compensation at one point of the analysis, with one chart or table grouping all phenomena, will not only represent deletion-compensation at least as clearly as Geller's system does but will also relate that phenomenon directly to other compensatory phenomena.

A final remark on all forms of length compensation: as I have noted previously,[63] and as the present sample text has borne out, the compensation as practiced does not lead to any form of quantitative equality of the

---

[62] Cf. Geller, *Parallelism*, pp. 319-363.

[63] "*mᵉrôrăt-pᵉtanîm* 'Venom' in Job 20:14," *ZAW* 91 (1979) 401-416, esp. pp. 403-405; n. 21; "A Philological and Prosodic Analysis of the Ugaritic Serpent Incantation *UT* 607," *JANES* 10 (1978) 73-108, esp. pp. 102-105.

half-lines, but only to an approximate one,[64] compatible with no form of quantitative meter other than perhaps a stress system (irrespective of syllable count).

5) *Distribution of parallelisms*. Various authors have made use of the concepts of inclusion (or 'inclusio' or 'envelope construction'—a poetic work or poetic unit beginning and ending with the same figure[65]) and chiasmus (i.e., the chiastic arrangement of a poetic work or poetic unit[66]) in discussing the larger structure of Northwest Semitic poetic works. My intention here is to discuss phenomena of parallelism in terms of the larger structure, rather than uniquely in terms of individual poetic units. This is one area of analysis that neither Geller's system nor Collins' touches in any way. Collins makes an attempt[67] to treat some extended poetic units, but always in terms of the individual poetic units, while Geller's system is entirely devoted to the analysis of the individual poetic unit (even a tricolon must be analyzed as two bicola: 1 + 2, then 2 + 3). From the analysis of *ʿnt* I, I have become convinced that any analysis of the parallelistic structure of a poetic text must include an analysis of parallelism at all distances. Repetitive macro-structures have been noted for some time (e.g., the command-fulfillment structure of the *krt* text; the house-motif in the *bʿl* epic) and these must, of course, continue to be noted. I am here, however, referring to parallelistic techniques much like the ones with which we are familiar from traditional studies and from more modern studies such as Collins' and Geller's but which are not restricted to the single poetic unit.

An obvious categorization of the distribution of parallelisms is the following: 1) Half-line parallelism; 2) inner-colonic ("regular") parallelism; 3) near parallelism (that of elements of contiguous poetic units); 4) distant parallelism (that of elements of two or more units separated from each other by at least one other poetic unit).

The second category, inner-colonic parallelism, is so well known that my only burden at this point is to make a very strong impression to the effect that it is not the only variety of parallelism.

Half-line parallelism[68] has no part in either Collins' or Geller's

---

[64] The precisely equivalent semantic, grammatical, and positional structure in *ʿnt* I 4-5 and 8-9 has two quite different quantities: 2/5/11 // 1/7/16 in ll. 4-5; 2/6/13 // 1/6/14 in ll. 8-9 (for this method of computing quantitative values [word count, syllable count, "vocable" count], see *ZAW* 91 [1979] 403; *JANES* 10 [1978] 73).

[65] M. Dahood, *Psalms III* (Garden City, N.Y.: Doubleday, 1970) *passim* (see index, p. 483).

[66] J. W. Welch, "Chiasmus in Ugaritic," *UF* 6 (1974) 421-436.

[67] *Line-Forms*, pp. 257-273.

[68] For an older treatment of the phenomenon in Hebrew poetry, see Newman, "Parallelism" (reference in n. 6; 1918) 155-158 (termed "reduplication or internal synonymity").

systems (Collins treats half-line parallelism of major constituents as a "variation" on his line-forms; Geller's formula has no way of noting it, being uniquely concerned with the relationship between half-lines). Half-line parallelism corresponds in part to Dahood's "juxtaposition" and "collocation,"[69] though both these forms of 'parallelism' may occur in distributions other than half-line parallelism.[70]

In the sample text upon which this discussion is based, there are three clear cases of half-line parallelism, all three cases of juxtaposition according to Dahood's terminology. Two are semantic/gramatical parallelisms, one is repetitive:

bk rb ʿẓm *rʾi* (l. 12)
rbt ymsk bmskh (l. 17)
qm ybd wyšr (l. 18)

In each case, the surrounding parallelistic features are not the most regular, indicating that half-line parallelism may be one device used to strengthen a structure otherwise lacking in cohesiveness: In the first case the bicolon is in syntactic continuity with the preceding and following bicola and does not itself exhibit "regular" parallelism. In the second case the grammatical parallelism *yqḥ* // *ymsk* does not rest on a strong semantic basis and the internal repetitive parallelism in the second half-line (*ymsk bmskh*) appears to be compensating for the weakness of the semantic link between *yqḥ* and *ymsk*. Finally, in the third example, l. 18 is half of a bicolon, but it represents the three-verb structure which twice above constituted a complete bicolon (ll. 4-5, 8-9); moreover, there is no "regular" semantic or grammatical parallelism in this bicolon (ll. 18-19). Thus, once again, the half-line parallelism appears to be supporting a structure otherwise lacking in cohesiveness. There is yet a fourth case of half-line parallelism, this of minor elements: *ʿl . . . b* in l. 21. The strength given to a structure by minor elements of this kind is probably not the same as that of major semantic and grammatical parallelisms, but it is nonetheless to be noted that this fourth example of half-line parallelism does occur in a bicolon lacking "regular" parallelism. Thus all four cases of half-line parallelism in this sample text appear to have a comparable function. A much larger sample is needed, of course, before a definitive statement can be made as to the function of half-line parallelism.

Passing now to near parallelism, it is worth noting immediately that three out of the four cases of half-line parallelism occur in bicola also characterized by near parallelism:

---

[69] *RSP I* (1972) 87.

[70] Dahood's methodological error lay in not making a clear distinction between prose texts and poetic ones when noting all forms of parallelism (cf. de Moor and van der Lugt, *BiOr* 31 [1974] 6; Pardee, *JNES* 36 [1977] 66-67).

rʾi . . . tphnh // *tʿn* (ll. 12, 14-15; cf. *rb* + *ʿẓm*, l. 12)
ybd . . . yšr (ll. 18, 20) and
yšr . . . yšr (ll. 18, 20; cf. *ybd* + *yšr*, l. 18, and *ʿl* + *b*, l. 21)
nʿm . . . ṭb (ll. 19, 20; cf. *ybd* + *yšr*, l. 18, and *ʿl* + *b*, l. 21)

This distribution appears further to strengthen my tentative conclusion that half-line parallelism is used to strengthen otherwise weak poetic units. It may now be added that near parallelism may also be used to shore up these same "weaker" units by providing semantic and grammatical links to surrounding structures, structures which may in some cases be stronger. (Or the intermingling of "irregular" parallelistic features may be sufficient to provide strength, as in the case of the two-bicola in ll. 18-22, which both lack "regular" parallelism, but which are characterized by half-line, near, and distant parallelism, repetitive, semantic, and grammatical).

Other cases of near parallelism:

ʿbd // *sʾid . . . yṯʿr* // *yšlḥmnh* (ll. 2-3, 4-5)
yʿšr // *yšqynh . . . ytn ks* (ll. 9, 10)
-h . . . -h . . . -h . . . -h // *-h . . . -h . . . -h* (ll. 5, 6, 9, 10-11, 14, 17)[71]
ks // *krpn . . . bk . . . ks* // *krpn . . . kd* (ll. 10-11, 12, 13-14, 16)
bʿl . . . bʿl (ll. 21, 22)

It is already clear from the two forms of "non-regular" parallelism already discussed, and it will become clearer from the following listing of distant parallelisms, that these near parallelisms may be quite independent of other attachments (*nʿm . . . ṭb*, ll. 19, 20) or they may be linked with other parallelistic devices as part of complex structures stretching over several cola.

Let us examine immediately the cases of distant parallelism:

bʿl // *bʿl . . . bʿl . . . bʿl* (ll. 3, 21, 22)
qm . . . ndd . . . qm (ll. 4, 8, 18)
yṯʿr // *yšlḥmnh . . . yʿšr* // *yšqynh* (ll. 4-5, 9)
w + *-nh . . . w* + *-nh . . . w* (ll. 5, 9, 18)
ks // *krpn . . . bk . . . ks* // *krpn . . . kd* (ll. 10-11, 12, 13-14, 16)[72]
-d- // *yd- . . . -d* (ll. 10-11, 19)
ytn (*ks*) . . . (*kd*) *yqḥ* (ll. 10, 16)
rʾi . . . tphnh // *tʿn . . . ytmr* // *yʿn* (ll. 12, 14-15, 22-23)

---

[71] The structural strength of the near parallelism in ll. 14 and 17 is especially dubious because the antecedent of the pronoun is different in each case.

[72] Note the combination of regular, near, and distant parallelism in this chain of like terms.

There are also cases of distant parallelism of other minor elements which do not occur in otherwise clear structures (the preposition *b* and the 3 m.s. suffix *-h*[73]).

Some time spent examining this list in the context of the entire poem and of the other distributions of parallelism will leave little doubt, I believe, that parallelism in its repetitive, semantic, and grammatical aspects may operate over three and more poetic units with no difficulty. It is doubtful, however, that the other types of parallelism (phonetic, that of minor elements) can function over distances without the help of intervening like structures and/or without the help of other structural devices in the distant units. For example, I am dubious that the phonetic parallelism of *ks* and *kd* in ll. 10 and 16 would be picked up without the intervening examples of phonetic, semantic, and grammatical parallelism in ll. 11-15. Or, for another example, the structural significance of *w* + *-nh* . . . *w* + *-nh* . . . *w* in ll. 5, 9, 18 is clear because of the structure of the three bicola (supported by repetitive, semantic, and grammatical parallelism), while the structural significance of the eight-fold repetition of the 3 m.s. suffix is blurred because it does not fit a single pattern in all eight occurrences.

We may see, therefore, in the use of distant parallelism, as opposed to the other types of parallelism which include elements of physical contiguity, a hierarchy of types of parallelism based on structural strength. Repetitive parallelism is the strongest form of parallelism and can provide an outline for a relatively small unit such as *ʿnt* I with no difficulty. (More extensive repetitive parallelism, such as command-performance sequences, is able to bind together much longer units.) Semantic parallelism is next in strength; it is most visible in the present text when linked with other forms of parallelism (e.g., *qm* . . . *ndd* . . . *qm*). Grammatical parallelism alone is of little significance (i.e., the fact that a verb occurs in l. 2 and another in l. 22 says very little about the structure of the poem), though it is very clearly linked with repetitive and semantic parallelism to form distant parallelisms in the same way that it contributes to the parallelism of individual poetic units. A grammatical analysis of the type done by Collins will produce "line-types" which may be used as diagnostic indicators of repeated syntactic structures. It is doubtful here also, though, that these line-types would be indicative of parallelistic macro-structures unless semantic and/or repetitive parallelism were included.[74]

---

[73] *-h* occurs in regular, near, and distant parallelism (ll. 5, 6, 9, 10-11, 14, 17, 23).

[74] My sample text was too small to determine whether either Collins' or Geller's formulae occur in groupings comparable to the structures formed by near and distant parallelism, but neither author makes such a claim and I am dubious that they would

Finally, from the sample text there are no clear instances of inclusio or chiasmus of macro-structure. There is one distant parallelism which is chiastic in form (*ytn ks . . . kd yqḥ*), but this is a rather obscure element of the overall structure. Though one might be tempted to see the repetitive parallelism of *bʿl* in ll. 2-3 and 21, 22, as an inclusio, the distribution of this particular repetition is probably owing to the state of the tablet rather than to the desire to construct an inclusio (i.e., it is likely that these repetitions of the divine name are sequential within the larger poem rather than initial and terminative within a particular lesser structure). There are some cases of A B A macro-structures which might be seen as envelope constructions (*qm . . . ndd . . . qm*; *ks // krpn . . . bk . . . ks // krpn*), but the last element in each case is followed by further elements in the structure and is thus not terminative (*qm . . . ndd . . . qm . . . yšr . . . yšr*; *ks // krpn . . . bk . . . ks // krpn . . . kd*). These A B A structures are not, therefore, discrete units, followed by different discrete units, though they may perhaps be described as overlapping envelope constructions.

Conclusion. From this presentation it should be clear that I am calling for a close and detailed analysis of the parallelistic structure of Ugaritic and Hebrew poetry. This position is based on considerations both theoretical (we need a detailed analysis to pierce the obscurity of distance in time and culture) and empirical (I have learned more from close analysis than I did from a more intuitive reading). At some point this detailed analysis of parallelistic structures needs to be allied with analyses from the perspectives of psycho-linguistics and theory of literature in order to determine to what extent the many devices which emerge from detailed analysis were explicitly recognized and consciously practiced.[75] Though such questions are of great interest, they are not necessarily relevant to an analysis with modern methods and insights, for such an analysis may proceed to identify "what is there" before, after, or during an analysis of what the poet perceived as "being there."[76]

---

be perceived as of structural significance without the aid of other parallelistic features (i.e., repeated line-types and formulae do occur in a given text, but a pattern will only emerge when the distant grammatical structure is supported by repetitive and semantic parallelism).

[75] The only explicit recognition of such problems with respect to Ugaritic poetry of which I am aware is by Greenstein, in the article cited above in n. 39 (*JANES* 6 [1974] 87-105).

[76] On this problem of descriptive analysis over against the "rich allusiveness of poetry," see Peter and Wendy Steiner's review (of Elmar Holenstein, *Roman Jakobson's Approach to Language: Phenomenological Structuralism*) in *PTL* 3 (1978) 357-370, esp. pp. 368-369. The problem with relying completely on the "allusiveness" is, of course that such

ʿnt I

Text[77]	*Translation*
[2]. . . *ʿbd . ʾalʾiyn* [3]*bʿl .*	He serves mighty Baal,
sʾid . zbl . bʿl [4]*ʾarṣ .*	Regales the Prince, lord of the earth.
qm . yṯʿr	He arises, prepares,
[5]*w . yšlḥmnh*	And causes him to eat.
[6]*ybrd . ṯd . lpnwh*	He cuts the breast before him,
[7]*bḥrb . mlḥt* [8]*qṣ . mrʾi .*	With a salted knife (does he cut) a slice of fatling.
ndd [9]*yʿšr .*	He arises, serves,
wyšqynh	And causes him to drink.
[10]*ytn . ks . bdh*	He puts a cup in his hand,
[11]*krpn . bklʾat . ydh*	A goblet in his two hands;
[12]*bk rb . ʿẓm . rʾi*	A large vessel, mighty to look upon,
dn[13]*mt . šmm*	Belonging to the furnishings of the heavens;
ks . qdš [14]*ltphnh . ʾaṯt .*	A holy cup (which) women may not see,
krpn [15]*ltʿn . ʾaṯrt .*	A goblet (which) ʾAṯirat may not eye.
ʾalp [16]*kd . yqḥ . bḫmr*	One thousand *kd*-measures he takes from the *ḫmr*-wine.
[17]*rbt . ymsk . bmskh*	Ten thousand he mixes into his mixture.
[18]*qm . ybd . wyšr*	He arises, chants, and sings;
[19]*mṣltm . bd . nʿm*	Cymbals (are) in the hands of the goodly one.
[20]*yšr . ǵzr . ṭb . ql*	The good-voiced youth sings
[21]*ʿl . bʿl . bṣrrt* [22]*ṣpn .*	For Baal in the heights of Ṣapan.
ytmr . bʿl [23]*bnth .*	Baal sees his daughters,
yʿn . pdry [24]*bt . ʾar .*	Eyes Pidra, daughter of light.

total reliance can lead to "mystical dillettantism" (D. I. Masson, "Vowel and Consonant Patterns in Poetry," pp. 3-18 in *Essays* [reference above, n. 56], quotation from p. 18). I would, in any case, certainly not want my pleas for a detailed analysis of parallelistic structures to be understood as implying that such "nuts-and-bolts" analysis can take the place of literary, aesthetic, or historical criticism. "Instead, the analyses are rigorous descriptions of the preconditions for criticism . . . " (Steiner and Steiner, ibid., p. 369).

[77] To save space, I have given only the text arranged according to poetic structure (and have omitted the few signs at beginning and end which, because of lacunae, cannot be fitted into the poetic structure). The arrangement of lines on the tablet can be easily determined from the line numbers given here in superscript.

APPENDIX II

TYPES AND DISTRIBUTIONS OF PARALLELISM IN UGARITIC AND HEBREW POETRY

Communication prepared for the Annual Meeting of the Society of Biblical Literature, New York, December 21, 1982

The purpose of this presentation is to describe two main schemas which may be used in the analysis of Ugaritic and Hebrew poems and to suggest how the overlapping or overlaying of the two schemas may give various insights into the structure of a given poem. The first schema consists of the various types of parallelism which have been observed over the years, that is, repetitive, semantic, grammatical, and phonetic. The second schema is that of the physical distribution of these types of parallelism over a poetic work. The discussion of overlapping will deal with how the various types of parallelism function in various degrees of proximity. I fully realize that a book could be written on each of my sub-topics—indeed several books have been written on several of these sub-topics. I am consciously attempting, therefore, to provide an overview which will place some of the sub-topics in a larger perspective. This procedure does force me, however, to be much briefer than I would wish to be in most instances. A final preliminary remark: I am going to assume that persons attending this session are acquainted with the major recent works on Hebrew poetry and will thus permit myself to refer to them by author's last name only.

The types of parallelism, then, which I wish to discuss, are repetitive, semantic, grammatical, and phonetic. I place repetitive parallelism first because it englobes all the others, at least partially. That is, a repetition of a same word will usually mean the same in both instances, be grammatically similar in both instances, and sound the same in both instances. Time will only permit a discussion of a few facets of repetitive parallelism, primarily ones of definition and of problematic features. First, repetitive parallelism has only fairly recently received recognition as a major constitutive feature of early Northwest Semitic poetry and is in a sense a misnomer. For, in the study of parallelism as a poetic device in other literatures, "repetition" is used to describe the entire parallelistic principle and not just verbatim repetition. Northwest Semitists must be careful, therefore, at least when writing for a larger audience, to make clear the sense in which they use the word.

Second, the problem of definition is a thorny one. O'Connor has recently held (p. 109) that repetitive parallelism must be *nearly* verbatim repetition and that all other forms of repetition of the same root are only *figurae etymologicae*. I have no quarrel with setting up a distinction between two types of repetition but do believe that repetitive parallelism in O'Connor's sense of the term and *figura etymologica* must be grouped as more like each other than like semantic or phonetic parallelism (in the sense of alliteration or assonance). For purposes of analysis, therefore, I would suggest that "repetitive parallelism" might be sub-classified as "verbatim repetition" and "weak repetitive parallelism," both being used to describe parallels of forms derived from a same root.

Finally, the question of the chronologically diagnostic or typological value of repetitive parallelism has not yet been established. Far more work must be done on poems the dating of which is beyond dispute before one can follow or reject Albright in this particular insight. On the basis of my very small sample, I would guess that repetitive parallelism may indeed have a higher incidence in Ugaritic than in Hebrew poetry but that this device is not alone a sufficient indicator of date.

Semantic parallelism is where the modern study of parallelism began, of course, and in recent years we have seen two separate paths taken in the analysis of semantic parallelism. That of Geller was to attempt a more refined analysis of the semantic relationship between the two half-lines of a bicolon, whereas Kugel's approach consisted in redefining parallelism as a rhetorical device the function of which was to "second" or "heighten" a statement. I will only permit myself at this point to wonder aloud if these two main approaches are as incompatible as Kugel would have them to be. I agree fully with Kugel's basic analysis of how parallelism functions but would emphasize the words "function" and "rhetoric" in my previous description. It appears to me that the position that parallelism functions as a rhetorical heightening device does not preclude analyzing the component parts of that device with regard to semantic, grammatical, and phonetic make-up. The indisputable fact that the permutations will be innumerable does not preclude trying to set up major categories of classification, such as Geller and others have done. The important thing, from Kugel's perspective, if I have understood him correctly, would be not to confuse the individual trees of the classification with the forest of the device known as parallelism.

Grammatical parallelism has come to the fore in less than five years, counting from publication date, with the major works of Collins (1978), Geller (1979), and O'Connor (1980), and with the lesser but very significant article by Berlin in 1979. The proximity of publication date indicates that these four scholars were working independently and, indeed, their work varies considerably. In a nutshell, Collins works with major constituents only (subject, object, verb, modifier) and observes their distribution in "line-types"; Geller works with both morphological and syntactic categories of grammar and blends grammar, semantics, and meter into one, and I speak for myself, nearly impenetrable notational system; O'Connor has replaced traditional meter with a system of syntactic constraints, though his study also includes an analysis of semantic parallelism and of macro-structure; Berlin has looked at the grammatical relationship between words that are in semantic or positional parallelism.

These studies are so new and so varied that it will take some time to assess their long-term value and I am not the person to do much of the linguistic assessment in any case. So I will limit myself to a few brief comments. Collins' study is of interest in that it establishes that certain line-types (that is, configurations of major constituents) are more frequent than others. I see three main areas of research that need to be carried out along these lines: 1) First, Collins' method is applicable, as he has set it up, to only about 40% of Hebrew poetry. (In my application of his method to the Ugaritic sample text, I got approximately the same results). The method should be expanded so that it can describe more of the corpus. Only then can we see how it describes the corpus. 2) Second, there should be an explicit comparison of line-types in poetry with configurations of major constituents in prose in order to determine if the distribution of line-types differs—of course the binary nature of much of the poetry will make a comparison somewhat difficult, but one should be able to set up such a study. If the distribution of line-types is not significantly different in prose and poetry, the significance of the poetic distribution will have to be re-evaluated. 3) Third, how may the analyses of Collins and O'Connor be compared? Are they similar enough to be worked into one system of analysis or are they looking at aspects of syntax too different to be united?

Geller, it appears to me, was mistaken in trying to include meter in his analysis and notational system. Collins, O'Connor, Kugel, and myself have all in recent years, working independently, rejected the notion of a meter, in the traditional and common sense of the term, in Hebrew poetry, and since I include myself in this list I obviously believe that Geller should not have made meter a part of his analysis. This does not mean that the analysis of what Geller calls "deletion-compensation" should be dropped, simply that this should be stated in terms other than narrowly metrical ones. Since Geller's system was burdened with the notion of meter, and since he included meter, semantics, and grammar in his notational system, it is a bit difficult to see just what his grammatical analysis, which included far more detail than did Collins', contributed to the overall perception of the poetic structure. My question regarding Geller's view of grammatical parallelism, then, is: Just how useful is a detailed notation of grammatical structure and how should such a notation dovetail with a notation of major constituents?

O'Connor's study has the great merit of rejecting meter as a structural device, stating rather that there were constraints on the number and combination of various types of syntactic units. From my own perspective, his system has the great advantage of producing what I have called "lines of approximately comparable length." I do not, however, have the linguistic expertise to judge the basic question of whether the whole approach is valid and has been correctly adumbrated. Kugel has pointed out that O'Connor's constraints occasionally produce poetic lines that appear rhetorically unlikely and I for my part will restate the query expressed above regarding Collins' system: To the extent that prose and poetry are comparable, would a comparison of the two using O'Connor's method produce significant differences? Is it not possible that the syntactic structure of a bicolon is owing to the rhetorical terseness of poetry rather than being the result of a set of line-type constraints or of syntactic constraints which would be significantly different in basic syntax from those found in prose?

Berlin turned grammatical parallelism, as viewed by Collins and Geller at least, on its head by studying the *differences* between parallel units rather than the similarities. Thus she defines grammatical parallelism as "The alteration of grammatical structure in parallel stichs, or, better, the pairing of two grammatical structures in parallel stichs" (p. 20). This study is important because it points up semantic parallelisms that might have been missed otherwise because of grammatical differences. It is, however, in my opinion, only half the picture, for the very opposite situation can occur; grammatical likeness can bind together segments that are semantically dissimilar. I cite as illustration of this point lines 15-17 of the sample text, where *yiqqaḥu* 'he takes' and *yamsuku* 'he mixes' are semantically different but grammatically alike. Here the grammatical similarity serves as one element binding the bicolon together.

Briefly summing up grammatical parallelism, I can readily see a place for an analysis such as Collins', for it can appear alongside and in a notational format much like that of semantic parallelism. I can foresee a usefulness in Geller's detailed analysis but wonder how detailed the analysis should be and what a readily comprehensible notational system would be once it is stripped of the metrical overburden and separated physically from the notation of semantic parallelism. I would like to see a detailed assessment of O'Connor's system by a professional linguist who knows biblical Hebrew very well. And I would agree with Berlin's study as long as grammatical dissimilarity is viewed as only one aspect of grammatical parallelism.

Passing now to phonetic parallelism (and by the term I do not mean 'meter'), I must be brief for relatively little has been done in recent years in the area of alliteration, assonance, etc. It is Margalit who has done the most with what he calls "alliteration," in this case an unusually high incidence of a given consonant or consonants in a unit of Ugaritic poetry. Though his use of this 'consonantism' is a bit marred by his reliance upon it to restore and even to emend, his contribution is important. I believe that he is correct in pointing up this consonantism and believe that it is a linking device between the half-lines of a bicolon. I have two main questions regarding this approach, however: 1) One, what was the role of the vowels in the Ugaritic phonetic repetition? I have analyzed my sample Ugaritic text and even with this artificially reconstructed vocalization have come up with very little on vowel patterning. 2) Second, can consonantism play a larger role than simply making two half-lines sound alike? I have found at least one fairly clear example of a larger consonantal structure, the repetition of /k/ in the "cup" section of the sample text: there are four words for vessels in lines 10-16 and each of them contains a /k/: *kāsu*, *karpanu*, *bīku*, and *kaddu*. In addition, the consonant /k/, along with /q/, occur in five other words in the four bicola in question. What we really need, however, is for someone trained in the methods of Roman Jakobson to look closely at Northwest Semitic poetry and teach us how to open our eyes to the patterns which may lie there.

Before passing on to the second major schema, I should state that the four major types of parallelism just discussed, with their sub-categories, do themselves provide a tremendous potential for interaction and variation, as I have already intimated in my remarks regarding grammatical versus semantic parallelism. Within any given poetic unit one may find virtually any given combination of the four types, ranging from a high incidence of repetitive parallelism to a very low incidence of any of the four types. On the whole it may be said that at least one of the major types of parallelism will usually occur within a unit and, if not, one of the types will occur between the unit in question and another unit in near or distant parallelism. Thus I certainly agree with the kernel of Kugel's assessment of grammatical parallelism, that it was "devised in the necessity of salvaging the principle of parallelism for lines where semantic similarities were obviously lacking," but disagree totally with the negative tone of the words "devise" and "salvage." I am convinced that it is no question whatever of salvaging a bankrupt system of analysis, but rather of expanding our analytical tools so as to be able to discern all the means whereby poetic units were bound together, on the level of micro-parallelism as well as of macro-parallelism—to which I now pass.

Though there have been many analyses of the macro-structure of Ugaritic and Hebrew poems, very few indeed have studied the macro-structure in terms of the types of parallelism we have just discussed, those used to form the structure of an individual poetic unit. My question, then, which led to the results I am about to outline for you, was: How are these types of parallelism distributed over an entire work? or, in slightly different terms, How do these micro-structural devices contribute to macro-structure?

I would suggest first, as a simple common-sense division of possible distributions, proceding from smaller to larger divisions: 1) half-line parallelism (that is, within the section that precedes the caesura); 2) "regular" or inner-colonic parallelism (that is, between the two half-lines of a bicolon); 3) near parallelism (defined as occuring between two contiguous bicola); 4) distant parallelism (defined as occuring between bicola separated from each other by at least one complete bicolon—this last category could, of course, be sub-divided according to the number of units separating the parallel structures).

I will now give examples of each of these distributions, then make some remarks about the structural function of these distributions and then, looking at them from another angle, at how the various types of parallelism discussed in the first part of the paper are distributed in these categories.

There are three relatively clear cases of half-line parallelism in the sample text:

1) *rabba* // *ʿaẓuma* (line 12), a case of semantic parallelism (+ grammatical).

2) *yamsuku bimaskihu* (line 17), an example of weak repetitive parallelism or *figura etymologica* (different major grammatical categories, verb vs. noun).

3) *yabuddu wayašīru* (line 18), another example of semantic parallelism (+ grammatical).

There is no need to provide examples of "regular" parallelism as it is the most prevalent in the sample text and the most widely recognized in general.

There are four relatively clear examples of near parallelism:

1) *ruʾi* in line 12 with *tiphânnahu* // *taʿīnu* in lines 14 and 15, three different verbs meaning 'to see' (a mixture of near and regular distributions).

2) *yabuddu wayašīru* in line 18 with *yašīru* in line 20, a mixture of repetitive, semantic, and grammatical parallelisms (also a mixture of half-line and near distributions).

3) *naᶜīmi* in line 19 with *ṭābu* in line 20, simple semantic parallelism + partial grammatical.

4) *baᶜlu* in lines 21 and 22, repetition of the divine name.

There are five clear examples of distant parallelism, usually consisting of mixtures of repetitive, semantic, and grammatical parallels and in combination with other distributions of these parallelisms:

1) *baᶜlu* in lines 3, 21, and 22.

2) *qama . . . nadada . . . qama* in lines 4, 8, and 18.

3) *yaṯᶜuru // yašalḥimannahu* with *yaᶜšuru // yašqiyannahu* in lines 4, 5, and 9.

4) a multi-leveled structure of the vessels: *kāsa // karpana* (lines 10-11) . . . *bīka* (line 12) . . . *kāsa // karpana* (lines 13-14) . . . *kaddi* (line 16).

5) another multi-leveled structure of the verbs 'to see': *ruʾi* (line 12) . . . *tiphânnahu // taᶜīnu* (lines 14-15) . . . *yîtamiru // yaᶜīnu* (lines 22-23).

On the basis of this small sample it appears that the major function of half-line and near parallelism was to bind together units not otherwise characterized by semantically strong parallelism in regular distribution:

— the half-line parallelism of *rabba* and *ᶜaẓuma* in line 12 occurs in a bicolon which has no real traditional parallelism between the two half-lines.

— the half-line parallelism of *yamsuku* and *bimaskihu* in line 17 occurs in a bicolon characterized by the weak semantic parallelism of *yiqqaḥu* and *yamsuku* and of *ḫamri* with *maskihu*.

— the half-line parallelism of *yabuddu* and *yašīru* in line 18 again occurs in a bicolon which lacks semantic or grammatical parallelism.

— the first element of the the near parallelism of *ruʾi* in line 12 with the verbs of seeing in lines 14 and 15 occurs in the same weak bicolon as *rabba* and *ᶜaẓuma*.

— the near parallelism of *yabuddu wayašīru* in line 18 with *yašīru* in line 20 occurs in bicola which are both grammatically and semantically weak.

— the near parallelism of *naᶜīmi* and *ṭābu* also occurs between these same bicola.

I would suggest on this rather small basis that the higher incidence of so-called "synthetic" parallelism in Hebrew poetry which Kugel, as compared with earlier scholars, has isolated should be re-examined to see if these secondary strengthening devices may not be present.

Distant parallelism, by its very nature as distant, seems to function primarily as a binder of larger structures. All of the cases listed above are macro-structural binders, with the possible exception of the divine name *baʿlu*, the occurrence of which probably owes more to narrative considerations than to specifically poetic ones. A clear case of macrostructural binding is that of *qama . . . nadada . . . qama*, a combination of repetitive, semantic, morphological, and syntactic parallelism, used to introduce each of the three main sections of the feast, eating, drinking, and singing.

It appears to me, however, that distant parallelism also participates in the binding of weak structures, both internally and to their surrounding structures, for most of the distant parallels cited above have at least one member in a weak unit: *baʿlu* in line 21, *qama* in line 18, *bīka* in line 12, and *ruʾi* in the same line.

As a conclusion to patterning of distributions, then, I would say that half-line and near parallelism may be coupled with regular parallelism but will more frequently have a complementary distribution with it. Distant parallelism will usually be part of a complex pattern with other distributions. Part of a distant structure will frequently be from a unit which is not itself characterized by strong parallelism, while the primary function of half-line and near parallelism in the sample text was to strengthen structurally weak units.

Finally, I will make a few more specific comments about the interrelationships of the two schemas of parallelism, the types of parallelism and the distributions of parallelism. My conclusion, once again on the basis of the present sample, is perhaps an obvious one but nonetheless one that bears stating. I will put it in terms of relative strengths in binding together units large or small. In these terms, repetitive parallelism is the strongest binder, though it will usually be linked with semantic parallelism as in the case of *qama . . . nadada . . . qama*, already cited above, where *nadada* is semantic while the two *qama*'s repeat. The complex structure describing the drinking contains a list of four vessels of which two, *kāsa* and *karpana*, are twice repeated. Repetitive parallelism can also be used, however, to bind together smaller structures and the sample text provides examples of half-line distribution (*yamsuku bimaskihu*), regular distribution (*baʿlu // baʿlu*) (line 3), and near distribution (*yašīru . . . yašīru*) (lines 18, 20).

Semantic parallelism is the next strongest binder, used in half-line, regular, near, and distant distributions, though my impression is that the greater the distance of distribution, the more likely it will be that semantic parallelism will be linked with repetitive parallelism.

Grammatical parallelism is not nearly so strong a binder as the previous two types and probably cannot operate beyond the near distribution without the support of repetitive and/or semantic parallelism and will not be a strong binder even in near distribution. The reason for this, I believe, is that the relatively few grammatical categories are not distinctive enough by themselves to serve as poetic recall devices in distant distribution.

The same appears to be true of phonetic parallelism: the high occurrence of a given sound almost certainly serves to bind a half-line and a bicolon together but a sound-element alone is not distinctive enough to bind larger sections unless it be linked with semantic or repetitive parallelism (as, for example, in the instance cited above of the four words for vessels).

Thus repetitive parallelism, because it englobes all the other types is the strongest; semantic parallelism is next in strength because of its broad lexical and ideational basis; grammatical and phonetic parallelism are largely limited to micro-structures, unless linked with one of the stronger types, because of the limited repertory in each of these categories.

In summary, I believe that the study of types of parallelism must continue, especially in the relatively new field of grammatical parallelism and in the relatively neglected field of phonetic parallelism. I am convinced, moreover, that, whatever further advances may be made along these lines, it will be useful to observe the contribution of these types of parallelism to the larger structure of any poem. We also need to observe, and this is one area that I have not myself even begun to study yet, just how the micro-structural devices serve to set up larger images and sets of images. This will be closely tied in with the study of distributions but will require going beyond the simple tabulation of the repetitions in a search for their rhetorical and imagistic function.

The conclusion to which this study of distributions has led me to date is that any notion that a poem may be studied, as a piece of poetry, only by reference to the bicolon or the tricolon must be abandoned. Though it should be abundantly clear from my own analyses of the sample text that I consider the bicolon or the tricolon to be the building-block of poetic structure, I hope that it will be equally evident that I consider it as insignificant to study *only* these building-blocks as it would be to study, for example, *only* the individual stones that went to make up the Parthenon. Because of the bulk of any complete study, I remain uncertain as to just how to go about producing a study which takes in all the varied aspects of parallelism, but am no less convinced that all facets must be the purview of any study aiming at comprehensiveness.

INDEX OF BIBLICAL PASSAGES

1.7.1 *Phonetic Parallelism: Repetition of Consonants*[74]

Regular and Half-line

I.	ʿbd . ʾalʾiyn [3]bʿl	ʿ, ʿ	b, b	d	ʾ, ʾ	l, l				
	sʾid . zbl . bʿl [4]ʾarṣ	ʿ	b, b	d	ʾ, ʾ	l, l				
II.	qm . yṯʿr	m	y							
	[5]w . yšlḥmnh	m	y							
III.	[6]ybrd . ṯd . lpnwh	b	r	d, d	l					
	[7]bḥrb . mlḥt [8]qṣ . mrʾi .	b	r, r		l	ḥ, ḥ	m, m			
IV.	ndd [9]yʿšr .	n	y	š						
	wyšqynh	n	y, y	š						
V.	[10]ytn . ks . bdh	y	t	n	k	b	dh			
	[11]krpn . bklʾat . ydh	y	t	n	k, k	b	dh			
VI.	[12]bk rb . ʿẓm . rʾi	b, b	r, r	m						
	dn[13]mt . šmm .			m, mm						
VII.	ks . qdš [14]ltphnh . ʾaṯt .	k	l	t, t	(lt)	p	h, h	n	ʾ	ṯ
	krpn [15]ltʿn . ʾaṯrt .	k	l	t, t	(lt)	p		n, n	ʾ	ṯ	r, r
VIII.	ʾalp [16]kd . yqḥ . bḫmr	k	y	b	m	r				
	[17]rbt . ymsk . bmskh	k, k	y	b, b	m, m	r	s, s	(msk, msk)		
IX.	[18]qm . ybd . wyšr	m	y, y	bd						
	[19]mṣltm . bd . nʿm	m, m, m		bd						
X.	[20]yšr . ǵzr . ṭb . ql	r, r	b	l						
	[21]ʿl . bʿl . bṣrrt [22]ṣpn	rr	b, b	l, l	ʿ, ʿ	(ʿl, ʿl)	ṣ, ṣ			
XI.	ytmr . bʿl [23]bnth .	y	t, t	r	b, b	ʿ	n			
	yʿn . pdry [24]bt . ʾar .	y, y	t	r, r	b	ʿ	n			

Near

	ʿ	l	y	n	r
I.	ʿ, ʿ	l, l	y	n	
	ʿ	l, l			r
& II.	ʿ		y		r
		l	y	n	

	y	r	d	n	w	h	q
III.	y	r	d, d	n	w	h	
		r, r					q
& IV.	y	r	dd	n			
	y, y			n	w	h	q

	t	n	k	b	d	r	ʾ
V.	t	n	k	b	d		
	t	n	k	b	d	r	ʾ
& VI.			k	b, b		r, r	ʾ
	t	n			d		

	k	s	q	d	l	t	p	h	ʾ	r
VII.	k	s	q	d	l	t, t	p	h, h	ʾ	
	k				l	t, t	p		ʾ	r, r
& VIII.	k		q	d	l		p		ʾ	r
	k, k	s, s				t		h		r

	q	y	b	š	r	(yšr)	ṣ	l	t	n	ʿ
IX.	q	y, y	b	š	r	(yšr)					
			b				ṣ	l	t	n	ʿ
& X.	q	y	b	s	r, r			l			
			b, b		rr	(yšr)	ṣ, ṣ	l, l	t	n	ʿ, ʿ

	q	m	y	t	r	w	l	ḥ	n	h
II.	q		y	t	r					
		m	y			w	l	ḥ	n	h
& III.			y	t	r	w	l		n	h
	q	m, m			r, r		l	ḥ, ḥ		

	n	d	y	r	h
IV.	n	dd	y	r	
	n		y, y		h
& V.	n	d	y	r	h
	n	d	y	r	h

	k	r	ʿ	ʾ	d	n	t	š
VI.	k	r, r	ʿ	ʾ				
					d	n	t	š
& VII.	k			ʾ	d	n	t, t	š
	k	r, r	ʿ	ʾ		n, n	t, t	

	l	d	y	q	b	m	r	t
VIII.	l	d	y	q	b	m	r	
					b, b	m, m	r	t
& IX.		d	y, y	q	b	m	r	
	l	d			b	m, m, m		t

	y	r	b	l	ʿ	(bʿl)	t	p	n
X.	y	r, r	b	l					
		rr	b, b	l, l	ʿ, ʿ	(bʿl)	t	p	n
& XI.	y	r	b, b	l	ʿ	(bʿl)	t, t		n
	y, y	r, r	b		ʿ		t	p	n

Sequences

I.	l, l	y	n								(ʾ, ʾ)	(b, b)	(ʿ, ʿ)
	l, l			r							(ʾ, ʾ)	(b, b)	(ʿ)
II.		y		r	q								(ʿ)
	l	y	n			w	h						
III.	l	y	n	r		w	h	d, d				(b)	
	l			r, r	q							(b)	
IV.		y	n	r				dd					
		y, y	n		q	w	h						
V.		y	n				h	d	t	k		(b)	
		y	n	r			h	d	t	k	ʾ	(b)	
VI.				r, r						k	ʾ	(bb)	(ʿ)
			n					d	t				
VII.	l		n		q		(h, h)	d	t, t	k	ʾ		
	l		n, n	r, r					t, t	k	ʾ		(ʿ)
VIII.	l	y		r	q			d		k		b	
				r			(h)		t	k, k	ʾ	b, b	
IX.		y, y		r				d				b	
	l		n					d	t			b	ʿ
X.	l	y		r, r								b	
	l, l		n	rr					t			b, b	ʿ, ʿ
XI.	l	y	n	r					t, t			b, b	ʿ
		y, y	n	r, r					t			b	ʿ

---

[74] The consonants are listed in order of appearance in the first half-line. "Phonological" would, of course, be a more precise term linguistically speaking than "phonetic," for I am outlining the appearance of "phonemes" (and even graphemes, in the case of the consonants!), rather than "phones." In line with common usage in ancient Near Eastern studies, however, I have preserved the term "phonetic" (cf., e.g., "phonetic complement").